The Esso CNG Offer

A subsidiary of Exxon Mobil Corporation, Esso CNG Ltd is one of the UK's largest suppliers of compressed natural gas. Esso CNG offers a comprehensive and competitive natural gas supply package.

■ A Bespoke Fuel Solution:

A CNG refuelling installation designed around individual needs
Refuelling point provided by Esso CNG
On-going programme of maintenance, training and technical support

■ A One Stop Advice Shop:

Information and guidance on how to get the best out of an investment in CNG, including:
Advice on vehicle developments and availability
Information on fuel management systems
The latest news on grants and incentives

■ A 'No Extra Cost' Refuelling Point:

On site refuelling facility with no capital outlay for the customer

■ A Pricing Mechanism Linked to Long term Inflation

Reducing uncertainties surrounding fuel price fluctuation

■ No Fuel Stock Holding

Protects against fuel theft
A minimal hydrocarbon inventory
Cost effective system: fuel is only paid for as it is used

■ The Mobil CNG Demonstrator Vehicle

Allows customers to experience CNG-powered technology at first hand

For further information contact :

Ella Misfeldt
Tel: 0800 917 4264
cng@email.mobil.com

The
DICTIONARY of
TRANSPORT
AND LOGISTICS

The
DICTIONARY of
TRANSPORT
AND LOGISTICS

DAVID LOWE

The Institute of
Logistics and Transport

KOGAN
PAGE

First published in 2002

Kogan Page
120 Pentonville Road
London N1 9JN

© David Lowe, 2002

British Library Cataloguing in Publication Data

A CIP record for this book is available from the British Library.

ISBN 0 7494 3571 2

Typeset by JS Typesetting, Wellingborough, Northants
Printed and bound in Great Britain by Biddles Ltd, Guildford and King's Lynn
www.biddles.co.uk

In this dictionary

The terms, abbreviations and acronyms included herein cover:

- heavy vehicle technology;
- road haulage and own-account transport operations;
- passenger vehicle and public service operations;
- legal aspects of transport;
- logistics;
- supply-chain management;
- freighting by rail, air, sea and inland waterway;
- passenger transport by rail, sea and air;
- transport policy and planning;
- related business, accounting and information technology.

An asterisk (*) is used to denote a cross-referenced entry.

Preface

Originally published in 1991 by *Headlight* magazine as a small dictionary of transport terms and abbreviations, this new edition has been updated and expanded to include many additional terms found in distribution, logistics, supply-chain operations, shipping, rail and air freighting, in passenger transport and in related transport planning, business and information technology functions. Thus with some 3,000 terms, abbreviations and acronyms now included, this becomes the most comprehensive dictionary of its type currently available and hopefully will prove to be a boon to readers from all sectors and at all levels, from students and junior staff to top management, all of whom may need to source the meaning or relevance of industry terms not generally found in standard English language dictionaries.

But why is such a dictionary needed at all? The answer lies in the fact that road haulage operations particularly and the broader aspects of freight and passenger transport and logistics as a whole have become so technically sophisticated that a whole language of technical and generic terms, jargon, abbreviations, acronyms and management buzzwords, to say nothing of legal terminology and definitions, has been generated.

For example, in the same way that a vacuum cleaner is almost always referred to as a 'Hoover' (have people never heard of other makes of carpet cleaners?), so in most people's minds a van is always a 'Transit', most curtain-sided vehicles and trailers are called 'Tautliners' although many of them are not of this make, and lorry-mounted cranes from a variety of manufacturers are invariably referred to as 'Hiabs', all of which provides excellent, and free, publicity for the respective manufacturer concerned.

But this is by no means all; there are many other conundrums such as why the Department of Transport, Local Government and the Regions (as this 'super ministry' is now called) is still referred to as the 'Ministry' and its enforcement officers as 'Ministry men', but is this really who they are? Answer, no. These days they are examiners from the Vehicle Inspectorate, an agency offshoot of the DTLR.

Similarly, demountable vehicle bodies are frequently called 'swop (or swap) bodies', but are these one and the same? And does everybody really know for sure that a 'fifth-wheel' is part of an articulated vehicle, or could it be something else? And what on earth is a 'towing dolly', or a 'composite trailer'? And what is the legal definition for each of these? What is a 'peripheral' or indeed a 'tri-axle bogie'? What do 'liberalization' and 'harmonization' mean in transport terms? Who or what is AETR, or TIR, or RHA? Where does the word 'derv' come from? What is a 'TREMCARD' and who would want one? What is a 'floppy disc', or come to that a 'hard disc', and who might use one? And what is that word 'DEKRA' featured so prominently on Michael Schumacher's cap when he wins yet another Grand Prix?

The list seems endless and covers every aspect of transport and logistics. New terms are added, old ones fall into disuse, many are overtaken by ever-newer technological developments, and from time to time organizations change their names (and the initials or acronyms by which they are commonly known), and new ones appear.

For anybody unconnected with transport or the wider fields of logistics and supply-chain management these terms and abbreviations present a bewildering language of 'in-words' and jargon; they must sound to the uninitiated like pure gobbledegook. Also, there must be many people already working in or associated with the industry who may not be familiar with all the terms or who may wish to know what a particular abbreviation stands for or what organization it represents.

The purpose of this dictionary is to identify these terms and abbreviations and to explain, in simple language, just what they mean or who they represent, or to give, translated into plain language, the legal definition. Where appropriate, company or product names (especially where they are becoming generic terms) are identified and official organizations are named.

As a work of reference this dictionary should be of interest and use to those with only an ancillary interest or involvement with the world of transport and logistics as well as to those wholly occupied with the business, for example anybody who is a member or intends becoming a member of the Institute of Logistics and Transport. It should also be of interest to newcomers to the industry, to those in the business who have only limited technical understanding and to anybody else who wants to become more knowledgeable in this area, particularly students at universities and colleges of further education undertaking logistics and transport-related studies. It goes without saying that those engaged in the practical operations of road haulage and/or road passenger transport would find the book to be an essential source of reference in preparing for the professional competence examinations in either or both of these disciplines.

The original idea for this dictionary came from discussions with a driver agency firm, whose young employees were regularly subjected to attempted bamboozles by boastful temporary drivers as to the type of vehicle they could handle with competence (was it a twin-steer, tri-axle, fifth-wheel bogie with a demountable, range-change, dolly gearbox? Or was it just a 3-ton bread van?). From this the idea developed that many people may wish to have a ready source of reference to such terms and many others, hence this book.

In compiling the text I have racked my brain and searched wide for suitable material but it is inevitable that some terms and abbreviations will have escaped the net, possibly even simple everyday ones. If this is the case, I would welcome hearing about them for inclusion in any future edition. Also to be noted is that many of the words or terms included have a number of meanings or other uses; here they have been defined only in the context of their usage in transport and logistics operations, leaving aside any other meanings or application they may have.

Generally, the masculine pronoun has been used in this book to avoid cumbersome language and to save space. No discrimination, prejudice or bias is intended by this. I fully recognize the key role played by the many female LGV drivers, staff, managers and senior executives in transport and logistics.

Acknowledgements

I have used many sources to cross-check my entries both to avoid glaring omissions and to validate my definitions against accepted standards. Many of the terms, abbreviations and acronyms in this dictionary have been culled from textbooks, trade journals, newspapers and both official and commercial publications too numerous to identify and acknowledge individually. However, I must mention a number of sources in particular.

First, the Institute of Logistics and Transport whose library staff at Corby have been especially helpful in identifying sources of reference. The Institute's journal, *Logistics and Transport Focus* has been the source of many relevant terms and, from its Supply-Chain Inventory Management Special Interest Group Internet Web site, I have included a list of inventory-related terms developed by the Group. Jon Harris, the ILT Director of Policy, very kindly contributed a number of transport planning entries.

The new (2000) edition of *The Handbook of Logistics and Distribution Management* by Alan Rushton, John Oxley and Phil Croucher (published by Kogan Page) contains a very useful list of logistics-related abbreviations that I have taken the liberty of selectively plundering to add to my own list in this book.

Two works on shipping by Alan E Branch, namely, *Elements of Shipping* and *Export Practice and Management*, both published by Chapman & Hall, London, have provided a source of confirmation for many of the shipping terms included, while the European Logistics Association's published list of terms and definitions, *Terminology in Logistics*, has been a source for cross-referencing many of my logistics definitions. For passenger transport references, Paul Fawcett's interesting work, *Managing Passenger Transport Logistics* (also published by Kogan Page) has proved useful. I also acknowledge in particular that the term 'fourth-party logistics', included herein because of its relevance, carries the registered trademark of Andersen Consulting LLP.

I must thank long-time friend and fellow writer on heavy truck issues, Gibb Grace, who kindly allowed me to cross-check with him my definitions for a number of the technical terms included.

Finally, but by no means least, my thanks are also due to yet another long-standing colleague, Professor John Hibbs, who undertook a very detailed reading of the manuscript. He suggested a number of valid corrections to some of my shaky interpretations and offered helpful ideas for a number of additional entries, particularly in regard to passenger vehicle and public transport operations, for which I am especially grateful.

As times change so does the use of words and I recognize that some of the terms included may be in much less common use today than hitherto, but I believe they still remain valid for inclusion.

In all cases where I have been unable to find formal or established definitions (or where a definition might breach established copyright) I have provided my own interpretation, which hopefully represents an accurate meaning for the words or terms used. I would certainly be pleased to hear from anybody who may wish to put forward an alternative inter-pretation in any particular case or indeed to suggest any terms I have omitted that could be usefully added to any future edition. Please e-mail me at LoweDvd@aol.com.

David Lowe
September 2001

List of sources

The following texts were examined in the quest to find as many relevant terms as possible for inclusion in this dictionary:

Aberdeen and Fairhurst Transportation Consultants, *Green Transport* (strategy document), Robert Gordon University

APICS, *Dictionary* (of logistics), 9th edition, 1998

Taylor Barnard, *Technical Terms for the Logistics Industry*, Suffolk

Alan Black, *Urban Mass Transportation Planning*, McGraw-Hill, 1995

Alan E Branch, *Elements of Shipping,* Chapman & Hall, 1996

Alan E Branch, *Export Practice and Management,* Chapman & Hall, 1997

ELA, *Terminology in Logistics*, Brussels, 1994

Paul Fawcett, *Managing Passenger Logistics,* Kogan Page, 2000

B Gunston, *Transport: Problems and Prospects,* Thomas & Hudson, 1972

S Hutcheson, *An Introduction to Air Transport,* National Library of Australia, 1996

ILT, *Glossary of Inventory and Materials Management Definitions*

Key Leasing, *A to Z of Transport and Finance Terminology*

David Lowe, *Dictionary of Transport Terms and Abbreviations,* Headlight, 1991

C A O'Flaherty (editor), *Transport Planning and Traffic Engineering,* Arnold, 1997

Philips, *Terminology for Logistics,* 1988

Plane Sailing Logistics, *A to Z Guide of Terms for the Clothing, Transport, Processing and Forwarding Industry*, Middlesex

Alan Rushton, John Oxley and Phil Croucher, *Handbook of Logistics and Distribution Management,* Kogan Page, 2000

P Shearman, *Air Transport – Strategy Issues in Planning & Development,* Pitman, 1992

J S Stephen, *Transport Strategy and Policy,* Blackwell, 1993

David Steward-David, *The Theory & Practice of Transport,* Heinemann, 1980

R S Tolley and B J Burton, *Transport Systems, Policy and Planning,* Longman, 1995

A T Wells, *Air Transportation – A Management Perspective,* 3rd edn, Wadsworth, 1993

Peter White, *Public Transport,* 3rd edn, UCL Press, 1995

Donald F Wood and James C Johnson, *Contemporary Transportation,* 5th edition, Prentice Hall, 1996

About the author

David Lowe, FCIT, FILT, has been actively involved in the transport industry for almost half a century, acquiring practical 'hands-on' road haulage and logistics experience, a detailed knowledge of UK and EU transport law and a wide understanding of transport issues across all modes. He practised for many years as a transport consultant with many 'blue chip' companies in his portfolio of clients and has addressed transport conferences in Europe, Japan and Southern Africa as well as lecturing extensively at both public seminars and at in-company training sessions. He is the sole author of *The Transport Manager's and Operator's Handbook* (published annually since 1970) and as a freelance writer has written many other books, guides, study manuals and magazine articles, all related to transport and logistics.

A long-standing and active member of both the former Chartered Institute of Transport and Institute of Logistics prior to their merger in 1999 and subsequently in their new guise as the Institute of Logistics and Transport (ILT), he is currently Champion of the Institute's Freight Transport Special Interest Group, a member of the Logistics Safety Forum and of the Institute's Working Party on Sustainable Distribution. He is a Liveryman of the Worshipful Company of Carmen and a Freeman of the City of London.

Aa

A   Nationality symbol for Austria – to be shown on the rear of vehicles from that country.

AA   Automobile Association – motoring organization providing roadside breakdown and other support services.

AA Roadwatch   Service of AA providing road reports, information on traffic delays, etc.

AAIB   Air Accidents Investigation Branch. DTLR* agency that investigates air accidents involving UK registered aircraft in the UK or abroad.

Abandoned vehicle   A motor vehicle that appears to the authorities to have been abandoned and which may subsequently be removed and disposed of under the provisions of the Road Traffic Regulation Acts.

ABC   Activity based costing. Accountancy/planning jargon used in the distribution industry.

ABC analysis   A form of Pareto* analysis applied to a group of products for selective inventory management controls. The inventory value for each item is obtained by multiplying the annual demand by unit cost and the entire inventory is then ranked in descending order of cost. However, the classification parameter can be varied; for example, it is possible to use the velocity of turnover rather than annual demand value. *(Source: ILT Supply-Chain Inventory Management SIG)*

ABC classification   The classification of inventory, after ABC analysis, into three basic groups for the purpose of stock control and planning. Although further divisions may be established, the three basic categories are designated A, B and C as follows:

■ A Items – items that, according to an ABC classification, belong to a small group of products that represent around 75–80 per cent of the annual demand, usage or production volume, in monetary terms, but only some 15–20 per cent of the inventory items. For the purpose of stock control and planning, the greatest attention is paid to this category of A-products. A items may also be of strategic importance to the business concerned.

- B Items – an intermediate group, representing around 5–10 per cent of the annual demand, usage or production value but some 20–25 per cent of the total, which is paid less management attention.
- C Items – products which, according to an ABC classification, belong to the 60-65 per cent of inventory that represents only around 10-15 per cent the annual demand, usage or production value. Least attention is paid to this category for the purpose of stock control and planning and procurement decisions for such items may be automated. *(Source: ILT Supply-Chain Inventory Management SIG)*

ABC curve   ABC analysis whereby, for example, products or product lines can be categorized into A, B and C groupings where A represents fast movers, B = medium movers and C = slow movers. D usually represents obsolete items. Frequently drawn as a graph (or curve). See also Pareto – a system of analysis taking account of the 80/20 rule whereby generally 80 per cent of sales are for only 20 per cent of products.

Abnormal load   A load which cannot, without undue expense or risk of damage, be divided in two or more loads for the purpose of carriage by road and which by virtue of its size and weight cannot be carried on a normal road vehicle under the provisions of the C&U regulations*. Such loads are normally carried on 'Special Types' vehicles under the provisions of the Special Types General Order*.

ABP   Associated British Ports. The UK's leading port business providing port facilities and services to shippers and cargo owners. Owns and operates 22 ports around Great Britain including the major container port of Southampton handling a quarter of the country's sea-borne trade. Owns other businesses as well including Slater's Transport.

ABS   Anti-lock braking system. *See also* Anti-lock braking.

ABTA   Association of British Travel Agents. Association of travel agents, which provides a bonding scheme to guarantee clients' (ie passengers') bookings.

ACAS   Advisory Conciliation and Arbitration Service. Statutory body providing conciliation in trade disputes, also advice to employers/ employees on industrial relations matters, etc.

Access The ability of people (typically public transport users) to get to essential facilities (eg schools, hospitals, shopping and leisure/sport facilities, etc) when necessary by convenient and economical means.

Accessibility The measure of how easy it is to reach a destination, assessed across all modes, with particular emphasis on the use of sustainable transport.

Accident In transport a road traffic accident (RTA*) involving a motor vehicle when the driver must stop and fulfil legal obligations regarding the provision of certain information to other persons and reporting to the police.

Accident book All firms must have one under RIDDOR* in which specified information must be recorded (eg accidents/people employed/ cleaning and painting records).

Accident evaluation The progress of a goods vehicle in terms of speed of travel and distance covered prior to and at the moment of impact in an accident can be accurately determined from its tachograph chart by a scientific process known as accident evaluation – a service provided by specialist firms with the aid of an electronic binocular microscope.

Accompanied vehicle/trailer Driver accompanied vehicle/trailer, usually on cross-Channel ferry service. *See also* Unaccompanied.

Accountant General of the Supreme Court With whom a deposit of securities must be lodged (value £500,000) where, subject to the authority of the Secretary of State for Transport, a firm/organization wishes to carry its own liabilities rather than take out motor insurance.

ACEA *Associations des Constructeurs Européens de l'Automobile.* Europe-wide organization concerned with performance testing of motor vehicles, components and lubricants, etc.

ACFO Association of Car Fleet Operators. Trade association for car rental companies.

ACL (1) The HSE *Approved Carriage List* for dangerous goods carriage.

ACL (2) Automatic chassis lubrication – a system whereby the moving parts of a goods vehicle suspension system, etc are automatically lubricated by oil pumped from a central reservoir.

ACOP/ACoP Approved Code of Practice (ie as typically issued by the HSE on health and safety matters).

ACPO   Association of Chief Police Officers of England, Wales and Northern Ireland. Leading campaigners on traffic enforcement, speed limits, etc.

Act   Common abbreviation for an Act of Parliament*.

Act of God   Any fortuitous act/action that could not have been prevented by any amount of human care and forethought. A term used in insurance and meaning an accident of, or caused by, nature, such as flood, storm, lightning or a combination of freak weather conditions. Many policies do not pay out in such eventualities.

Act of Parliament   Document setting out Parliamentary law following debate and voting on a Bill by both Houses of Parliament (ie the Commons and the Lords) which then receives the Royal Assent. Acts are enabling legislation which detail new law or give relevant government Secretaries of State powers to create subordinate legislation in the form of regulations published in Statutory Instruments or Statutory Orders.

Activa   Model designation for Mercedes medium-weight truck range.

Active inventory   An inventory from which items are currently being drawn or will be drawn within a short space of time.

Activity-based modelling   Concept used to 'test' a variety of alternative activity strategies using varying quantitative information.

Activity mode switch   Component on front of tachograph instrument by which the driver legally indicates his activities (ie driving, other work, break and rest periods) to ensure they are correctly recorded on the tachograph chart.

ACTRAN   Assessment Centre for Transportation NVQs*.

Actros   Model designation for Mercedes heavy-weight truck range.

ACV   Air cushion vehicle (ie a hovercraft).

Ad valorem   A term meaning 'in proportion to the value' and used in customs circles where tax or duties are levied on goods as a percentage of the declared value.

Adaptor gearbox   Component of a tachograph installation that ensures the drive cable from the vehicle gearbox rotates at correct speed to provide accurate indication and recording of speed and distance at the tachograph instrument head.

Added value   Provision of service beyond the basic – what the customer is looking for; ie that something extra above the norm.

ADE   Atlantis Diesel Engine. Produced in South Africa as part of that country's indigenous (ie local content) truck building programme.

ADEEP   Aligned Documents and Electronic Equivalents Project. System for computerization of international trading documents.

ADF   Automotive Distribution Federation. Organization representing manufacturers and distributors of automotive components and products to the aftermarket.

ADI   Approved Driving Instructor (by the Driving Standards Agency – DSA). Only ADIs may provide driving instruction for payment, but this does not apply to instruction for driving HGVs (ie goods vehicles over 7.5 tonnes gvw) – *RTA 1988* s 123.

Adjacent axles   Re closely-spaced, multi-axle bogies, adjacent axles are those near to each other (ie as in a tri-axle bogie the three axles are all adjacent to each other).

Adjoining axles   As above; in closely-spaced, multi-axle bogies, adjoining axles are those immediately next to each other and joined by the suspension units.

ADM   Automatic drive-train management. System developed by Steyr of Austria.

Admission to the occupation   Abbreviation for EC Directive 'On admission to the occupation of road haulage operator in national and international transport operations' – legal requirement for standard operators' licence applicants in the UK to be 'professionally competent'.

ADR (1)   Derived from French title of the 'European Agreement on the International Carriage of Dangerous Goods by Road' which ensures that dangerous goods carried in a road vehicle on an international journey have been suitably packed, are being carried safely and in all other respects conform to the agreement.

ADR (2)   Alternative dispute resolution. Means of resolving disputes over non-payment of monies due.

ADSL   Asymmetric digital subscriber line. Telephone line that enables subscribers to download data at up to 20 times normal speed – uses frequencies 300 times greater than those used to transmit voice and faxes.

Advanced driving test   Advanced level driving test organized and conducted by the Institute of Advanced Motorists (available for car, motorcycle and goods vehicle drivers) and intended to ensure exceptionally high standards of driving competence and road safety.

Advice note   A document that provides details of goods, their consignor and consignee.

AETR   The 'European Agreement Concerning the Work of Crews of Vehicles Engaged in International Road Transport' under which a set of hours rules are applied when drivers travel to or through states which are party to the agreement (other than EU states where the EU rules apply).

AEVR   *Approved requirements for the construction of vehicles intended for the carriage of explosives by road.* HSE publication.

Affreightment   A contract for the carriage of goods by sea for shipment expressed in charter party or bill of lading.

AFRL   Automated First Registration and Licensing System. Computer at DVLA* Swansea dealing with vehicle registrations and providing online facility for motor manufacturers and dealers.

AFT-IFTIM   *Association pour le développement de la Formation professionnelle dans les Transports and Institut de Formation aux Techniques d'implantation et de Manutention.* French road haulage and logistics professional training organization based at Monchy St Eloi, France.

AFV   Alternative fuel vehicle, also known as bi-fuel vehicles*. Vehicles (mainly cars and light vans, currently) designed to run on both conventional unleaded petrol or liquefied petroleum gas (LPG*).

Agency card   A form of credit card (usually supplied by fuel companies) issued to drivers to enable them to draw fuel from retail outlets (ie filling stations) away from base.

Agency driver   A temporary driver hired from staff/employment agency firm (eg Manpower organization) to cover for staff shortages/holidays/illness, etc.

Agent   One who represents a principal, or buys or sells for another. A person who acts for or on behalf of another person or firm, usually under a contractual agreement which sets out and limits the extent to which they are permitted to act on behalf of that other party.

Aggregate inventory management   The size of many inventories requires that they be broken down into groupings for the purpose of control. Aggregated inventory is the further collection of these groupings into a single entity to enable the establishment of operating policies, key performance indicators, targets and reports. Aggregate Inventory Management enables such things as the overall level of inventory desired to be established and then appropriate controls implemented to ensure that individual operating decisions achieve that goal, at optimum cost. *(Source: ILT Supply-Chain Inventory Management SIG)*

Aggregation   A term used to mean combining of goods (or consignments) perhaps into a container or trailer load.

Aggregator   Firms that aggregate individual load demands and 'buy' freight train services to carry them as whole trainloads.

AGR Convention   International convention concerned with route marking – in particular the trans-Europe 'E' route system.

Agricultural machine   Defined in the *Vehicles Excise Act*. Includes tractors (see also land tractor), ploughing engines and such like used in agriculture for haulage-type work between farms and other agricultural land. Reduced rates of VED apply. Also defined in C&U regulations* as an agricultural trailed appliance which is a trailer used off roads for the purposes of agriculture, horticulture or forestry.

AGV   Automated guided vehicle. A load/personnel carrying computer-controlled vehicle that follows an automatic guidance system (invariably laid in the floor) without manual steering or control – usually found in warehouses and large stores.

AICC   Autonomous Intelligent Cruise Control. Part of the European Prometheus* road safety project. *See also* CoPilot.

Aiding and abetting   A phrase usually associated with the aiding and abetting of a crime or offence by another person. In general terms it is an offence to assist or encourage another person to commit an offence.

AIL   Abnormal indivisible load. *See also* Abnormal load.

AIM   Alternative investment market. Public stock market operated by the Stock Exchange for smaller, growing companies, management buy-outs, etc (ie useful source of funds for the smaller business).

Air dryer   Component part of heavy goods vehicle inserted in air brake system to eliminate (ie dry) condensation in air pipes/reservoirs, etc.

Air-lift axle   Retractable (ie lift-up) axle on vehicle/trailer lifted from road surface by means of compressed air to reduce rolling resistance (for fuel economy reasons) and tyre wear.

Air management   Systems added to goods vehicle driver cabs to improve airflow and consequently improve fuel consumption – eg cab-top air deflectors, front air dams, side skirts and cab-to-body collars.

Air pollution   Pollution of the atmosphere (ie the air we breathe) by vehicle exhausts. A comparison of the emission factors between road and rail shows the following general relativity of emissions in grammes per tonne kilometre:

	Road (g/tkm)	Rail (g/tkm)
Carbon dioxide	183.00	30.00
Carbon monoxide	2.08	0.05
Nitrogen oxides	3.86	0.55
Hydrocarbons	3.60	0.07
Sulphur oxides	0.26	0.23
Respirable particles	0.67	0.11

(Source: Railtrack plc, 'A Guide to Railfreight' April 1999)

Air receiver   Correct name for the air storage tank on air compressor in a vehicle workshop/factory, etc. These have to be regularly inspected by an approved engineer under safety legislation.

Air suspension   Heavy vehicle suspension system that relies on compressed air stored in air bags to provide smooth suspension – mainly used on vehicles carrying goods susceptible to damage or on tanker vehicles where vibration may cause damage to tanks/tank mountings (also on luxury coaches to provide greater passenger comfort).

Air tank/reservoir   Storage tank for compressed air used in heavy vehicle air braking systems.

Air/water separator   Term used for anti-spray* equipment on goods vehicle – refers specifically to 'cats whisker' type of nylon bristle which surrounds the mudguard valance to prevent water from spraying out but allows air to pass through.

Air waybill   A form of consignment note used in air freighting. *See also* Waybill.

Airsprung axle/bogie   Axle or set of axles with suspension provided by air bags (*see* Air suspension).

AL   Nationality symbol for Albania – to be shown on the rear of vehicles from that country.

Alcohol problem   Motor vehicle drivers convicted for having an excess of alcohol in their breath/blood may be officially classed as having an 'alcohol problem' if the levels of alcohol found are particularly high or the offence is repeated. Such persons have to prove they no longer have a 'problem' before their driving licence is restored.

Alcolmeter   Equipment used by police to test motor vehicle drivers for excess alcohol in their breath – as with a breathalyzer*.

Alert   *See* Scania Alert.

Aligned documents   Documents used in international trade which are standardized as to size and layout and capable of being produced in a one-run unified set from a single master document for ease of understanding and speed and efficiency of completion.

All risks cover   A form of insurance cover providing protection against 'all risks' as opposed to specified individual risks.

All-time order   The last order for a particular product in the last phase of its life cycle. This order is of such a size that the stock provided will satisfy all expected future demand (see all-time requirement below) for the product concerned. Sometimes known as a life of type order. *(Source: ILT Supply-Chain Inventory Management SIG)*

All-time requirement   The total requirement for a particular product to be expected in the future. Normally used for products in the last phase of their life cycles, when production is (nearly) stopped. *(Source: ILT Supply-Chain Inventory Management SIG)*

All-time stock   The stock resulting from the assessment of an all-time requirement and delivery of an all-time order. If necessary, controls can be set for such stock to avoid consumption of items for reasons over and above those for which usage was predicted. *(Source: ILT Supply-Chain Inventory Management SIG)*

ALLMI   Association of Lorry Loader Manufacturers and Importers. Trade association for such. Publishes code of practice on the application and operation of lorry loaders.

Allocated stock   A part that has been reserved, but not yet withdrawn or issued from stock, and is thus not available for other purposes. *(Source: ILT Supply-Chain Inventory Management SIG)*

Allocation   Term used in connection with distribution planning (eg allocation of orders/consignments to a vehicle or route).

ALREM   Association of Load Restraint Equipment Manufacturers. Trade association for such.

Ambient barrier   Term used in temperature controlled transport operations to refer to the temperature below that of normal air at which point mechanical (or other) means of cooling/chilling is necessary for satisfactory carriage of food, etc.

Ambient temperature   The temperature of the surrounding air.

Amortization lease   A form of financial lease where the full cost of the asset and interest is covered (ie amortized) in the lease payments leaving no residual value to be recovered.

AMT   Air mail transfer. A term used in international trade when a remittance is purchased by a debtor from a banker.

ANA   Article Number Association. An independent non-profit making body which provides standard numbers for all traded goods which are displayed in the form of bar codes.

ANAC   Analysis Centre. An oil analysis service and database operated by French company Elf.

AND   Nationality symbol for Andorra – to be shown on the rear of vehicles from that country.

ANF   Arrival notification form – advice to consignee of goods coming forward.

Animo   Code name for Europe-wide computer database on live animal movements.

Annual testing 1 (goods vehicle)   A scheme for testing goods vehicles over 3,500 kg gvw, articulated vehicles and certain goods-carrying trailers annually from the anniversary date of first registration at Goods Vehicle Test Stations. On passing a 'test certificate' is issued which must be produced when applying for vehicle excise licences and at the request of police and enforcement authorities.

Annual testing 2 (passenger vehicles)   Passenger vehicles are subject to annual testing in much the same way as goods vehicles described above, the actual requirements depending on the classification of the vehicle. Basically, passenger vehicles seating not more than eight persons fall within scope of the Class IV 'MOT' test conducted at approved garages displaying the white triangular symbol on a blue background or at designated Council garages. This test requires a first examination after three years and then annually thereafter. Passenger vehicles seating not more than 13 persons which are not PSVs* are also subject to this test except that the first such test is required after the first anniversary of the date of original registration. Passenger vehicles with more than 12 seats and those used as works buses and permit minibuses which are non-PSVs, and PSVs with no Certificate of Initial Fitness (CoIF*) such as Community buses and certain school buses are tested after the first year and then annually either at approved council workshops or at DTLR* heavy goods vehicle testing stations. Other PSVs with more than eight seats are tested annually at DTLR heavy goods vehicle test stations or at approved council workshops.

Anti-jack knife/device   A device fitted to articulated vehicles to prevent jack-knifing whereby the tractive unit and semi-trailer hinge in the middle causing the semi-trailer to push the towing unit round in a circular movement out of control. Such devices may be designed to lock the tractive unit and trailer in the straight-ahead position but more commonly prevent the tractive unit rear wheels from locking under braking, which is a fundamental cause of jack-knifing accidents.

Anti-lock braking (ABS)   Anti-lock braking system. A safety system by which vehicle brakes are prevented from locking the road wheels thereby preventing skidding. Works by rapidly applying and releasing brakes so as to prevent wheel lock-up, which would induce a skid.

Anti-spray   A system employed on heavy vehicles to prevent excessive spray being thrown up from the wheels in wet weather conditions. *See also* BS AU 200 and Air/water separator.

Anti-theft device/alarm   Equipment fitted to vehicle to prevent unlawful interference and theft of it or its contents.

Anticipation stock   Inventory held in order to be able to satisfy a demand with seasonal fluctuations with a production level that does not fluctuate at all or that varies to a lesser extent than the demand; or to cope with erratic production or deficiencies in production capacity. *(Source: ILT Supply-Chain Inventory Management SIG)*

AOL   Auto-Oil Programme*.

AORTL   Association of Road Transport Lawyers. Specialist lawyers dealing with road transport/traffic law cases.

APA   Accreditation of Prior Achievement. A method of obtaining a qualification by demonstrating previously acquired qualifications and experience – as used by the CIT* for experienced candidates seeking its Diploma in Transport. *See also* APEL.

APEL   Accreditation of Prior Experiential Learning. Qualification relating to past experience. *See also* APA.

API   American Petroleum Institute.

Approval mark   Mainly referring to European Type Approval marks whereby vehicle components are marked to show they meet established standards (eg the 'E' mark).

Approved list   Under legislation controlling the carriage of dangerous goods* by road, the relevant 'dangerous goods' are identified in Approved Lists published by the Health and Safety Executive (HSE*).

Approved workshop/fitter   A workshop or fitter approved by VI* to test, repair, calibrate (*see* Calibration) and fit tachograph equipment to vehicles. It is illegal for any other workshop or person to undertake such work. Approved workshops must be quality approved to BS 5750/ISO 9000*.

APPS   Approved personal pension scheme. A pension scheme taken out by a self-employed person – available also to employed persons in certain circumstances and subject to laid-down conditions.

APR   Adjustable pallet racking. Pallet rack with beams adjustable for height on side frames usually in increments of 75 mm.

APS   Advanced Planning System. Computer software package that views the whole supply chain and allows decisions to be made on a chain-wide basis rather than on a restricted, local basis.

APT   After peak tank. Tank on ship for carrying fuel, water, etc located in stern of vessel. Usually forms aft-most watertight bulkhead.

Aqueduct   Bridge carrying water (usually a canal). Best known in the UK is the Pontcysyllte Aqueduct in north Wales (306 metres long).

Arbitration   A widely employed means of settling disputes via an arbitrator, ie an independent person or authority (eg an advocate or judge) whose final decision is usually binding on the parties concerned.

Archiving service   New concept whereby logistics operators provide customers with secure storage and recovery services for archived documentation.

Armitage Report   A report published by the DoT (now DTLR*) in 1980 entitled *'Report of the Inquiry into Lorries, People and the Environment'* based on the work of a committee headed by Sir Arthur Armitage which recommended increased lorry weights for the UK.

Artic   Colloquialism for an articulated vehicle.

Articulated vehicle   A goods vehicle comprising a powered tractive unit (ie the drawing vehicle) and a semi-trailer superimposed upon it in such a way that when the trailer is uniformly loaded, not less than 20 per cent of the weight of the load is borne by the tractive unit. Certain buses and coaches are also articulated where they are in two parts (ie hinged) and where the passenger can pass from one part to the other.

Articulation   The function whereby two parts of a vehicle are flexibly joined to provide a more manoeuvrable whole. *See also* Bendibus.

ARTM   *Approved requirements and test methods for the classification and packaging of dangerous goods for carriage*. HSE publication.

As and Ds   *'Applications and Decisions'* – booklet produced fortnightly by the Traffic Area* offices detailing applications to the Traffic Commissioners* for new and varied 'O' licences* plus results of the TCs' decisions on applications (and disciplinary proceedings) – source of information for bodies which have statutory rights of objection to licence applications.

ASA   Air service agreement. A reciprocal (bilateral) agreement between two countries governing air traffic rights (eg the frequency and capacity of services, fare and tariff agreements, etc).

ASCII   American standard code for information interchange (ie via computer).

ASR   Anti-skid technology. Product of Mercedes-Benz on its 'Actros' range of disc-braked heavy trucks fitted with the 'Telligent'* braking system.

AS/RS   Automated storage and retrieval system. System used in auto-mated warehouses, usually computer controlled handling systems – may be carousels, cranes or AGVs*.

Assembly   Term used in distribution in connection with load assembly (ie compiling a number of individual consignments into a full vehicle/container load).

Asset-based   Term often used in logistics where a firm is expanding its operations by buying other established businesses (ie buying the assets) as opposed to forming strategic alliances*.

Associate company   In 'O' licensing*, a company where the parent/holding company has an equity holding no greater than 50 per cent and therefore is not a subsidiary company* for these purposes. Vehicles specified on the restricted 'O' licence of a parent/holding company cannot carry goods for the business of an associate company, and those on the 'O' licence of an associate company may not legally carry goods for the business of the parent/holding company or any of its subsidiaries.

ATA   American Trucking Association. Virtual equivalent of our Road Haulage Association.

ATA carnet   A Customs carnet (ie clearance document) used in inter-national transport operations for the purposes of allowing goods to be temporarily imported into a country (eg for exhibition purposes) without payment of, or deposits against, import duties. Obtainable from Chambers of Commerce.

ATC (1)   Technical Committee of Petroleum Additive Manufacturers in Europe (Belgium).

ATC (2)   Air Traffic Control.

ATCC   Air Traffic Control Centre.

ATCO   Association of Transport Co-ordinating Officers. Brings together Local Authority transport officers.

ATIEL   *Association Technique de l'Industrie Européenne des Lubrifiants.*

Athens Convention   An international convention governing carrier's liability for passengers and their baggage when carried by air.

ATOC   Association of Train Operating Companies. Set up in 1994 by Britain's privatized passenger train companies. The Association's aim is to support and represent these companies and provide membership services. The train companies were, on formation, Anglia; Cardiff Railway; Central Trains; Chiltern; Connex South Central; Connex South Eastern; Gatwick Express; Great Eastern; Great North Eastern; Great Western; Island Line; LTS Rail; Merseyside Electrics; Midland Main Line; North Western Trains; Northern Spirit; Scotrail; Silverlink; South West Trains; Thameslink; Thames Trains; Virgin Trains; Wales & West; and West Anglia Great Northern.

ATP (1)   From French title: European Agreement on the International Carriage of Perishable Foodstuffs to which the UK is a signatory. It sets specified temperature conditions and standards of thermal efficiency for the movement of prescribed perishable foodstuffs on international journeys. Not currently applicable for UK domestic transport of such foods.

ATP (2)   Automatic Train Protection. A system to prevent trains passing signals at danger (ie red signals). *See also* TPWS, SPAD and ERTMS.

ATR   *Approved tank requirements* – ie for dangerous goods carriage. HSE publication.

Attendance at work   Term used to describe the activity of goods vehicle driver (and shown on his tachograph chart*) as being work for his employer other than driving.

Attendant   Extra person required to be carried when vehicles/loads exceed certain dimensions. When three or more such vehicle/loads travel in convoy, attendants are required on the first and last vehicles only. *See also* Statutory attendant – *RV (C&U) 1986.*

Audible warning instrument   An instrument required on a motor vehicle, other than a bell, gong or siren, and capable of giving audible and sufficient warning of the approach or position of the vehicle. Also includes reversing alarms* which are devices intended to warn persons that a vehicle is reversing or is about to reverse.

Audited accounts   The (annual) accounts of a business which have been examined and approved by an 'auditor'. In the case of limited liability companies such accounts are required by law (see Registrar of Companies) and must have been prepared by an independent 'chartered' (ie professional) accountant.

Auditor   A person/accounting firm who officially audits company accounts in accordance with legal requirements – must be a 'chartered' accountant.

Authorized examiner   Under *RTA 1988* s67 a person who is: a certifying officer or PSV examiner; appointed as an examiner under the *RTA 1988*; appointed to inspect public carriages (ie hackney carriages); appointed by the Secretary of State for Transport*; a constable appointed to act by or under the instruction of a chief officer of police; appointed by the police authority for a police area to act as such. Authorized examiners may test a motor vehicle on a road, including driving it where necessary, to ensure the law is complied with in regard to brakes, silencers, steering, tyres, lights, reflectors, and the emission of smoke, fumes, vapour and noise.

Authorized vehicles   The maximum number of vehicles (ie over 3.5 tonnes gvw) which may be operated under an 'O' licence. This is the total number authorized by the Traffic Commissioner* and must not be exceeded (see also 'specified vehicles' and 'margin').

Auto/Oil   European Commission programme aiming to reduce the five most harmful emissions from vehicle exhausts, ie particulate matter – volatile organic compounds (VOCs*), black smoke, carbon monoxide (CO)*, nitrogen dioxide and nitric oxide (NOx)*.

Auto-reverse brakes   On light trailers with overrun brakes*, a system which allows the driver to reverse vehicle by overriding the overrun mechanism without leaving his seat (ie provides instant reverse facility which is otherwise not possible). Legally required on new trailers since 1 April 1989.

Autoguide   New technology which provides drivers with recommended routes to their destination via vehicle-mounted display prompted by roadside beacons which transmit advice data from a central computer – pilot scheme introduced in London in 1990.

Automated store ordering   Process where store replenishment orders are generated automatically, based on data capture of sales, stocks and deliveries due.

Automated warehouse/order picking   Type of warehousing whereby stocking and order picking is carried out by remote (ie computer) controlled handling equipment – often operated totally without human intervention and without lighting.

Automatic coupling   Type of coupling for articulated vehicles (no longer in widespread use) whereby the action of reversing the tractive unit under the semi-trailer results in automatic raising of the landing gear and release of the trailer brakes to provide swift coupling and uncoupling without the driver leaving the vehicle cab.

Automatic tachograph A tachograph instrument which automatically records driving mode on a chart when the vehicle is moving – saves driver having to turn the activity mode switch* to 'drive mode' every time he starts to drive the vehicle.

Auto-Oil Programme (AOL) An EU-inspired programme for setting fuel quality and vehicle emission standards with the specific intention of reducing pollution from road traffic by 2010, and generally the environmental impact of transport.

Autoroute Plus Computer software program comprising a road network database with at least 33,000 place names and 67,000 miles of road identified.

Availability The primary measure of system performance relating to the expected percentage of the supported system that will be available at a random point in time and not out of service for lack of spares. *(Source: ILT Supply-Chain Inventory Management SIG)*

Available stock The stock available to service immediate demand. *(Source: ILT Supply-Chain Inventory Management SIG)*

Available to promise (ATP) The uncommitted portion of a company's inventory and planned production, maintained in the master schedule to support customer order promising. The ATP quantity is the uncommitted inventory balance in the first period and is normally calculated for each period in which an MPS receipt is scheduled. In the first period, ATP includes on-hand inventory less customer orders that are due and overdue. *(Source: ILT Supply-Chain Inventory Management SIG)*

AVC Additional voluntary contribution. Term used in regard to pension arrangements. *See also* FSAVC.

Average Term used in shipping and insurance in connection with the apportionment of loss or damage to goods or vehicles/vessels (eg apportionment of loss between joint owners or insurers).

Average bond A bond in which cargo owners agree to pay their share in the general average losses, each individual contribution being determined by the average/loss adjuster.

Average deposit Shipping term where a cash security is deposited by the consignee pending an assessment of the general average contribution.

Avionics Electronics used in aviation (flight instruments and navigation aids, etc).

AVL   Automatic vehicle location. System that monitors a vehicle's position and state (eg loaded/empty). *See also* AVM.

AVM   Automatic vehicle monitoring. *See also* AVL.

AVR   *Approved Vehicle Requirements* – ie for dangerous goods carriage. HSE* publication.

AWLREM   Association of Webbing Load Restraint Equipment Manufacturers. Trade association for manufacturers concerned with standards and safety aspects.

Axial   Leading name in UK and European new car delivery. Currently (2001) part of Tibbett & Britten Group and formed by merger of former key players Toleman and Silcock Express.

Axle interspace   Legally specified minimum ground clearances for trailers. The distance from point of support on the tractive unit in the case of semi-trailers, or the centre line of the front axle in the case of other trailers, to the centre line of the rear axle or the centre point between the rear axles if more than one.

Axle load indicator   A built-in device for indicating the weight of the load borne by a goods vehicle axle – intended to help prevent axle overloading.

Axle spread   Distance between the centre lines of the outermost axles (ie the foremost and rearmost axles) on a goods vehicle (see also relevant axle spacing).

Axle weight   Sum of the weights transmitted to the road surface by all the wheels of a vehicle axle.

Axle weight calculation   Theoretical exercise (used mainly in CPC* examinations) to determine the weight on an axle when other given weights are known. Formula (P x D)/W applies when P = vehicle payload, D = the distance from the load centreline to the axle and W = the vehicle wheelbase.

Bb

B Nationality symbol for Belgium – to be shown on the rear of vehicles from that country.

B2B Business-to-business. Trading jargon in e-commerce.

B2C Business-to-consumer. Trading jargon in e-commerce.

BA British Airways. Britain's national airline.

BAA British Airports Authority. Operator of Heathrow and other UK airports.

BACAT Barge-aboard-catamaran.

Back haul (or load) An alternative term for return loading, a back load or return load. A load arranged to fill empty capacity on a vehicle on return from an outward loaded journey – often at an inferior haulage rate, or at cost.

Back order A previously unfulfilled order that is carried forward for fulfilment when stocks of the item become available.

Backflushing The deduction from inventory, after manufacture, of the component parts used in a parent part by exploding the bill of materials by the production total of parents produced. *(Source: ILT Supply-Chain Inventory Management SIG)*

Backlog Usually meaning a list of previous orders to be fulfilled or tasks to be completed when stocks are available or the facilities/equipment/labour is in place to finish the job.

BAF Bunker adjustment factor. An adjustment factor incorporated in shipping costs to reflect the current cost of bunkering (ie refuelling the ship).

Bail bond Necessary when taking a vehicle to Spain in case it is impounded and the driver held by police following a road traffic accident or incident. The bond (normally valued at £1,500 and obtainable from vehicle insurers and motoring organizations in UK) secures release.

Bailment   Legal term in freighting which refers to the holding of goods until charges are paid (see also lien – the right to hold goods). The holder of the goods is the 'bailer'.

Balance of trade   A financial statement indicating the balance of a country's visible trade exports and imports.

Balance sheet   Annually (usually) prepared statement showing assets and liabilities of a business at the year-end. The 'bottom line' figure indicates the 'worth' of the business. Under company law a balance sheet must be prepared for the shareholders of a limited liability company. A copy must also be sent to the Registrar of Companies* (along with other financial information).

Balloon lease   Form of financial lease* whereby a large payment is made either at the beginning or the end of the lease period, usually with the intention of reducing the interim monthly or quarterly repayments.

Baltic Exchange   London-based organization (founded in the 18th century) that trades in shipping (ie bulk cargo chartering).

Band 3 radio   Radio channels operating on the old 405-line black and white television VHF wavelength. Available for mobile communication between a base station and mobile unit for brief messages only. Currently operated by two official franchise holders, GEC and Band Three Radio, each with 200 channels. Although limited in use it is cheaper to operate than the cell-phone system.

Banker's/bank draft   Form of cheque provided by a bank which guarantees payment because the funds have already been taken from the payee's account (ie the most secure form of payment next to cash).

Bankruptcy   When a person/business cannot meet its liabilities a court may rule them to be 'bankrupt' in which case all their assets are seized and disposed of to pay off creditors.

BAR   British Association of Removers. Trade association for furniture removal firms.

Bar coding   Numerically-based system for storing information about an item (price, location, minimum stock level, etc). Shown on item in form of a bar code which can be electronically read when passed across a scanner.

Barge   Freight-carrying craft/vessel used on inland waterways.

Barriers (ie removal of)   In connection with the Single European Market* and '1992' – the removal of barriers to trade and to the movement of people, goods, capital and services between the member states of the European Union.

Base rate (bank)   A minimum level of interest chargeable on loans and overdrafts, etc. Set by the Bank of England (ie minimum base lending rate).

BASEEFA   British Approvals Service for Electrical Equipment in Flammable Atmospheres. Standards approval and certification body. In transport, deals with electrical wiring standards for dangerous goods road tanker vehicles.

Batch number   A code used to identify the specific production point, for a product or an assembly, in a manufacturing or assembly process. *(Source: ILT Supply-Chain Inventory Management SIG)*

BATNIEC   Best available technology not involving excessive costs (also known as BATNEEC – Best available technology not entailing excessive costs). A series of 'green' solutions the cumulative effect of which leads to reduced costs.

Battery vehicle   Vehicle powered by batteries (ie electric vehicle).

BDI   Both days included. Term used in ship chartering, etc.

Beacons (ie rotating/flashing lamps)   Defined in *RVLR 1989* as 'Warning beacon – a lamp that is capable of emitting a flashing or rotating beam of light throughout 360 degrees in the horizontal plane'. Usually roof mounted on vehicles carrying wide or abnormal loads, breakdown vehicles, gulley emptiers, etc.

Bead   Inner rim of vehicle tyre which sits on/in wheel rim. Made of steel, covered with rubber compound and to which the ply cords are moulded.

BEN   Motor and Allied Trades Benevolent Fund. Charitable organization within the motor industries.

Benchmarking   A system of establishing standards or best practice (or comparing standards from other firms or industries) against which future operations are measured (ie against the benchmark). In transport such standards may relate to fuel consumption, reductions in empty vehicle running and improving load capacity.

Bendibus   Populist name for an articulated bus*. Many seen in European cities.

Berne Gauge   European standard rail loading gauge (not to be confused with track gauge).

Beyond economic repair (BER)   Where the projected cost of repair, normally for a repairable or rotable* item, exceeds a management-set percentage of the replacement value of the item concerned. *(Source: ILT Supply-Chain Inventory Management SIG)*

BG   Nationality symbol for Bulgaria – to be shown on the rear of vehicles from that country.

Bhp   Brake horse power. Imperial measure of the output of an engine in horsepower. *See also* DIN.

Bias belted   Vehicle tyre constructed so that the ply cords are laid at alternate angles (of less than 90 degrees) and overlaid with a circumferential belt of at least two layers of inextensible cord also at alternate, but smaller, angles. Like diagonal ply tyre*.

Bibendum   Name given to the Michelin Man*, logo for the Michelin tyre company. He was 100 years old in 1998. Bibendum is a Latin word that means 'let's drink' as in *'Nunc est bibendum'*, 'Now for the drinks'. Not very appropriate in the driving or transport context!

BIFA   British International Freight Association (previously Institute of Freight Forwarders). Trade association for freight industry and particularly freight forwarding firms.

Bi-fuel vehicle   Vehicles (mainly cars and light vans, currently) designed to run on both conventional unleaded petrol or liquefied petroleum gas (LPG*). Also known as alternative fuel vehicles (AFV*).

Bi-lateral agreement   A treaty between two national states (eg on road haulage movements). *See also* Multi-lateral agreement.

Bi-lateral permit   Road haulage permit* authorizing goods vehicle to enter or transit a foreign state with which the country of its registration has negotiated such rights – obtainable from International Road Freight Office*.

Bilateralism   Trading activities between two countries.

Bill (1)   Popular terminology for an invoice or request for payment ('Can I have the bill please?')

Bill (2)   A Parliamentary Bill containing government proposals for a new law, usually following on from publication of one or more consultation Green* and White* papers. A Bill is debated and voted on in both the House of Commons and the House of Lords and is often subject to considerable change before being finally passed, receiving the Royal Assent and becoming an Act of Parliament*.

Bill of exchange   A written request from a creditor to a debtor ordering the debtor to pay a specified sum to a specified person or bearer at a certain date.

Bill of lading   Legal document of title. In other words, a receipt for goods shipped by sea. It is signed by the representative of the shipping line (or his agent) that contracts to carry them, and states the terms on which the goods are carried.

Bill of material   A listing of components, parts and other items needed to manufacture a product, showing the quantity of each required to produce each end item. A bill of material is similar to a parts list except that it usually shows how the product is fabricated and assembled. Also called a product structure record, formula, recipe, or ingredients list. *(Source: ILT Supply-Chain Inventory Management SIG)*

Bill of sight   Customs import form that is used when an importer cannot complete the Customs requirements due to a lack of information from the shipper.

BIM   British Institute of Management. Professional body for managers concerned with the study and application of management techniques in business and industry.

BIMCO   Baltic and International Maritime Council. A Copenhagen-based organization to which many ship owners belong that represents their interests and assists by preparing standard charter parties and other shipping documents and providing other advisory services.

Bi-modal   A vehicle that can use two forms of transport, eg road and rail. Bi-modal trailers are usually equipped with both road wheels and facilities to mount on a rail bogie for long-haul trunking by rail.

Bi-modal trailer   Specialized road semi-trailer which converts into a rail wagon for rail transit. On the road the trailer runs on its own wheel and tyre bogie, but when connected to rail it rests on special rail bogies at each end with the road-wheel bogie retracted. These trailers are strengthened to withstand the forces generated in rail shunting.

Bi-modal transport   The carriage of goods by two separate modes of transport, usually road and rail. Certain special trailers have retractable running gear and actually ride on rail bogies for long-haul rail journeys.

BITA   British Industrial Truck Association. Trade organization that sets construction and safety standards for industrial trucks built by members.

Black box   Electronic device which provides similar functions to tachograph* (ie recording time, speed, etc) plus other facilities. Has storage capacity and can be downloaded to computer. *See also* ICS Black Box.

Block changing   Term used to describe the action of gear changing in a multi-ratio gearbox on a heavy vehicle when one or more intermediate gears are omitted in the upward or downward gear-changing process (also sometimes referred to as skip changing). This practice depends on the vehicle load and the road gradient and requires intelligent application by the driver (it is not intended as a shortcut for the lazy driver). When properly adopted it reduces fuel consumption, wear and tear on the vehicle transmission and on the driver himself (bearing in mind the many hundreds of gear changes that a driver may make during a day).

Block stacking   Simple stacking without racks, pallets are stored directly on the floor. Usually stored up to three pallets high depending upon load stackability and crush factors. Each row must only contain one product code.

Block train   A constantly-linked train of wagons usually running on a merry-go-round* system. Also a freightliner train that carries ISO containers* between sea ports and inland terminals.

Blood alcohol limit   Statutory maximum limit for the alcohol content of blood of motor vehicle drivers above which (ie 80 mg alcohol per 100 ml blood) an offence is committed.

Blower   Cargo discharge pump on tanker/tipper type bulk-carrying vehicle or for the super/turbocharger mounted on an engine to increase power output. *See also* Turbocharger.

Blue book   Freight industry (particularly shipping) term for Department of Trade and Industry publication, *The Carriage of Dangerous Goods in Ships*. Contains information about the classification, methods of packing and freighting of dangerous goods (including road freighting where sea/ferry crossings are involved).

Blue tooth   Latest technology that permits items of electronic equipment to communicate with each other without connection by wire (it uses infra-red technology).

BNRR   Birmingham Northern Relief Road. Projected (and much needed) £1.8 billion road project to be constructed under the government's DBFO* initiative. Subject to significant criticism by the anti-road building campaign and others.

BOC   British Oxygen Company – commercial firm with major interests in supplying gases for industrial use (eg oxygen and acetylene to vehicle workshops) and in road haulage (eg temperature-controlled transport and contract distribution).

Bogie   A number of wheels or axles mounted on a pivotal sub-frame (eg on a rail locomotive or on aircraft landing gear, or a set of suspension-linked wheels/axles for a road vehicle/trailer. *See also* Tandem and Tri-axles bogie.

Bolero   As in www.bolero.net. Web site created by world's leading banking and logistics communities to transfer world trade on to the Internet. The system allows importers, exporters, banks, Customs and shippers to 'talk' to each other seamlessly and for documents and data to be exchanged online between all parties in the trade chain.

BOM   Bill of materials. Term used in manufacturing logistics.

Bond   Form of guarantee made to customs for specified amount of duty to be paid.

Bond Line   The point (ie line) in a bonded warehouse* beyond which customs duties become payable.

Bonded warehouse   Warehouse where goods are stored under Customs control and released only on payment of any duties due.

Bonnet (truck)   Term for engine cover. A bonneted truck has the engine ahead of the driver (eg American style, called normal control) as opposed to common European design of being under the driver (called forward control) and where the engine cover (ie bonnet) is inside the cab.

BOO   Build, own and operate. A strategy used in, for example, the development of distribution centres whereby the developer buys the land, builds the facility and then operates it.

BOTB   British Overseas Trade Board.

Box   Common parlance for an ISO-type container.

BPR   Business process re-engineering. Modern jargon for reshaping the business to meet current and future demands, or being 'done over' by consultants.

Bracket tariff   In EU member states where tariffs used to be applied to road haulage rates the bracket is the spread between the upper and lower tariff limits.

BRAKE   An independent road safety organization working to prevent death and injury on the road and to support traumatized road accident victims and their families.

Brake fade   A phenomenon whereby brake linings and drums (discs even) overheat under constant (heavy) use on long or steep downhill gradients and gradually lose performance. Can be overcome by the use of retarders, exhaust brakes, etc.

Braking efficiency   Legal minimum standard for the efficiency of vehicle braking systems as set out in the C&U regulations*. Also measure of the efficiency of a vehicle braking system usually established on a rolling road (ie roller brake tester) and shown as a percentage figure.

BRB   British Railways Board. Responsible for non-operational railway land (through British Rail Property Ltd). Also responsible for British Transport Police. British Rail was divested of all its railway operating functions by 1977 under the *Railway Act 1933*. Now encompassed within the Strategic Rail Authority (SRA*).

BRC   British Retail Consortium. Trade association for major retailers. Concerned with logistics as well as all other relevant issues.

Break bulk   Breaking down of bulk consignment (eg from a trailer or container) into individual consignments for delivery.

Break-bulk cargo   Freight shipped loose in the vessel's hold (ie not in a container).

Break-bulk ship   A vessel built to carry non-containerized cargo such as loose pallet-loads, crates, etc.

Break-even chart   Used in accounting and financial calculations for illustrating when, for example, income/revenue crosses the point of maximum costs so it is possible to see when costs have been fully recovered (ie the 'break-even point').

Breath alcohol limit   Statutory maximum limit (ie 35 mg alcohol in 100 ml of breath) for the alcohol content of the breath of motor vehicle drivers above which an offence is committed. *See also* Breathalyzer and Blood alcohol limit.

Breathalyzer   Means by which the police test motor vehicle drivers for excess breath alcohol levels (*see* Breath alcohol limit, above). On the roadside this is done with a breathalyzer bag or instrument and is later confirmed at a police station by use of a Lion intoximeter*.

BRF   British Road Federation. Body concerned with the condition and development of the UK road system. It issues regular reports on matters relating to road building and road use statistics for example. *NB:* The BRF closed shop in April 2001 after nearly 70 years of lobbying for better roads.

Bridge plate   Metal plate laid across gap between loading bay and vehicle to allow fork lift trucks*/pallet trucks* to load/unload.

Bridleway   A 'way', or path, over which the public have rights but only on foot, leading a horse or on horseback and to drive animals along the way.

Brit-disc   Proposed British equivalent for the Eurovignette*. A means of charging foreign road hauliers for the use of UK roads. Thought to be necessary because of the lower rates of VED* paid abroad.

British domestic hours rules   The rules applicable to EU-exempt road transport operations in the UK as contained in the *TA 1968* as amended.

Broken stowage   Space wasted in a ship's hold due to irregular-sized/ shaped consignments. Same applies when stowing ISO containers*.

Broker (ie freight broker)   Intermediary between consignors of freight and carriers (eg road hauliers). More commonly referred to in the UK as clearing houses*.

BRS   Formerly British Road Services, state-owned road haulage operator, part of National Freight Corporation/Consortium (NFC*), etc. Now truck rental arm of Volvo trucks with over 300 vehicles at 40 depots.

Brussels   Capital of Belgium. Heart of the European Union and home to the European Commission from which much of our current legislation emanates.

BS   British Standard. Standards determined by the British Standards Institution (see also BSI). Each standard has an individual identifying reference number prefixed by 'BS' (see below).

BS 5750   British Standard for quality approval – applied for and granted to firms which meet the British Standard (ie BS 5750) for the quality of their administration and services under the Registered Firms scheme. *See also* ISO 9000, which superseded BS 5750 in 1994.

BS (AU 141a)   British Standard applied to smoke emissions from heavy vehicles in accordance with legal requirements (ie *RV (C&U) 1986*).

BS (AU 200)   British Standard applied to anti-spray (ie spray suppression) devices fitted to heavy goods vehicle in compliance with legal requirements (ie *RV (C&U) 1986*).

BSC   British Shippers' Council.

BSI (British Standards Institution)   National body in UK which sets and approves standards (see above) and runs its Kitemark, Safety Mark and Registered Firms schemes.

BST   British summer time. Period during 'summer' months (March to October) when clocks are advanced one hour ahead of Greenwich Mean Time (GMT) to provide extra daylight hours.

BTA   British Tourist Authority. Works to promote an attractive image of Britain. Provides impartial tourism information and gathers essential market intelligence for the UK tourism industry.

BTAC   Breweries' Transport Advisory Committee. A committee comprising brewery transport managers and fleet engineers who meet regularly (and hold symposia) to discuss key issues.

BTC   British Transport Commission. Created by the *Transport Act 1947* to own and operate the railways and canals and some docks, road haulage (other than local journey operations), bus and coach services and London Transport. Proved to be unmanageable and was wound up by the *Transport Act 1962*, its assets being transferred to the British Railways Board (BRB), the London Transport Board, the British Docks Board and the British Waterways Board. Road haulage and bus services were transferred to a new Transport Holding Company (THC*).

BTRA   British Truck Racing Association. Body controlling truck racing in the UK.

Budgetary control   Financial planning device for controlling expenditure within pre-set limits (ie the budget).

Buffer stock   *See* Safety stock.

BUG   Bike Users Group. Group comprising individual cyclists and/or motorcyclists (often regular commuters by these modes) who get together to comment and lobby on relevant issues.

Builders' skips   Metal bins used for carrying rubble/rubbish and such like and capable of being lifted on/off road vehicles by means of hydraulic arms – usually available for hire.

Bulk   Term used in connection with the carriage of goods in bulk – ie without individual packagings.

Bulk unitization   Means by which multiple packages or items are consolidated into a single-load device.

Bullet train   Japan's famous high-speed (180 mph) train, more properly known as the Shinkansen, which runs between Tokyo and Osaka (320 miles).

Bumper   Part of vehicle, mounted to protect front of cab/bodywork from impact damage also at rear on certain heavy vehicles as required by law (ie rear underrun protection*).

Bund wall   An inner protective lining.

Bunded tank   A tank with an inner liner to safeguard against leakage in the event of puncturing.

Bunker   A fuel tank on a ship. Also a verb to describe the process of refuelling a ship.

Bunkering   Shipping term for refuelling also applied to the refuelling of road vehicles.

Bus   Legally defined as a vehicle constructed or adapted to carry more than eight seated passengers in addition to the driver.

Bus and rail groups   The major UK bus and rail groups are: Arriva, FirstGroup, Go-Ahead, National Express, Prism, Stagecoach and Yorkshire Traction.

Bus lane   Area of public road marked and restricted for use normally only by buses (but may also be used by taxis and pedal cyclists) during the times of operation as indicated on nearby signs.

Business name   Name (other than that of the proprietor or partners) used by a person/firm (not a limited liability company) for trading purposes (eg International Truckers). It must be shown on business premises and documents together with the names of the proprietors so that customers and others know with whom they are dealing.

BV   Bureau Veritas. A French industrial and shipping classification society.

BVRLA   British Vehicle Rental and Leasing Association. Trade association for vehicle rental and leasing firms.

BW   British Waterways. Responsible for Britain's inland waterways. Carries over 3 million tonnes of freight annually.

Cc

C88   Official designation code for the Single Administrative Document (SAD*) used for Customs entry of relevant data.

C&U   *Road Vehicles (Construction and Use) Regulations 1986,* as amended. UK Regulations which govern the construction and use of all road vehicles from invalid carriages and pedestrian-controlled mowers to maximum weight articulated goods vehicles.

CAA   Civil Aviation Authority. DTLR's* Aviation Directorate controlling and licensing aviation in the UK.

Cab (1)   Abbreviated term for the driver's compartment of a lorry (ie cabin).

Cab (2)   Colloquial term for a taxi (ie hackney carriage that can be hailed in the street).

CAB (3)   Citizen's Advice Bureau. From where useful legal information can be obtained (on working conditions and employments terms, etc).

CABAF   Currency and bunker adjustment factor. Shipping term meaning a combination of CAF (currency adjustment factor) and BAF (bunker adjustment factor).

Cable car   Passenger-carrying vehicle carried on a suspended cableway, usually up a mountain. Commonly seen in ski resorts. One of the most famous is that taking visitors to the top of Table Mountain in South Africa.

Cabotage   The act of picking up and delivering goods in one country by a vehicle registered in another country. At one time totally illegal but now permitted within the EU. Also applies to European passenger road transport (with limitations) and to air transport.

Cabover   Term for North American-style heavy truck with driver's cab mounted over the engine (as mainly in UK and Europe). *See also* Conventional and Bonnet.

CAC Central Arbitration Committee. Arbitration body that deals with wage/pay disputes and assists in collective bargaining.

CAD (1) Computer aided design. Use of computer software to produce designs and repetitive plans/drawings (eg in motor vehicle design).

CAD (2) Cash against documents. Term used in shipping.

CAF Currency adjustment factor. An adjustment factor to reflect currency exchange fluctuations.

Caisse mobile French name for swap body* built to standard dimensions for intermodal freighting.

Calibration The task of correlating the accuracy within which a piece of equipment operates, ie to a pre-determined standard. In transport, the calibration of tachograph installations (ie following installation in vehicles and repair and at six-yearly intervals) to ensure that the operation of the instrument and the recordings made conform to legal requirements; the measurement of tank capacities for road tanker vehicles; the measurement of bulk-carrying vehicle bodies.

CAN Customs assigned number.

CAN-bus Controlled area network databus. A control system for electronics which, in heavy truck technology terms, replaces conventional wiring systems and allows such as engine performance data (fuel consumption, temperatures and operating hours, etc) to be displayed, recorded and downloaded – Volvo calls its system 'TEA' (Truck electronic architecture); Mercedes-Benz calls its system 'Telligent'*.

Canal Manmade inland waterway. In the UK BW* manages and conserves 3,200 km of canals and inland waterways, including a number of major rivers used for freight haulage and leisure boating.

Cantilever Term used for vehicle tail-lifts (see also Tail-lift) to describe the action whereby the load platform is lowered on arms which swing under the rear of the vehicle. Alternative to vertical method of operation.

CAP Common Agricultural Policy. One of the EU's 'common' policies intended to ensure harmonization throughout the Community (see also Common Transport Policy). Certain CAP-related goods are specially assessed by Customs for export and import purposes.

Capacity management A new term introduced in the late 1990s to describe the provision of additional hire vehicles (usually with driver) on a short/medium-term basis to supplement core owned-fleet at times of increased trading. BRS Ltd, the Volvo-owned former NFC road haulage company and now a major truck rental operator, is a key player in this market.

Capital allowance   In financial/accounting calculations, the amount of depreciation which the Inland Revenue will permit to be set against profits in respect of capital purchases (eg motor vehicles).

Car-derived van   A vehicle defined in legislation for the purposes of speed limits; a goods vehicle constructed or adapted as a derivative of a passenger vehicle and having a maximum laden weight not exceeding two tonnes (ie this includes both closed-van type vehicles and open-back or pick-up type vehicles). *See also* Pick-up truck.

Car pooling   The sharing of cars by a number of commuters, frequently organized by an employer, a resident's group, or the local authority.

Car pound   A secure parking area to which police (or their contractors) remove illegally parked vehicles and those causing obstruction. The driver/owner has to pay a fixed penalty and removal fees before the vehicle can be taken away. Often manned by Traffic Wardens* and is the only occasion when they can demand to see a driver's licence.

Car sharing   A facility authorized under the *Public Passenger Vehicles Act 1981* * whereby vehicles with eight or less passenger seats may be used non-commercially (ie when the fares paid amount to less than the running cost of the vehicle, including depreciation).

Cargo   Another word for freight, used primarily in the shipping and air freight sectors.

Cargo manifest   An inventory of cargo loaded and shipped.

Cargo pump   Pump fitted to vehicles for blowing liquid/power/granular materials from the vehicle into a receiving tank/hopper/silo, etc. *See also* Blower.

Cargo-Sprinter (or Cargosprinter)   German freight train system operated by DB*-Cargo which uses small electro-diesel multiple rail units (ie Freight Multiple Units*). More flexible than full-scale freight trains. It carries standard containers on flat-bed wagons with loads up to 160 tonnes (ie five large lorry-load equivalents). *See also* Mini freight train.

Carman In the days of horse-drawn transport, the man who drove the wagon. In the City of London, a bye-law controlling Carmen was passed in 1272. *See also* Carmen.

Carmen The Worshipful Company of Carmen. The City of London Livery Company (founded 1517 as the 'Fraternyte of Seynt Katryne the Virgin and Marter of Carters') representing the interests of modern day transport men and women. *See also* Carman.

Carnet Legal document or permit as with *Carnet de passage* described below, or a ticket or voucher authorizing travel on public transport.

Carnet de passage *Carnet de passage en douane pour l'admission temporaire.* Document permitting the temporary importation of a foreign vehicle (ie not the load it carries) into a country without payment of import duties, deposit against duty or guaranteed Customs documents. Available from the AA*, RAC* and RSAC*.

Carousel A mechanized system where stock is held in shelving or bins suspended from chains driven by electric motors which enable the stock to be brought to the operator as required. May be vertical or horizontal and invariably computer controlled.

Carriage forward Goods consigned with the carriage charges paid or to be paid by the consignee (ie the recipient of the goods).

Carriage paid Goods consigned with the carriages charges already paid or to be borne by the consignor (ie the sender).

Carriageway Part of highway (ie road) on which vehicles travel. Not specifically defined in law. *See also* Road.

Carrier A transport operator – an alternative term for a road haulier or rail operator – tends to be used in legal texts (carrier's liability, etc).

Carrier's lien Legal term for the carrier's right to hold goods until carriage charges have been paid. Particular lien means that a specific consignment of goods may be held until the charges relating to that (and only that) consignment have been paid – this is a standing right in law. General lien relates to the holding of any goods until charges for previous consignments have been paid – this is a right only if provided for in the carrier's conditions of carriage.

Carrier's right to sell goods Carriers do not normally have a right to sell goods consigned via their services except where there is an 'agency of necessity' in which case three conditions have to be satisfied: the customer must have given consent for the carrier to have possession of the goods; there must be a real emergency with, for example, perishable goods; and it must be impossible for the carrier to have been able to obtain the customer's instructions regarding their disposal. The carrier must obtain the best possible price for the goods and pay over to the customer the proceeds of the sale less his expenses.

Cartel   Firms joining together for the purposes of fixing prices and restricting competition between them to the disadvantage of customers and outsiders (eg Shipping conferences).

Cash flow   The movement of cash through a firm's bank accounts (ie money in/money out). Poor cash flow (ie more going out than coming in) is a precursor to financial problems in business.

Cash flow budget   A budget or plan to control the cash flow through a firm's bank account to ensure funds are available to meet needs as they arise.

Category management   The management of groups of products that are interchangeable or substitutable in meeting consumer needs as opposed to the traditional concentration on individual products and brands. *(Source: ILT Supply-Chain Inventory Management SIG)*

Catenary   The structure of overhead wires/power cables on an electric railway from which the train draws its electric power via the pantograph* mounted on its roof. Also applies in tram* and trolleybus* operation.

Caterpillar   Renowned American manufacturer of heavy truck and plant diesel engines and of heavy duty earthmoving plant.

Catwalk   Grid, usually found mounted behind the driver's cab of articulated tractive units to enable the driver to safely walk across to connect brake hoses and electrical connections, etc. Often comprising safety cover for long-range fuel tanks mounted across vehicle chassis behind cab.

Cause (ie the use of)   An illegal act whereby one person persuades another by instruction or direction to breach the law (to overload vehicle, use defective vehicle on road, exceed driving hours, falsify tachograph charts, etc).

CB (1)   Citizen's band radio. Mobile radio system used in vehicles to allow communication between vehicles and with base stations. Less efficient for business use than private mobile radio and cellular telephone systems because of undisciplined use by CB enthusiasts. A CB licence (obtainable from Post Offices) is required to operate such radios.

CB (2)   Container base, where containers are assembled prior to or following shipment.

CB truck   Counterbalanced fork-lift truck. Lift truck with forks (ie tines) ahead of the front axle, which needs a counterbalancing weight at the rear. Advantage is their ability to get close to the warehouse racking or road vehicle, but they require a wide turning area as opposed to reach trucks, which withdraw their forks within the wheelbase.

CBI   Confederation of British Industry. Britain's business voice. The UK's leading independent employers' organization, representing public and private sector companies employing 10 million of the workforce. The CBI's objective is to help create and sustain the conditions in which the UK can compete and prosper. Through its network of offices around the UK and in Brussels, it represents its members' views on all cross-sectoral issues to the government and other national and international policy-makers. It supplies advice, information and research services to members on key public policy issues affecting business and provides a platform for the exchange and encouragement of best practice.

CCC   Customs clearance certificate.

CCLT   Cranfield Centre for Logistics and Transportation. Specialist teaching and research facility at Cranfield School of Management, Bedfordshire, England.

CCT (1)   Compulsory competitive tendering. Local authorities, public utilities, etc must seek competitive tenders from external sources (eg private enterprise industry) to undertake public services.

CCT (2)   Common customs tariff.

CCTV   Closed-circuit television. Used extensively for security protection in distribution warehouses and transport premises.

CD   Compact disc. A disc capable of storing and playing large quantities of music (ie audio CD). *See also* CD-ROM.

C&D   Collection and delivery.

CD-ROM   Compact disk – read only memory. Similar to audio CD disc but containing information/programs for business/education/entertainment (up to 270,000 pages of text or up to eight hours of sound) that can be played through a computer with suitable equipment.

CDGCPL2 *The Carriage of Dangerous Goods (Classification, Packaging and Labelling) and Use of Transportable Pressure Receptacles Regulations 1996.*

CDGRoad *The Carriage of Dangerous Goods by Road Regulations.*

C&E Customs and Excise. *See also* HMC&E.

C&F Cost and freight. Freighting term whereby the exporter arranges and pays for freighting leaving the buyer to arrange insurance cover for the goods while in transit. *See also* Seller's interest.

CEC (1) Commission of the European Communities.

CEC (2) Co-ordinating European Council for the Development of Performance Tests for Transportation Fuels, Lubricants and Other Fluids.

CEEC Central and Eastern European Countries. The CEE countries of Belarus, Bulgaria, Czech Republic, Estonia, Hungary, Latvia, Lithuania, Moldova, Poland, Romania, Russia, Slovakia, Slovenia and Ukraine are now working towards harmonization with the European Union (EU*).

CEFIC European Council of Chemical Manufacturers' Federations – representative organization for national chemical industry associations (CIA – Chemical Industries Association in GB). Responsible for uniform Europe-wide system of transport emergency cards (TREMCARDs*).

Cellular ship Ship designed to carry ISO containers*(ie container ships*) and provided with cells below decks into which the containers are slotted, being kept in place with vertical guide rails.

Cellular telephone Mobile telephone system with direct-dial connection to national and international telephone networks. Telephone equipment can be vehicle-mounted or carried in briefcase/suitcase or jacket pocket.

Cellnet British Telecom cellular telephone network – one of two operators licensed by the government to provide such services.

CEN *Comité Europeen d'Normalization.* European inspection and standards setting organization for tanks and transportable pressure receptacles (eg cylinders used for transporting gases).

CENT Controlled Engineering Tribology. An oil analysis service provided by Century Oils, Hanley, Stoke-on-Trent.

Central Railway Proposed new freight-only railway running from Leicestershire to the Channel Tunnel.

Central ticket office   Usually at a police headquarters (or elsewhere) where fixed penalties* for traffic/motoring offences have to be paid. Address is to be found on the fixed penalty notice.

Centre field   Central area of tachograph chart wherein driver must enter his name, vehicle number, date of use and other details. It is an offence to fail to (correctly) complete this part of the chart.

CENTREX   Centres of Training Excellence. New name for former RTIETB Services and prior to that the RTIETB*.

CENTRO   West Midlands Passenger Transport Executive (PTE*).

Certificate in Transport   A qualification available from the Institute of Logistics and Transport* that gives exemption from both the national and international examinations for professional competence in road freight transport.

Certificate of Conformity   Under Type Approval* legislation, a certificate issued by a vehicle manufacturer to indicate to the first purchaser that it has been built to a Type Approved standard. The certificate is needed to first register a vehicle after which it has no further relevance.

Certificate of Incorporation   Issued by the Registrar of Companies* when a business has become a limited liability company. The certificate shows the date of incorporation and the company's registered number and must be displayed at the registered office of the company.

Certificate of origin   A certificate (document) indicating the country in which goods originated. Used for customs purposes in international trade.

Certifying officer   An examiner appointed under the *Public Passenger Vehicles Act 1981* to examine passenger vehicles and deal with associated matters of law enforcement.

CF 2000   Customs computer system for freight. Now superseded by CFSP*.

CFC   Chlorofluorocarbon. An ozone-depleting substance used as a refrigerant. *See also* HFC, HCFC and ODP.

CfIT   Commission for Integrated Transport. Commission established in 1999 to provide independent advice to government on the implementation of integrated transport policy, to monitor developments across transport, environment, health and other sectors and to review progress towards meeting the objectives set out in the Government's 1998 Integrated Transport* White Paper,* 'A New Deal for Transport – Better for Everyone'*.

CFPB   Crime and Fraud Prevention Bureau. Body established by the insurance industry to combat insurance crime.

CFS   Container freight station. Place for packing and unpacking LCL* consignments.

CFSP   Customs Freight Simplified Procedures. Customs computer system designed to simplify freight clearance, operational from 1998.

C/fwd   Carried forward (eg figures carried forward onto another page or into another accounting period), or carriage forward (where carriage charges are to be paid by the consignee – ie the recipient of the goods).

CG (1)   Consumer goods – sometimes FMCG* – fast moving consumer goods. Term used in distribution circles to describe products handled – ie goods that are used directly by (and distributed direct to) the consumer.

CG (2)   Centre of gravity (of load, etc).

CH   Nationality symbol for Switzerland – to be shown on the rear of vehicles from that country.

Channel Tunnel   Tunnel, 51 km long, under the English Channel between Cheriton (Folkestone) and Coquelles (Calais) providing a rail link between the UK and France, opened in May 1994. Operated by Eurotunnel with Le Shuttle* rolling motorway* type services. Also used by through-freight and passenger train services between London, Paris, Brussels, etc.

Chart (1)   Tachograph chart on which recording of vehicle speed and distance are shown against time together with the driver's working activities, breaks and rest periods – a legal document which must be retained for 12 months after use.

Chart (2)   A map or plan of water and seaways used by ship's navigators and pilots, particularly to locate appropriate safe channels to follow and dangerous waters and obstacles to avoid. Also indicates depths and currents, etc.

Charter   Term to describe a non-scheduled service where the whole vehicle/ship with driver/crew is hired by an individual or group for an exclusive journey, cruise or excursion*.

Charter party   In shipping, the name given to a contract for the hire of a vessel, where the ship owner places his ship, or part of it, at the disposal of a shipper (ie the charterer) for the carriage of goods from one port to another, the contract term being either for a single journey (port to port) or for a given period of time. The terms and conditions, and any exceptions, are set out in the charter party. *See also* C/P.

Chelsea tractor   Derogatory term (by farmers, etc) for 4 × 4 jeep-style vehicles used only on city streets and for the school run and shopping trips.

CHIEF   Customs Handling of Import and Export Freight. Customs computer system.

Chilled transport   Specialized transport operations using insulated* but not necessarily refrigerated* vehicles for carrying fresh (as opposed to frozen) produce.

Chinese-six (wheeler)   Three-axled (ie six-wheeled) goods vehicle with twin steering axles and a single-drive axle at rear (no longer a popular configuration).

CHIP   *The Chemicals (Hazard Information and Packaging) Regulations 1994.* Require suppliers of chemicals to label any hazardous substances they supply.

Chunnel   Slang term for the Channel Tunnel*.

CI   Compression ignition. Describes the method by which a diesel engine operates by compressing fuel in the cylinder to such an extent that ignition takes place without the addition of a sparking device.

CIA   Chemical Industries Association – trade association for chemical manufacturers concerned with (among other things) the safe carriage of dangerous goods by road. Produces a Code of Practice for such operations. *See also* CEFIC.

CIF   Cost, Insurance and Freight. Freighting term whereby the exporter is responsible for arranging freighting and insurance cover to the agreed destination.

CILT   Chartered Institute of Logistics and Transport. The new name (from 2001) for the Institute of Logistics and Transport, which resulted from the 1999 merger of the Chartered Institute of Transport (CIT*) and Institute of Logistics (ILT*), under which the combined Institute will have 'chartered' status.

CIM (1) *Convention Internationale concernant le Transport des Marchandises par Chemin de Fer* (known as the COTIF Convention). Rules covering the international carriage of goods by rail.

CIM (2) Computer Integrated Manufacturing. Computerized systems to integrate and control individual manufacturing processes.

CIP Carriage and Insurance Paid. Freighting term normally used in shipping.

CIPS Chartered Institute of Purchasing and Supply. Professional body (with Royal Charter) for individual purchasing officers and such like. Examining body providing recognized professional qualifications.

CIRHS Continuous International Road Haulage Survey (of UK vehicles). Statistical survey carried out by government. *See also* CSRGT.

CIS Commonwealth of Independent States. Formed on the break-up of the old Soviet Union (USSR).

CIT Chartered Institute of Transport. The premier professional body for individuals engaged in transport whether by land, sea or air. The Institute holds a Royal Charter and its patron is HRH the Princess Royal. The CIT in the UK is now merged with the Institute of Logistics to form the Institute of Logistics and Transport (ILT*). *See also* CILT.

CITB Construction Industry Training Board.

City diesel A cleaner form of diesel fuel which helps to reduce toxic exhaust emissions (ie ultra-low sulphur diesel).

Civil Code of Practice Home Office Code to be followed by truck drivers and road hauliers to avoid the civil penalty for aiding the entry of illegal immigrants (see also clandestine entrants) to the UK.

Civil penalty Home Office penalty imposed on truck drivers and road hauliers found with illegal immigrants in their vehicles – currently set at £2,000 per immigrant found. No appeal – only defence is that the Civil Code of Practice* was followed.

Clandestine entrants Legal terminology (used in *Immigration and Asylum Act 1999*) to describe illegal immigrants (or 'illegals' for short) into the UK where hauliers and drivers may have to pay a penalty if caught with such persons on their vehicles.

Classification Society   An independent organization which surveys and inspects ships to ensure their sea-worthiness (eg Lloyd's Register of Shipping).

Clear Pass   A commercial product (by Monsanto) that prevents vehicles throwing up excessive spray from wet roads. Manufactured to conform to legal requirements. *See* Anti-spray and BS AU 200.

Clearing banks   The major banks which deal with commercial banking, cheque clearance, etc.

Clearing house   A firm that undertakes haulage contracts by (mainly) sub-contracting the work to other vehicle operators. Many have a poor reputation as a result of paying low rates and taking a long time to settle sub-contractor accounts. Now referred to in modern terminology as 'freight exchanges' or 'electronic market places'.

Clearway   Part of highway designated (and signposted) as such where vehicles are not permitted to stop – see Highway Code* for details and illustration of sign.

Climate change levy   New (from April 2001) government tax on the use of energy by industry, commerce and the public sector – and including road hauliers, bus and coach operators (predicted to increase user energy costs by between 10 and 20 per cent).

Close-coupled   Relates to trailers with two (non-steerable) wheels on each side with their centres of contact with the road surface not more than one metre apart.

Close-proximity mirror   Rear-view mirror fitted to goods vehicle exceeding 12 tonnes pmw and used since 1 October 1988 in addition to normal mirrors to provide driver with close proximity and wide-angle vision.

Closely-spaced axles   Where two axles are spaced with their centres not more than 2.5 metres and not less than 1.02 metres apart, and where three axles are spaced with the centres of the outermost axles not more than 3.25 metres apart and each of which has a plated weight no greater than 7,500 kg.

Closing date   Latest date cargo accepted for shipment by (liner) ship owner for specified sailing.

CMPE   Contractor's Mechanical Plant Engineers. Provides driver training on lorry loaders.

CMI (1) *Comité Maritime International.* International committee of maritime lawyers.

CMI (2) Co-managed inventory.

CMR *Convention on the Contract for the International Carriage of Goods by Road* (ie CMR Convention) concerned with the international carriage of goods by road for reward between states, one of which is a party to the Convention (except UK – Eire and not the Channel Islands). The Convention applies automatically so haulage operators involved in such traffic should ensure their liabilities are fully covered by appropriate insurance.

CMR consignment note Requirement of CMR operation (see above) is that a CMR consignment note is used for the whole transit and besides all other relevant details, shows the name of every carrier party to the movement (ie who each share liability proportionate to the freight charges).

C/N Abbreviation for consignment note.

CNG Compressed natural gas. Under test as a fuel for heavy vehicles because of its lower emissions. *See* Natural gas.

CO Carbon monoxide. Scientific designation for this (highly poisonous) product of vehicle exhaust emissions. A so-called greenhouse gas* contributing to global warming. *See also* CO_2, HC, NOx and PM.

CO_2 Carbon dioxide. Scientific designation for this product of vehicle exhaust emissions. A so-called greenhouse gas* contributing to global warming. *See also* CO, HC, NOx and PM.

Coach A passenger vehicle constructed to carry more than 16 people besides the driver, weighing more than 7.5 tonnes gross weight and capable of exceeding 60 mph. The term usually implies a vehicle more comfortably furnished than the spartan fittings found in most service buses. Many, especially those used for long-distance touring holidays, are positively luxurious having on-board toilets, cooking facilities (ie microwave ovens) and TV for showing video films, PA systems for the tour guide's commentary and radio/tape music played to individual seats (as on aircraft) for listening with headphones.

C/O Certificate of origin. Document needed in export/import trade.

CoD Cash on delivery. Carriage charges (and sometimes payment for the goods themselves) payable by consignee (ie recipient) before the delivery is completed. No payment invariably means no delivery.

CoF   Certificate of fitness. Applicable to passenger vehicles under the *Public Service Vehicle (Conditions of Fitness, Equipment, Use and Certification) Regulations 1981* – as amended.

COGSA   *Carriage of Goods by Sea Act.* In the UK the 1924 version (Hague Rules) now superseded by 1971 version of the Hague-Visby Rules.

COI   Central Office of Information. Government department dispensing official information.

CoIF   Certificate of initial fitness. Issued in respect of PSVs* at the time of or shortly following manufacture.

Cold chain   Term used in refrigerated food storage/transport to indicate the complete 'chain' of operations from original production to the retailer's display.

Cold start (device)   A device provided on diesel-engined vehicles to provide extra fuel to the engine for starting (as with the choke on petrol-engined vehicles). It is illegal for a cold start device (referred to as excess fuel device in regulations) to be within reach of any person in the vehicle when it is moving. Use of such devices on a moving vehicle produces black smoke which is an offence under the C&U regulations.

Collapsible containers   Freight containers, usually built of wood, which can be folded down into a flat pack for ease of transport prior to and after use.

Collector's office   Customs accommodation where declaration(s) (entries) are scrutinized and amounts payable collected.

COM   Customer order management. Development in logistics where suppliers not only deliver to specific customer order, but also proactively anticipate and action order demand.

Co-managed inventory (CMI)   Practice whereby the retailer and supplier are jointly responsible for setting and maintaining inventory levels.

Combi   Abbreviated term used where a mode of transport carries both passengers and freight – eg in air transport.

Combination weight   The combined weight of a powered vehicle and a goods-carrying trailer (ie as in gross combination weight for articulated vehicles).

Combined mode A term meaning intermodal freighting, particularly road-rail operations, where each mode is used to its best advantage to provide overall economy and efficiency for the whole journey.

Combined test A combined driving test taken on a goods vehicle whereby the learner driver may gain both ordinary and large goods vehicle driving licences on passing the test. This facility is no longer available in the UK.

Combined transport Transport system involving use of multiple modes (eg road/rail, road/water, road/sea, road/air). *See also* CTO.

COMECON Council for Mutual Economic Aid. Affiliation of countries in the erstwhile 'Communist Bloc' in central Europe which were committed to assist each other economically.

Comitology Euro-jargon for a committee comprising, for example, officials from member state governments, trade union representatives, technical people from relevant manufacturers plus representatives from trade associations, etc and chaired by an official of the European Commission (eg as with that currently dealing with the specification for digital tachographs*).

Commercial Motor Leading UK weekly road transport journal, founded 1905.

Common carrier Haulier who has not limited his liability against claims for loss or damage to goods by operating under the terms of 'Conditions of Carriage'. *See also* Private carrier.

Common Transport Policy One of the basic tenets of the Treaty of Rome* was that member states (originally 6, now 15) would develop a 'common transport policy' to provide harmonization of legislation standards, etc across the Union. This has not yet been achieved but developments towards SEM* in 1992 were leading in this direction.

Community Transit Customs system for dealing with the movement of goods between EU member states where Customs duty barriers no longer exist and where common tariffs are applied against non-EU goods. *See also* Customs union.

Compactor body Vehicle body type used in refuse collection. Equipment within the body can be operated (hydraulically) to 'compact' the refuse loaded from the rear.

Compensated rest   Rest taken by a goods vehicle driver operating under EU rules to compensate for reduced daily or weekly rest periods as required by law. Such compensated rest may only be added to other rest periods of at least eight hours' duration. Compensation by payment is not permitted.

Competent authority   The precise meaning of the term varies in accordance with the particular context in which it is used. In the case of tachograph fitment, calibration and repair, for example, the nationally approved authority in the UK is the DTLR*. In passenger transport terms, EU documentation implies that it means 'any authority competent to franchise passenger services by road, rail and inland waterway'.

Component   A part, ingredient, or sub-assembly that is both a component to a higher level part, and a parent part to other components. *(Source: ILT Supply-Chain Inventory Management SIG)*

Component part   Raw material, ingredient, part, or sub-assembly that goes into a higher level assembly, compound, or other part. *(Source: ILT Supply-Chain Inventory Management SIG)*

Composite trailer   In legal terms, a road trailer comprising an articulated semi-trailer mounted on a towing dolly. As such this counts as only one trailer when determining the number of trailers a goods vehicle may draw under the C&U regulations.

Comprehensive loss underwriting exchange   Scheme for direct selling of insurance at discounted premiums by American firm Equifax*.

Condition monitoring   Diagnostic scheme whereby, for example, monitoring of engine condition by analysis of lubricants allows for accurate pinpointing of high levels of wear – ie above normal limits.

Conditions of carriage   Terms of business defined by a haulage contractor to limit his liabilities for loss or damage to goods entrusted to his care. Hauliers may devise and publish their own conditions or, if members, trade under the standard conditions of the Road Haulage Association*. The same applies to passenger vehicle operators in respect of passengers carried and their personal belongings and chattels. Similarly, the railways have always had conditions of carriage for their freight, parcels and passenger traffic – the terms usually being referred to on passenger tickets and other documentation and invariably displayed on wall posters. The conditions must be communicated (ie made available on request) to customers prior to the negotiation of any business. *See also* Common and Private carrier. Passenger carriers and carriers by sea and air operate under conditions of carriage the details of which are usually shown on passenger tickets or freight documents, etc.

Conduct of driver   Re PSV*/PCV* operations, legal requirements relating to drivers whereby they must conduct themselves in an orderly and civil manner.

Conference   Organization of ship owners offering services on particular sea routes under agreed conditions. Shipping Conferences are usually classic examples of the operation of a cartel*.

Configuration of axles   Term used in goods vehicle operations to describe both the type, number and layout of axles on a vehicle/trailer (eg 4 x 2 describes a four-wheeled two-axle vehicle of which only two wheels are driven; 6 x 4 describes a six-wheel, three-axle vehicle with two driven axles – ie 4 wheels driven; 3+2 describes a three-axle tractive unit with a tandem, ie 2-axle semi-trailer, while 2+3 describes the opposite, a two axle tractive unit with a tri-axle semi-trailer).

Congestion charging   A concept whereby road users are charged for the use of certain roads where traffic congestion is a problem – the objective being to price-out frivolous or unimportant use and thus concentrate use for essential purposes only. This is just one example of the wider concept of road pricing*. Charging is usually via tolling (ie with access via toll gates where vehicles stop and pay) or by automated electronic charging systems.

Consequential loss   The losses (ie financial) incurred as a result of another event (eg the road haulier's loss of business/profits from his vehicle being off the road due to an accident). It is possible to insure against such losses.

Consideration   One of the essential ingredients of a legally binding contract (whether written or not) is that there shall be 'consideration'; in other words one or both parties must gain a benefit (ie consideration – not necessarily money) from the contract.

Consignee   The recipient of goods – ie person/firm to whom they are consigned.

Consignment note   Document used in transport/delivery operations. Indicates to driver what to deliver and to whom, plus other relevant details to identify goods and any special delivery instructions. Usually in multi-part sets to enable copies to be left at collection and delivery points as advice notes and for consignee to sign in confirmation of receipt (ie this becomes carrier's proof of delivery – POD*).

Consignment stock   The stock of goods held by an external customer which is still the property of the supplier but for which payment is only made when stock is sold or used by the customer. *(Source: ILT Supply-Chain Inventory Management SIG)*

Consignor   The sender of goods – ie the person/firm by whom they are consigned.

Consolidation   The operation of combining small units into a large unit (eg small consignments consolidated to fill a large trailer/container for onward transport).

Conspicuity tape   Reflective tape ideally used around the perimeter of vehicle bodies to increase their visibility at night and in daytime. Available in red for fitting to the rear, amber for the sides and white for the front.

Constable   Police constable. For the purposes of road traffic law all police officers irrespective of rank are 'constables'. But it is not a good idea to refer to an inspector or superintendent as such – or even a sergeant!

Constant mesh gearbox   Vehicle transmission whereby the gear trains remain constantly meshed to give smooth, silent, gear changing. Major technical advance in its day from old-type 'crash' gearboxes where double declutching was essential to allow gears to mesh and change smoothly and silently.

Consul   The commercial representative of a country residing officially in another country to facilitate business developments and represent the interests of trade between the two countries.

Consular invoice   Particular type of invoice used in export trade and given legal status by the Consul of the importing country in advance of shipment. Usually required so that Customs of the importing country can verify the nature and the origin of the goods prior to importation.

Consumable   A classification of stock used to describe items or products that are totally consumed in use, eg paper, oil, grease. *(Source: ILT Supply-Chain Inventory Management SIG)*

Consumer goods   Goods destined for use (consumption) by individual persons (ie the consumer) rather than by industry or commerce. Usually, the consumer is the ultimate or final customer.

Container ship   Ship specially designed and built to carry ISO containers in 20 ft and 40 ft modules in cells (ie cellular ship*).

Contingency stock   Stock held to cover potential system failure situations which can be mathematically modelled. *(Source: ILT Supply-Chain Inventory Management SIG)*

Continuous improvement (CI)   A term that describes the many management practices and techniques used to find and eliminate waste and to general improvements in business processes, quality or costs. *(Source: ILT Supply-Chain Inventory Management SIG)*

Continuous replenishment   System whereby stock in stores or distribution centres is replenished automatically (ie orders are usually generated automatically).

Contract   Legally binding and enforceable contracts exist whether in writing or not provided three basic requirements are met: there is an offer and an acceptance; there is a consideration (ie benefit or payment to one or more parties); there is an intention by the parties to be legally bound by the contract (this is always assumed unless there is a written provision to the contrary).

Contract hire   The operation whereby an owner hires a vehicle to the customer for his exclusive use for a given period. Usually contract hire vehicles are painted in the customer's livery and may be driven by the owner's driver or the customer's driver (depending on the contract terms). Contracts invariably provide for maintenance of the vehicle by the owner and temporary replacement to cover breakdowns, etc to relieve the customer of these worries as well as saving him the capital and replacement costs for the vehicle – the essence of contract hire.

Contract maintenance   Maintenance of vehicles by a specialist repairer (often the vehicle supplier) on a contracted, regular basis to save the operator incurring the costs and involvement with his own repair facilities.

Contract of employment   A contract, not necessarily (but preferably) in writing between an employer and an employee setting out the terms of the employment. It is a legal requirement that within 13 weeks of starting employment the employee must be given the main terms in writing (legislation specifies the items to be included in such contracts).

Contract (bus) services   Bus services provided on a regular basis under contract to an organization, a school, college or a firm, for example. These are invariably required to ferry workers or pupils to and from work or school, but they may also be provided for leisure purposes.

Contracted out   A situation where an employer provides a satisfactory (to the Occupational Pensions Board) occupational pension scheme and may 'contract out' of part of the state pension scheme benefits.

Control group cycle counting   The repeated physical inventory taking of a small 'control group' of parts, in the same locations, within a very short time frame to verify the design of a new inventory process. It is the only form of cycle counting not truly used to measure inventory record accuracy. *(Source: ILT Supply-Chain Inventory Management SIG)*

Control of fumes   Legal provisions make it an offence for crankcase gases from petrol-engined vehicles to escape into the atmosphere except through the exhaust system. Vehicles made before 1 July 1971, vehicles with two-stroke-engines and those complying with Community directives are exempt.

Controlled parking zone   A restricted parking/access zone for specific categories of vehicle, normally operated by a fee-paying permit or 'Pay and Display' system. Usually patrolled to detect non-payers. Zoned categories may include, for example, residents' vehicles, service vehicles, the general public on a short-stay basis and buses.

Controlling interest   Term used when a company acquires sufficient of the shares of another company to have control (ie not necessarily acquiring all the shares).

Conventional   Term for North American-style heavy truck where engine is ahead of the driver's cab. *See also* Bonnet.

Convergence   In logistics terms, the progressive merging of information technology (IT) and telecoms (ie computers and communications).

Converter dolly   Two-wheeled axle (ie in law a trailer) which has a drawbar for towing purposes and on which is mounted a fifth-wheel plate for coupling to an articulated semi-trailer to form a drawbar-type trailer (ie in law a composite trailer).

Convoi Exceptionel   French vehicle marking to indicate wide, large, heavy load – as with 'Special Types' operation in UK.

CoP (1)   Code of Practice.

COP (2)   Custom of port. Shipping term

COP (3)   Conformity of Production. Document issued to international hauliers whose vehicles have a lower NOx* emission than older vehicles. Needed for road transit in Austria.

COP Value   See COP (3) above. COP value is a figure representing the vehicle's NOx emission value plus 10 per cent, a standard by which the number of ECO stamps* for goods vehicle entry to Austria is determined.

CoPilot   A system for intelligent cruise control of heavy trucks and coaches. A product of German manufacturer MAN and part of MAN's contribution to the Prometheus* European road safety project.

Corporate manslaughter   A charge which can be brought against the directors of a company following an accidental death resulting from their negligence. Government proposal is for three levels of charge: killing (where this results from an unforeseen event); killing by gross carelessness (where conduct leading to the death falls far below what could be expected); reckless killing (where conduct would clearly cause death or serious injury).

Corporation tax   Tax payable on trading profits, income and capital gains of UK limited liability companies (ie not partnerships/sole proprietorships/ self-employed persons).

Corrector box/gearbox   In tachograph installations where mechanical drive (as opposed to electronic operation) is used, corrector gearbox 'adjusts' the turning rate of the drive cable to produce correct speed/distance indication/recording at the instrument head.

COSHH   *The Control of Substances Hazardous to Health (COSHH) Regulations 1988.* These require employers to assess the risks presented by the use of hazardous materials in the workplace and adopt suitable control and monitoring procedures. Employees who may be exposed must be given information on the hazards and trained in preventive measures.

Cost-benefit analysis   Assessment of the costs of a project against the value of benefits to be gained from its implementation. May be extended to include environmental and other benefits more difficult to measure.

COT   Customer's own transport. Shipping term meaning that the customer collects from/delivers to freight station or other specified point.

COTIF   Convention concerning international carriage by rail – the COTIF Convention. *See also* CIM.

Council of Ministers   Body within the EU comprising respective departmental ministers from all EU member states (eg European Council of Ministers of Transport – ECMT).

Counterbalanced fork-lift truck   A type of fork-lift truck in which the extended forks are counterbalanced by the heavily weighted rear-end of the truck.

Counter cheque   Issued by bank when payee has already transferred funds to bank (or funds have been debited from his account). As with bank/banker's draft, guarantees clearance and is thus a 'safe' cheque (ie will not 'bounce').

Counterpart   That part of the new EU-style 'unified' driving licence on which penalty points and disqualifications from driving are recorded.

Courier   An individual or firm that provides a fast, direct service, usually for small and urgent consignments – often vital documents, contracts, films, tenders, etc. Also a person who acts as a guide conducting tourists around historic sights and other places of interest, or gives a running commentary on a coach tour.

C/P   Charter party*. In shipping, a contract for the charter of a vessel.

C/Pd   Carriage paid (eg by the consignor/shipper of the goods).

CPC (1)   Certificate of Professional Competence. Evidence that holder meets statutory requirements for professional competence in road freight/passenger transport operations. Original CPCs issued by Traffic Area* offices – qualification now only by exemption or examination.

CPC (2)   Cruise power control. System of engine management to provide economy cruising power but high horsepower when needed (eg by engine manufacturers Caterpillar, Cummins and Detroit Diesel).

CPD (1)   Continuing professional development. The process whereby qualified people keep abreast of new thinking and new developments in their chosen professional field. Involves the keeping of an ongoing record by individuals of their education, training and work experience plus further training needs, etc, usually expressed as 'CPD days' and counting towards the award of professional status (eg gradings within the Institute of Logistics and Transport – ILT*).

CPD (2)   Charterer pays dues. Term used in ship chartering to define who pays ships dues.

CPI   Consumer price index. *See also* RPI.

CPL   *The Carriage of Dangerous Goods Classification, Packaging and Labelling and Use of Transportable Pressure Receptacles Regulations 1996.*

CPRE   Council for the Protection of Rural England. National lobbying organization that campaigns to protect the countryside. Also seeks to achieve more sustainable use of land and resources. Campaigns against over-development of roads and road traffic.

CPS   Crown Prosecution Service. Body of lawyers who prosecute offenders on behalf of (or instead of) the police.

CPT (1)   Carriage paid to. An Incoterm* used in combined transport operations.

CPT (2)   Confederation of Passenger Transport. Successor to the Bus and Coach Council. National trade organization representing UK bus and coach operators, also light rail and metro operators. Claims to be the voice of the passenger transport industry, officially recognized by government. Principal consultative body on national, local and EU legislative and regulatory matters.

CPU   Central processing unit – the 'brain' of a computer.

CPZ   Controlled parking zone (around schools, hospitals, etc). Infringement of the Zone provisions will result in the issue of a PCN*.

Credit transfer   Direct transfer of funds through the banking system from payer's account to payee's account.

Creditor   Person/firm to whom money is owed.

Critical path analysis   A form of network planning that determines all the activities to be carried out during a project, linked in sequence and timed (ie the critical path) to produce the required result at the right time. Usually produced in the form of a plan on paper or on a computer screen.

CRN   Customs registered number. Number issued by Customs to regular exporters for use on all relevant documentation and especially where goods are to be pre-entered* under the simplified clearance procedure. *See also* SCP.

Cross docking   Term used, mainly in parcels sector, to describe a technique where bulk loads of parcels arrive at a hub depot and are unloaded, sorted and reloaded to delivery vehicles across a loading bank or dock.

Cross ply/tyre   Vehicle tyre constructed with the ply cords laid at alternative angles (less than 90 degrees) to the peripheral line of the tread.

Same as a diagonal ply/bias belted tyre. Now largely replaced by use of radial ply tyres. *See also* Radial [ply] tyre.

Crossed hammers   On tachograph recordings, a symbol shown on the activity mode switch and on part of the recording area of tachograph charts. Indicates 'active' as opposed to 'passive' work. Its use is not part of UK legal requirements but may be used voluntarily for work other than driving.

Crown court   Court (higher than magistrates court) within English judicial system concerned mainly with criminal jurisdiction and where indictable (ie more serious) offences are tried before a judge (or recorder) and jury.

CRP   Continuous replenishment. A system of continuous stock flows replenishing goods removed from stock (ie for delivery or sold in the case of supermarket shelves).

CRS   Computer reservation system. Computerized airline booking system providing real-time (ie live) information on flight times, seat availability and fares, etc. Accessed normally by airlines and travel agents via computer terminals in their own premises.

CRT   Continuously regenerating trap. An exhaust after-treatment device (product of Eminox) combining a particulate trap and a specially-developed catalytic converter in the same 'can' and designed to reduce PM* and NOx* emissions in vehicles, particularly those using ultra-low (ie 0.002 per cent or less) sulphur fuels.

CSC   *International Convention on Safe Containers (1972).* Sets approval standards and requirements for the safe handling and movement of freight containers. Such containers must display valid CSC safety approval plate issued in UK by the HSE*.

CSDF   Cold Storage and Distribution Federation. Representing firms in this industry.

CSR   Customer service requirement. Demands of customers, usually for ever-more efficient and cost-effective delivery of goods, including the need to meet stringent JiT* schedules, or allocated delivery time-slots.

CSRGT   Continuous Survey of Road Goods Transport. Statistical survey carried out by DTLR* of UK domestic haulage based on weekly sample of over 3.5 tonne LGVs. *See also* CIRHS.

CT (1)   Combined transport*. The use of a combination of transport modes, principally road and rail.

CT (2)   Community transport. Passenger transport operated by and for voluntary and community groups, schools, colleges and local authorities and for door-to-door transport for people who are unable to use other public transport. It is estimated that over 100,000 minibuses serve over 10 million passengers on this basis annually.

CTA   Community Transport Association. National charitable body representative of the voluntary sector transport operators providing community transport. Concerned with training and the provision of information and at the forefront of promoting minibus safety.

CTC   Coach Tourism Council. Established in 1989 to promote travel and tourism by coach. Its members are coach operators and suppliers. Concerned with ensuring the coach-travelling public gets good value and fair dealing.

CTD   Combined transport document. Form of consignment note used in combined transport operations.

CTK   Capacity tonne/kilometre. A measure of performance used in shipping, etc.

CTL (1)   Combined Transport Limited. Private freight train operator providing through the Chunnel* intermodal* services.

CTL (2)   Constructive total loss. Term used in shipping referring to the English law doctrine of this name and occurring in CMR* on the international carriage of goods by road.

CTO   Combined transport operator. One who is engaged in combined transport operations involving the use of road, rail, sea and air systems under the provisions of the TCM* Convention 1969 and using TCM combined transport documents.

CTP   Common Transport Policy. Europe-wide policy for transport to achieve efficiency, economy and environmental improvements.

CTR   Central Trailer Rentco. Major trailer and semi-trailer hire company (claims to be largest in Europe).

CTRL   Channel Tunnel Rail Link. The high-speed (300 km/hr or 185 m/hr) rail link between central London and the Channel Tunnel.

CTU   Cargo transport unit. Shipping term for containers, tank containers, etc shipped by sea.

Cube out   Expression used to indicate that the volumetric capacity of a vehicle body/container is reached before its weight limit.

CUE   Claims and Underwriting Exchange. Body established by the insurance industry to combat insurance crime.

Current ratio   Financial calculation used to indicate ratio of current assets to current liabilities (ie the ability to pay current demands out of available funds) – same as working capital ratio.

Current value   Same as present/present-day value – in terms of depreciation calculations, etc what it would cost to replace an asset at today's prices or the price that would be obtained if an existing asset were to be sold today.

Curtainside/curtainsider   Vehicle/trailer having enclosed body with fixed roof and 'curtain' (ie flexible canvas/plastic-coated material) sides which can be drawn forward or to the rear to provide access to the load space from either side (for fork-lift loading/off-loading, etc), also rapid means of providing weather protection for goods.

Customer response centre (CRC)   Local centres where goods may be collected or from where goods are delivered to customers locally.

Customized truck   Goods vehicle specially painted (often with elaborate murals) and fitted with chrome/stainless exhaust stacks, bumpers and other trim, alloy wheels, etc and high levels of cab interior trim. Owned/operated/driven by truck enthusiasts and mainly seen at rallies for such and often entered in 'custom' competitions.

Customs and Excise (C&E or CE)   Her Majesty's Customs and Excise. Crown service which controls the import and export of goods. Controlling authority for Value Added Tax (see also VAT). Also monitors legal/illegal use of fuel in diesel-engined road vehicles. *See also* DERV, Duty free fuel and Gas oil.

Customs clearance   Process of clearing import/export cargo through Customs (ie by examination of the documentation and/or the goods themselves).

Customs' Union   An agreement between the Customs of member states of the full European Union (in this case), that there shall be no duty barriers between them and that they will all adopt a common tariff against non-Union goods.

CV or cv   Commercial vehicle. Vehicles used in connection with trade or business (eg trucks and buses).

CVR   *Convention on the Contract for the International Carriage of Passengers and Luggage by Road 1973.*

CVRS   Computerized vehicle routeing and scheduling – usually referring to computer software designed for this purpose.

CWE   Cleared without examination. Customs terminology used where a consignment is cleared on the basis of information given in the documentation rather than by a physical examination of the goods. *See also* CWO.

CWO   Cash with order. Trading term whereby the goods must be paid for at the time of ordering rather than later.

CWR   Continuously welded rail. Used on rail tracks to provide a smoother ride for passengers and reduced maintenance requirements.

CxHx   Hydrocarbons emanating from vehicle exhausts.

Cycle counting   Cycle counting is the physical counting of stock on a perpetual basis, rather than counting stock periodically. A cycle is the time required to count all items in the inventory at least once. The frequency of cycle counting can be varied to focus management attention on the more valuable or important items or to match work processes. Some of the systems used are:

■ ABC system with the highest count frequency for items with the highest annual usage value.
■ Reorder system when stocks are counted at the time of order.
■ Receiver system with counting when goods are received.
■ Zero balance system to count items when a backorder situation is reached to confirm that no stock is held.
■ Transaction system where stocks are counted after a specified number of transactions. *(Source: ILT Supply-Chain Inventory Management SIG)*

Cycle stock   *See* Working stock.

CZ   Nationality symbol for Czech Republic – to be shown on the rear of vehicles from that country.

Dd

3D   Three-dimensional.

4D   Four-directional. As in four-way entry pallets for example.

D   Nationality symbol for Germany – to be shown on the rear of vehicles from that country.

D1/2D   Despatch money payable at half demurrage rate. Shipping term.

D/A (1)   Deposit account. Bank account used where monies are reserved for future rather than current use – usually at preferential rates of interest.

D/A (2)   Documents against acceptance. Shipping term.

DAF (1)   Delivered at frontier. An Incoterm* usually used in providing transport quotations where the price is for delivery at frontier rather than at final destination (eg where there are restrictions on entry to a country).

DAF (2)   Doorne's Anhangwagen-Fabriek. Literally translated: van Doorne's trailer works. Dutch manufacturer of heavy trucks. Took over British truck maker Leyland and now part of giant American truck manufacturer Paccar (which also owns UK manufacturer Foden Trucks).

Daily rest period   Required by goods vehicle drivers under EU law on days when they drive relevant vehicles. Normally 11 hours but may be reduced to nine hours three times in week provided reduced time is compensated* (ie made up).

Daisy-wheel   Type of printer used with computers – gives letter-quality printing but at slower speed than with dot matrix types. Letters are actually carried on a 'daisy' wheel. *See also* Dot-matrix printer.

DAM   Drivers Action Movement. Non-political pressure group acting on behalf of full-time LGV* drivers. Founded 1994 principally to campaign for drivers' rights and public safety.

DAMP Driver Assessment and Monitoring Project. An ongoing, European-funded study project being conducted by the University of Huddersfield.

Danger labels/signs Diamond-shaped labels carrying officially-designated symbols and markings to indicate the hazards of dangerous goods. Fixed on packages and vehicles as required by law.

Dangerous goods Commonly used term – more correct to refer to such materials/products as dangerous substances (see below).

Dangerous Goods Adviser Proposed by EU (EC 91/C185/05) that carriers of dangerous goods by road should appoint a suitably qualified person as such (see also RPO – Risk Prevention Officer).

Dangerous substances Substances defined as dangerous for the purposes of carriage by road as defined in legislation, eg *The Road Traffic (Carriage of Dangerous Substances in Packages, etc) Regulations 1985* – but not only this, and as specified in the HSE* 'Approved List'. *See also* Approved list.

Darkness (ie hours of) Defined in *RVLR 1989* as being from half-an-hour after sunset to half-an-hour after sunrise – when headlights on vehicles must be switched on. Not to be confused with 'lighting-up time' – not specifically defined but meaning from sunset to sunrise, when obligatory lights on vehicles must be used.

Data interchange System for the interchange of information (ie data) via computer by electronic means (electronic data interchange – EDI*).

Data logger Instrument that logs data (eg vehicle-mounted top record engine/ transmission operating data).

Data Protection Act *Data Protection Act 1984* under which computer users who hold personal data about individuals on their files (other than exempt data) must register with the Data Protection Registrar (from whom all relevant information can be obtained). Failure to register as required when holding relevant data is an offence. The register is public and can be examined (free) on request to the Registrar.

Day In context of EU drivers' hours law, a rolling period of 24 hours during which a driver drives vehicles to which the regulations apply.

Day cab Term used to describe goods vehicle cab with no sleeping/bunk facilities (but see also sleeper pod). Generally this means a shorter cab allowing greater load platform length on the chassis.

dB Decibel*. A measure of noise or more precisely the intensity of a sound (ie one-tenth of a bel). Under current legislation maximum noise levels for goods vehicles are as follows: under 3,500 kg pmw =81 dB(A), over 3,500 kg pmw =86 dB(A), over 12,00 0 kg pmw with engine power at least 200 bhp DIN* =88 dB(A).

DB Deutsche Bahn – German national railway system. *See also* Cargo-Sprinter.

DBFO Design, build, finance and operate. Department of Transport's (DoT*) private finance initiative for awarding road building, design, maintenance and operating contracts.

DC Distribution centre. Premises where goods are stored and from which they are distributed locally, regionally, nationally or internationally. *See also* NDC.

DCF Discounted cash flow – means of determining the present day value of future cash flows – or financial returns (eg emanating from a project to be inaugurated at some future date). It is usual to apply a rate of discount of eight per cent per annum, but it is not unusual for investment that fails this test to be authorized in the public sector if it can be claimed to be 'in the public interest'. An essential factor in cost-benefit analysis*.

DDA (1) *Disability Discrimination Act 1995.* An Act to protect the interests of disabled persons at work or who want to work (eg at home).

DDA (2) Duty deferment account. Term used in connection with payment of customs duty.

DDO Despatch money payable on discharging only. Shipping term.

DDP Delivered duty paid. Incoterm* used mainly in shipping to indicate that the shipment will be delivered to a named destination with all relevant duties paid. See also DDU below.

DDU Delivered duty unpaid. Incoterm* used mainly in shipping to indicate that the shipment will be delivered to a named destination without prior payment of relevant duties. *See also* DDP.

De-coupling stock Inventory accumulated between dependent activities in the goods flow to reduce the need for completely synchronized operations. *(Source: ILT Supply-Chain Inventory Management SIG)*

Dead freight Space reserved on ship, but not taken up.

'Dead' (and 'light') working Situation where a bus or train, for example, has to be worked (ie run) back to its base or terminal either to operate the next service or for maintenance. Invariably these operations are conducted without carrying fare-paying passengers and are thus dead or light so far as revenue earning is concerned.

Deadweight Term used in shipping to indicate the all-up weight of the cargo, equipment, fuel, provisions, water and spare parts of a ship when loaded to the maximum draught (ie when the Plimsoll line is on the water).

Debenture Long-term (usually) fixed interest loan to a business for which a 'debenture' (ie certificate) is issued. May be secured against the firm's assets (or a specific asset) in case the firm goes into liquidation – or may not be secured.

Debtor Person/firm who owes money. *See also* Creditor.

DEC Drug Evaluation Classification programme. Training package for police forces to detect drug drivers. *See also* DIRT and FIT.

Decibel Logarithmic measure of noise (see also dB) on the decibel scale. An increase/decrease of 10 dB equates to a doubling/halving of the noise level. A weighted scale (ie dBA) is used for comparative purposes The human threshold of pain occurs at around 140 dB(A). A jet plane just overhead is around 110 dB(A), a heavy lorry passing close by would be around 85/87 dB(A) while a very quiet room would record around 42 dB(A).

Deck (1) The floor of a ship (a passenger ship may have a number of decks). The top deck is usually open to the elements.

Deck (2) The floor of a loading bay, colloquially called the 'deck'.

Declaration of intent Form of legal/binding 'promise' made by applicant for 'O' licence (when signing Form GV 79) and which if not subsequently adhered to may lead to penalty against the licence (eg curtailment*, suspension* or revocation*).

Dedicated distribution A term denoting the operation of exclusive distribution contracts for a single client – ie contract hire. The opposite of shared user* distribution.

Dedicated warehousing System where a warehouse is devoted to holding stock only for one customer.

Deduct point   The point in the production process up to which all the parts assumed to have been used (as defined in the bill of material) are 'backflushed' (automatically deducted) from the inventory records. Also see backflushing. *(Source: ILT Supply-Chain Inventory Management SIG)*

Defect notice   Official notice (Form GV 219) given by DoT* (ie Vehicle Inspectorate*) examiners when a vehicle is found to have defects which need attention but not of such a serious nature as to warrant prohibition (*see* PG 9).

Defence   Means by which a charged offender can put forward a pre-established reason why something occurred to avoid conviction (eg with tachographs* that a defect in the system occurred while on the journey in which the contravention of the law was detected – ie by police, etc; or with vehicle overload, driver was on his way to the nearest available weighbridge). *See also* Due diligence.

Deferred rebate   Rebate on freight rates given to shippers for regular bookings over a period.

DEKRA   Broadly translated as German Motor Vehicle Certification/ Standards Association. Founded in Berlin in 1924 for setting and certifying vehicle standards and testing, etc. *See also* TÜV.

Del credere   Guarantee given by shipping agent or broker to a principal for the solvency of person to whom goods are being sold.

Delay   In context of drivers' hours law, unforeseen delay to driver due to emergency situation that may cause him to exceed statutory limits. *See also* Emergencies.

Delivery order   An order to deliver goods (ie a document detailing instructions for delivery of goods to a consignee).

Demand management   A distribution term relating to the methods of managing customer demands (ie goods ordered with instructions as to where and when required for delivery, etc).

Demountable body   Goods vehicle load-carrying body which can be detached from the chassis (to stand independently for loading/transfer, etc). Interchangeable (ie swap body*) bodies/body types to give speed of vehicle turn-round and greater flexibility in operation.

DEMU   Diesel electric multiple unit. Train driven by diesel-electric power. Usually comprising a small number of coaches for local service use. *See also* DMU and EMU.

Demurrage   Term meaning payment (due or charged) when load is delayed/held-up/not loaded/off-loaded, etc when agreed. Also applies if vehicle/ship/rail wagon delayed when empty. Most frequently found in shipping/rail transport.

Denver boot   Slang term for wheel clamp used in metropolitan areas (mainly London) to catch and deter those who park vehicles illegally or cause obstruction. Driver has to pay fixed penalty and release fee to secure release (usually after a long wait).

Dependent demand   A classification used in inventory control where the demand for one item has a direct mathematical relationship with the demand for another higher level or parent component and where the demand for that item is ultimately dependent on the demand for the higher level or parent item. *(Source: ILT Supply-Chain Inventory Management SIG)*

Depot   Base or centre of operations for transport/logistics business, for example, and from which bus and coach operations are conducted. Also a place where vehicles are based or garaged when not in use (in 'O' licensing* terms, an 'operating centre'*).

Depreciation   The practice of reducing the book value of an asset (eg a vehicle) over a period of time to indicate wear and tear and possible obsolescence. May be by 'straight line' method (ie where equal amounts are charged over a period of, say, five or ten years), or loaded to increase/ decrease over a period. New cars, for example, generally depreciate by up to 50 per cent as soon as they are driven from the showroom.

DEQ   Delivered ex-quay duty paid. Price for goods delivered to the customer from the quay after unloading from ship and after payment of any duties due.

DERA   Defence Evaluation and Research Agency. Tests and evaluates military and civil hardware (ie every piece of equipment used by the British armed forces, including of course the full range of logistics vehicles).

Derived demand   Means demand derived from some function other than itself. Thus transport is not in demand for its own characteristics, but for the facility it provides to move people or goods. For example a manufacturing firm's demand for transport exists only because demand for its products exists and as demand for these increases so too does its demand for transport. In other words, the demand for transport derives from the demand for the manufacturer's products.

Derogation   Term used in EU legislation to mean exemption (eg from specific provisions of a regulation). In effect, taking away the need for a country/transport operation to observe particular aspects of the law (eg the UK has a derogation – temporarily – from the EU 40-tonne maximum vehicle weight requirement).

DERV   Diesel-engined road vehicle – diesel fuel for such vehicles which is commonly referred to as derv.

DES   Delivered ex-ship. Incoterm* used to describe conventional port-to-port sale of goods.

Design weight   The maximum weight (and axle weights) for which a vehicle is designed by the manufacturer to operate safety and efficiently. Contrasts with DTLR* plated weight which may require the same vehicle to operate at lower weight due to statutory limits (eg where a 40-tonne tractive unit has to comply with current UK limit of 38 tonnes).

Desktop (computer)   Term for small, personal, micro-computers which due to their size sit easily on a desk. As opposed to a mainframe (ie large), laptop* (now the essential tool of the travelling businessman and others), or a palm-top/hand-held (hold-in-the-hand) computer.

Desktop publishing   Term for system where small but powerful desktop micro-computers can be used to prepare text, layout, design, etc ready for printing (often by laser printer) without involvement of traditional printing methods. Desktop publishing programs are available for use with a variety of computer hardware.

Despatch (1)   Means to send a vehicle or consignment on its way.

Despatch (2)   Money paid by ship owner to charterer for earlier loading or discharging of cargo as scheduled in charter party.

Detention   Shipping term to describe the charge for detaining a container or trailer at customer's premises for longer than the period of time pre-scribed in the tariff.

Deterministic inventory control models   An inventory control system where all the variables and parameters used are known, or can be calculated with certainty. The rate of demand for items, and the associated inventory costs, are assumed to be known with assurance and the replenishment lead time is assumed to be constant and independent of demand. *(Source: ILT Supply-Chain Inventory Management SIG)*

DETR Department of the Environment, Transport and the Regions. Government's so-called 'super' Ministry (formed in 1997) with wide ranging portfolio including all aspects of transport by road, rail, sea and air, relevant licensing and statutory controls and infrastructures – formerly the DoT/DTp. Since the June 2001 election and government re-shuffle this department is now the DTLR* (Department of Transport, Local Government and the Regions).

DF Direction finder. Piece of navigation equipment used on ships.

DFDG Defence Freight Distribution Group. One of a number of sub-groups operating within the DLO* and responsible for carrying anything and everything for the combined services, from tap washers to ammunition.

DfEE Department for Education and Employment (since the May 2001 government reorganization, the DfES – the Department for Education and Skills). Ministry concerned with, among other matters, industrial relations, health and safety and training.

DGN Dangerous goods note. Document used in shipping.

DGSA Dangerous Goods Safety Advisor. EU requirement that firms which transport, load and/or unload dangerous goods should employ or appoint suitably qualified person as such, ie the holder of a vocational training certificate (VTC). *See also* Risk Prevention Officer (RPO).

DGVII European Commission Directorate General No 7, responsible for transport, environment and safety issues.

DHL Major worldwide airfreight and courier specialist company, now owned by Deutsche Post.

Dial-a-ride Door-to-door bus services providing accessible transport for people who cannot use, or find it difficult to use, public transport.

DIC Driver identity card. Smart card to be used in new-style digital tachographs from 2003. Another acronym or abbreviation may be chosen due to the impolite connotations attached to this one.

Diff-lock Differential locking system in heavy vehicle drive line by which wheel-slip (ie wheel spin) by one set of wheels, or one axle, relative to another is detected – automatic locking is effected until traction is regained.

Digging machine Defined as a vehicle designed, constructed and used for trench digging or any kind of excavating or shovelling work, which travels on public roads only to get to and from a place where it is to be used for that purpose and at such time carries no load other than for its own propulsion or its own equipment – *V(E)A 1971*.

Digital input   Means by which data is input digitally into computer.

Digital tachograph   New generation tachograph using digital technology with driver smart cards, etc, instead of paper-based chart recording. *See* Tachograph for a more detailed explanation.

Dim-dip lighting   Vehicle dipped-beam headlight operating at reduced intensity (between 10 and 20 per cent of normal intensity) for the purpose of use during the daytime (ie running lamps – seen as standard on Scandinavian cars).

DIN   *Deutsche Industrie-Normung*. German Standard for measurement of vehicle engine power output.

DiPTAC   Disabled Persons' Transport Advisory Committee. Official body concerned with the design and use of buses (and bus services) for elderly and disabled people.

Direct costs   In transport, the costs that directly relate to the operation of a vehicle as opposed to indirect costs that are ancillary to the vehicle operation.

Direct injection diesel   Compression ignition (ie diesel) engine in which fuel is injected direct into the combustion chamber – as opposed to indirect injection where it is injected first into a pre-combustion chamber.

Direct store delivery   System where goods are delivered from manufacturer direct to the retailer, ie not going via a warehouse or distribution centre.

DIRFT   Daventry International Rail Freight Terminal. Daventry (Northants) intermodal terminal.

Dirigible   Lighter than air vessel (eg an airship) which can be steered as opposed to a balloon which cannot.

DIRT   Drug Influence Recognition Training. Element within police training package for detecting drivers under the influence of drugs. *See also* DEC and FIT.

Disabled workers (employment of)   Under employment law, requirement for employers of more than 20 persons to employ a quota (3 per cent) of persons who are registered as disabled.

Disc brakes On motor vehicles, brakes using hardened steel discs and pads to provide the braking surface rather than the old type of asbestos/ fibre lining in a steel drum. They provide greater efficiency, cool operation, lighter weight and ease of access for maintenance purposes.

Discrimination (race/sex) Legislation makes it illegal (mainly for employers but others also) to discriminate against persons on grounds of their colour, race, nationality, ethnic origins. Also illegal to discriminate on grounds of sex (either against females or males).

Disk (computer) Special disk used for the external (ie back-up) storage of computer data (to avoid loss). Normally either in 3.5 in or 5.25 in size (single or double-sided floppy disks*). Also hard-disk* which is an internal storage disk within (or attached as a peripheral to) the computer.

Disposal of waste Strict legislation controls the disposal of (poisonous/ hazardous) waste and makes it an offence for transport operators to carry such waste without a licence and to 'dump' waste in non-authorized locations. Heavy fines may be imposed and vehicles impounded.

Disqualification (of driving licence holder) Driving licence holders can lose the right to drive for a given period when disqualified by the Courts following conviction (or indictment) for certain road traffic (and other) offences (eg drink/driving) or in other cases when the licence holder has incurred 12 penalty points on his or her licence within three years.

Distribution Regarding goods distribution, the process of storage, handling, loading and delivery (mainly by road) of goods/products to retail outlets or the final consumer. In practice many other individual functions may be involved (order processing, order picking, inventory control, etc).

Distribution requirement planning (DRP 1) The function of deter-mining the need to replenish inventory at branch warehouses over a forward time period. A time-phased order point approach is used where planned orders at branch warehouse level are exploded via MRP* logic to become gross requirements on the supplying source enabling the translation of inventory plans into material flows. In the case of multi-level distribution networks, this explosion process can continue down through the various levels of regional warehouses, master warehouse, factory warehouse, etc and become input to the master production schedule. *(Source: ILT Supply-Chain Inventory Management SIG)*

Distribution resource planning (DRP 2)   The extension of MRP* into the planning of the key resources contained in a distribution system. *(Source: ILT Supply-Chain Inventory Management SIG)*

DK   Nationality symbol for Denmark – to be shown on the rear of vehicles from that country.

DKV   Provider of on-road services for heavy diesel vehicle operators holding the DKV Card (diesel, repairs, 24-hr emergency breakdown, etc).

DLO (1)   Defence Logistics Organization. UK Ministry of Defence off-shoot (formed April 2000) which provides joint (ie combined services) logistics support to the Armed Forces in the frontline on operations at home and overseas. Part of the Defence Storage and Distribution Agency (DSDA)*.

DLO (2)   Despatch money payable loading only. Term used in shipping.

DME   Dimethylether. An alternative low-emission fuel for use in diesel-engined vehicles which is energy-efficient and made from natural gas (but can be made from renewable raw materials) – it becomes gas at room temperature.

DMU   Diesel Multiple Unit. Linked train comprising a number of passenger coaches and powered by a diesel engine. See also DEMU and EMU. Concept now being adopted for trials in the UK with small container-carrying freight multiple-unit trains (*see* Cargo-Sprinter). Similar system operated in Germany by DB*.

D/O   Delivery order. Instructions for delivery of goods/consignment.

Doc   Commonly used abbreviation for document.

Dock leveller   Equipment (hydraulically or manually operated) used to equalize the differing heights of a loading bay and road vehicles to make loading by fork lift truck*/pallet truck* possible.

Doctor's beacons   Form of warning beacon (ie fixed or rotating light) – green in colour – which doctor (ie medical practitioner registered by General Medical Council) may use for an emergency.

Document de suivi   Tracing note, signed by the consignor of a load, which must be carried by all carriers moving goods to, from or within France in addition to the standard CMR* consignment note. It must be produced to the police on demand. Not required for through transit loads.

Documentary credit   The most secure form of payment for exported goods if confirmed by a UK bank. Once the requisite documents are presented within the period of their validity (ie of the period of credit) the bank will honour the payment irrespective of any default by the payer or other problem (eg political upheaval in country of destination).

DOE   Department of the Environment – in Northern Ireland all road transport licensing and related matters are handled by the DOE in Belfast, not the DTLR* as in Great Britain.

DOG   Daily order generation. Distribution industry jargon.

Dolly   Also towing dolly. Single-axle bogie (may be fitted with fifth-wheel* coupling) used to support trailer/semi-trailer. Forms part of a composite trailer*.

DoT   Department of Transport. Now part of DTLR*.

Dot-matrix (printer)   Type of printer used with computers which prints on the paper with series of 'needles' which form the letters by means of a dot matrix.

DoT plate   Document (ie Ministry plate*) issued by Goods Vehicle Centre, Swansea indicating the pmw* for goods vehicle/trailer in accordance with current legal limits. Must be securely fixed in cab/on chassis frame and weights shown (ie gross/train/axle) must not be exceeded in Great Britain.

DoT register (of tachograph seals)   Tachograph installations must be mandatorily sealed following calibration/two-yearly checks with lead, customs-type seals. In fixing the seal a number and the approved fitting station code is impressed. This information is recorded in the DoT register for future reference (eg for enforcement purposes).

Double bottom   Form of articulated combination with two semi-trailers, the first mounted on the tractive unit, the second on a towing dolly*.

Double-decker   As in double-deck bus (ie with an upper deck carrying additional passengers) – common in the UK although rarely seen in Europe. Also double-deck trailers where an additional deck virtually doubles-up load capacity. Frequently used in livestock-carrying vehicles for the carriage of sheep and pigs. *See also* Tri- (triple) decker.

Double deep racking   Pallet racks with frames for two pallets deep using standard automatic pallet racking thereby reducing the number of gangways. Requires a modified fork-lift truck using double length forks. Selecting and putting away stock is slower than single pallet operations.

Double-drive/bogie   On heavy vehicles with two or more rear axles, where at least two of the axles forming a bogie are driven (as opposed to trailing axle/s which is/are not driven). This gives improved traction (eg for use on rough/steep terrain).

Double-manned   Vehicle with two-man driving crew (usually) for long-distance/ international operations). EU law makes provision for this by way of reduced rest periods for such operations.

Double reduction axle   Vehicle rear axle with gearing (ie crown wheel and pinion – differential) designed to provide normal and lower drive ratio. Also double reduction hubs – in heavy goods vehicle to reduce stress on differential and half- (ie drive) shafts. *See also* Hub reduction.

DP (1)   Designated premises. Designated (ie VI* approved) operator vehicle workshops where annual goods vehicle testing may be carried out instead of at the VI's own goods vehicle testing stations

D/P (2)   Documents against payment. Term used in shipping meaning that the official shipping documents will be handed over only when payment has been made.

DPP   Direct product profitability. Concept where all the costs relating to an individual product (eg material, manufacture, packaging, delivery, etc) to provide comparisons and identify inefficiencies in product marketing.

Drawbar   The connection between a vehicle and a trailer (comprising a steel bar).

Drawbar trailer/combination   Trailer with four or more wheels drawn by a rigid vehicle to form a drawbar combination. Currently in UK may be up to 32,520 kg maximum gvw and 18 metres long (to be increased to 18.35 metres).

Drawing vehicle   Term used in legislation for a motor vehicle which draws a trailer.

Drink-driving limit   Statutory limit in UK for alcohol in the breath of vehicle drivers above which it is illegal to drive or be in charge of a motor vehicle (currently 35 mg of alcohol in 100 ml of breath, which equals 80 mg of alcohol in 100 ml of blood or 107 mg of alcohol in 100 ml of urine – *RTA 1988* s11{2}).

DRIVE   Dedicated Road Infrastructure for Vehicle Safety in Europe. An EU* research programme on the application of telecoms and information technology* to road transport.

Drive 2 initiative   EU project concerned with developing vehicle monitoring equipment. *See also* Project Samovar.

Drive-in racking   This comprises vertical uprights linked by cantilever pallet supporting members at appropriate pallet heights. The fork truck drives into the racks to access pallets.

Drive line   Term which describes in two words the combination of essential components needed to drive a motor vehicle (ie engine [power unit], clutch, gearbox, propeller shaft and differential in rear axle and, where appropriate, double reduction hubs).

Driveline asset manager   High-tech terminology to describe the job of a truck driver – believed to have been originated by UK manufacturer, Foden Trucks.

Driver and Vehicle Licensing Agency   Executive body of the DTLR* that has taken over the driver and vehicle licensing work of the DVLC*.

Driver defect report   Required under provisions of 'O' licensing. Licence holders must undertake to ensure they have a proper system for drivers to report defects in their vehicles – failure to do so could lead to penalty against the licence.

Driver employment agency   Employment agency specializing in the provision of licensed LGV drivers (eg Overdrive).

Driver number   UK driving licences feature an identifying code known as the driver number which contains the first five letters of the driver's surname, or if their surname has less than five letters the remaining spaces are filled by the number 9 (eg the surname Cox would appear as COX99). Their initials are also shown.

Driving Standards Agency   Executive agency of the DoT* which is responsible for all driver and driving instructor testing and for monitoring Approved Driving Instructor (ADI) standards.

Drop-frame trailer   Semi-trailer in which the chassis (ie frame) can be lowered to ground to allow easy loading (of wheeled/tracked plant, etc).

Dropped trailers   Articulated semi-trailers detached from the towing vehicle (ie tractive unit) and left for loading/unloading. This allows the expensive part, ie the unit and driver to be usefully employed on other duties while these activities take place. Dropped trailers are sometimes used as a temporary extension of the storage facility.

Dropside (vehicle body)   Open-bodied goods vehicle on which the sides (sideboards) are hinged to drop down for ease of loading/unloading or to permit the carriage of wider loads – or which may be totally removed.

DRP   Distribution resource planning. Also Distribution requirements planning. A term relating to the planning of distribution resources with the object of ensuring that goods are available for supply to customers as and when they are required. A task usually performed by computer program, which can take account of all the inherent variables.

DRR   Demand-responsive replenishment. Distribution phrase implying that response to demand is by means of developing trading partnerships, instigating an internal strategy to facilitate continuous replenishment and improving the use of information flows.

DRS   Direct Rail Services. Rail freight operator principally engaged in moving nuclear materials for British Nuclear Fuel Limited (BNFL).

Dry cargo   Dry goods as opposed to liquid cargo.

DSA   Driving Standards Agency. Government agency dealing with driving standards and conducting practical and theoretical driving tests.

DSDA   Defence Storage and Distribution Agency. Government agency dealing with all military (ie multi-service) storage and distribution operations.

DSS   Department of Social Security. Government department concerned with the collection of national insurance contributions from employers and self-employed persons and payment of relevant benefits to claimants.

DTI (1)   Department of Trade and Industry. Government department concerned with trade matters.

DTI (2)   Direct trader input. Procedure for customs entry clearance via computer.

DTLR   Department of Transport, Local Government and the Regions. Successor to the DETR* following the 2001 general election and government reshuffle. Undertakes all of the transport-related functions of its predecessor.

DTMA   Defence Transport and Movements Agency. Government agency responsible for moving military stores, materials and equipment, etc.

DTp   Department of Transport. Former name for what became part of the Department of the Environment, Transport and the Regions and now, since June 2001, the DTLR*.

DTR2   *The Carriage of Dangerous Goods by Road (Driver Training) Regulations 1996* (SI 2094/1996).

Dual braking system   On motor vehicles whereby if one system (or one part of a system) fails a second (dual part) operates to provide braking power on at least half the wheels.

Dual kingpin   Re articulated semi-trailers, where two kingpins are provided instead of the normal one, to give a choice of coupling positions on the tractive unit – for the purposes of controlling drive-axle weight on the tractive unit or overall combination length.

Dual-purpose vehicle   A vehicle specifically defined in law. It may be generally described as being constructed or adapted to carry both passenger and goods, does not exceed 2,040 kg ulw and has either four-wheel drive or has a permanently fitted roof, is permanently fitted with one row of transverse seats (cushioned or sprung and with upholstered backrests) behind the drivers seat, and has a window on either side to the rear of the driver's seat and one at the rear. The majority of estate cars, hatchbacks, station wagons (including Range Rovers and certain models of Land Rover) are dual-purpose vehicles under this definition.

DUCT tape   Heavy duty, waterproof, cloth tape useful for all types of automotive repairs, etc – 'The tool kit on a roll'.

Due diligence   Term meaning that every possible care was given to ensure that something was right (RHA* has pressed government to insert a 'due diligence' defence* clause in legislation relating to vehicle weight offences/ overloading, etc). Also used to describe the process by which a detailed examination is carried out of the financial status of a firm prior to takeover or merger.

Dunnage   Pieces of wood, mats and other materials used to help secure the load on a vehicle or trailer or to facilitate the stowage of cargo in a ship.

Dutiable cargo   Cargo which attracts some form of duty (ie Customs and Excise* duty or VAT*).

Duty (1) Legal charge payable to Customs in connection with goods imported or exported.

Duty (2) The time spent by an employee (eg an LGV* driver) working for his employer. Includes driving, loading/unloading and waiting time. Also rostered duties for bus drivers. *See also* Changed duty sheet.

Duty free fuel Diesel fuel (ie rebated heavy oil*) on which reduced duty has been paid. Such fuel is commonly called gas oil or red diesel and is intended for use in off-road vehicles, contractors plant, farm vehicles, etc. It is illegal to use it in normal road vehicles – full duty-paid diesel fuel must be used in these.

Duty to give information The driver of a vehicle who is involved in a road accident* (where injury or damage is caused, other than to the driver himself or his vehicle) must give to anybody having reasonable grounds for requiring it, his own name and address, the name and address of the vehicle owner and the registration number of the vehicle. If this is not done at the scene, the accident must be reported to the police as soon as reasonably practicable but in any case within 24 hours. A driver who is alleged to have committed an offence under the *Road Traffic Act 1988* must give his name and address when required to do so by a police constable. Failure to give such information is an offence.

Duty to stop In the case of a road accident, where injury or damage is caused other than to the driver himself and his vehicle, the driver must stop. Failure to do so is a serious offence carrying heavy penalties.

DVD Digital versatile disk. A device that replaces the video recorder and shows films on DVDs (ie like CDs) with 'broadcast quality' sound.

DVLA Driver and Vehicle Licensing Agency. Executive agency of the DTLR* that handles all vehicle and driver licensing matters. Based at the Driver and Vehicle Licensing Centre at Swansea (see below). Has greater autonomy than when operating as a government department.

DVLC Driver and Vehicle Licensing Centre. Centre at Swansea where all vehicle and driver licensing matters are administered by DVLA*.

DVO Driver, vehicle and operator. As in DVO Strategy Board established by the government to promote better cross-agency coordination, and to establish a strategic framework, between the DVO organizations (ie the DSA*, DVLA*, VCA*, VI* and the TAN*) and the DTLR*.

DVPA   Driver and Vehicle Performance Analysis system. Set of modular hardware components and a software reporting suite that provides detailed operational information on drivers and vehicles – product of VDO Kienzle UK Ltd.

DWA   Driving without awareness. A syndrome that affects drivers by the onset of tiredness, but may include more complex conditions such as a loss of concentration and even going into a trance. Under grant-aided research by Exeter University and Devon County Council.

Dwell time   The time when a vehicle is waiting at a terminal. Term also used to represent time spent in an air terminal by passengers changing planes especially in hub-and-spoke operations. Dwell time is also defined as the period in a terminal when money is spent, but operators would prefer to minimize this.

DWT   Deadweight tonnage. The maximum weight a ship can carry including bunker fuel and stores. *See also* Tonnage.

Dynamic weighing   A system for weighing goods vehicle used by the police/ enforcement authorities under the *Weighing of Motor Vehicles (Use of Dynamic Axle Weighing Machines) Regulations 1978*. Dynamic axle weighing machines are set into the surface (usually at DoT roadside weigh-stations) and the vehicle is driven across at very low speed to give its individual axle weights and an aggregated gross/train weight. A weighing tolerance of plus or minus 150 kg per axle is allowed, multiplied by the number of axles to determine the tolerance for the gross/train weight.

Ee

E   Nationality symbol for Spain – to be shown on the rear of vehicles from that country.

'E' or 'e' (mark)   Marking on goods (vehicle components – light bulbs, lenses, etc) to indicate that they have been Type Approved (*see* Type Approval) in accordance with European legislation.

e-   Meaning electronic when used in the context of doing business via the Internet.

e-business   Term describing the increasing trend towards the conduct of business electronically over the Internet.

e-commerce   Same as above, but includes retail selling via the Internet – see also e-shopping below. A way to execute transactions and share information with other businesses, consumers or with government by using computer and telecommunication networks, including the Internet. *(Source: ILT Supply-Chain Inventory Management SIG).*

e-fulfilment   Fulfilment of orders and customer demands via the Internet.

e-logistics   Logistics and supply-chain operations being conducted via the Internet, especially the matching of shippers and carriers of goods and the transmission of documentation.

e-mail   Mail transferred electronically between computers via the Internet.

e-shopping   Term for the business by which individual consumers (ie shoppers) order goods over the Internet for home delivery. *See also* Internet shopping.

e-tailing   Retailing of general or specialized goods direct to the public via the Internet, usually with a promise of prompt or timed delivery.

'E' routes   System of principal route marking to be extended across Europe under the *AGR Convention 1975* whereby major national routes (m-ways/autoroutes) are given additional E-route numbers, eg French national route A1 Calais/Paris, A6 Paris/Lyon, A7 Lyon/Orange, A9 Orange/ La Jonquera (on Spanish border) is additionally designated the E15 throughout.

EAN European article number. Bar code numbers used for identification, pricing and tracking of stock.

EASA European Aviation Safety Authority. Proposed authority to harmonize aviation control and licensing standards in the EU.

EAT Employment Appeals Tribunal. A panel of High Court judges, plus appointed lay members, that hears appeals arising from Employment Tribunal decisions.

Eaton Manufacturer of heavy vehicle axle and transmission components.

EBS Electronic braking system. Designed and fitted to ensure tractor-trailer brake compatibility. Independent electronically controlled brake valves are fitted to each wheel.

EC (1) European Community. *See* EU.

EC (2) European Commission. The so-called 'powerhouse' of Europe. The executive of the EU, independent of national governments (ie of member states) and answerable only to the European Parliament in its power to initiate and execute policy. The fount from which all EU legislation comes.

EC 98/76 EU Directive, 'On admission to the Occupation of Road Haulage Operator in National and International Operations', under which the system of professional competence* for transport managers was established.

EC 3820/85 EU regulations concerned with social matters regarding the working conditions of goods and passenger vehicle drivers (ie by controlling their hours of driving and setting minimum rest periods, etc).

EC 3821/85 EU regulations concerned with the fitment of tachographs in certain goods and passenger vehicles and their use by drivers to control and monitor driving times, rest periods, etc.

EC directive Means by which the European Commission requires member states to conform to a set of broad principles. Each member state must enact its own domestic legislation to give effect to the provisions (unlike EC regulations which are binding as written).

EC regulation   Means by which the European Commission imposes its specific requirements on member states. Such regulations are binding in all states as written and require no domestic legislation for their enactment (unlike EC directives).

ECAS   Electronically controlled air suspension. Suspension system for heavy trucks to provide smoother ride and less damage to goods carried and road surfaces.

ECBL   European Certification Board for Logistics. Certifying body for logistics qualifications. The Institute of Logistics is the UK body providing accreditation and certification to ECBL qualifications.

ECE   Economic Commission for Europe. A United Nations body based in Geneva. It includes the Inland Transport Committee which established the Common Transport Policy.

ECGD   Export Credit Guarantees Department. Branch of Department of Trade and Industry that guarantees debts due by overseas purchasers to UK exporters.

ECHR   European Court of Human Rights. Founded in 1959 and sits in Strasbourg to hear cases brought under the European Convention on Human Rights.

ECM   Electronic control module – as used in dual fuel (diesel/natural gas) engines to regulate the relative proportions of each fuel.

ECML   East coast main line. Main rail route from London to Scotland and the north via the east coast route (Peterborough, Doncaster, York and Newcastle upon Tyne).

ECMT   European Conference of Ministers of Transport. An inter-governmental organization established by protocol in 1953. It is actually a forum comprising transport ministers from all EU member states who cooperate on (mainly inland) policy concerned with improving transport utilization and ensuring the rational development of European transport systems of national importance.

ECMT permit   Permit issued under the auspices of the European Conference of Ministers of Transport (ECMT*) and valid for road haulage operations between the states, which are party to the Conference but with exceptions due to shortages of supply. Such permits are available in limited numbers only; applications to the IRFO*, Newcastle upon Tyne.

Ecomatic   A product of Volkswagen (on its Golf vans) which switches the vehicle engine off when the accelerator is lifted to improve fuel consumption thus making urban driving more economical and quieter.

Economic order interval (EOI)   In fixed order interval systems, the interval between orders that will minimize the total inventory cost, under a given set of circumstances, obtained by trade-off analysis between the cost of placing an order and the cost of holding stock. *(Source: ILT Supply-Chain Inventory Management SIG)*

Economic order quantity (EOQ)   In fixed order quantity systems, the size of an order that minimizes the total inventory cost, under a given set of circumstances, obtained by trade-off analysis between the cost of placing an order and the cost of holding stock. *(Source: ILT Supply-Chain Inventory Management SIG)*

Economic stock   The sum of the physical stock and the goods ordered but not yet received, minus the goods sold but not yet delivered for which a company carries risk in respect of a drop in price and unmarketability. *(Source: ILT Supply-Chain Inventory Management SIG)*

Economies of scale   Economic theory which appears to dictate that 'big' is economically better (ie bulk buying gives lower cost per unit; large firms can operate more efficiently than small ones; two lorries can be operated more economically than just one, etc).Where a firm has a high proportion of direct costs* any increase in output that can be sold so as to achieve a satisfactory return will have the effect of lowering unit costs*. This advantage appears to be very limited in road freight transport and the coaching trade, but this does not account for the growth of larger bus firms. There are also diseconomies of scale (eg resulting from over-bureaucratic management) which will offset growth beyond a certain point.

Ecopoint stamps   Stamps worth one Ecopoint* each issued by IRFO* to road hauliers for entry into Austria and based on the COP value* for the vehicle. Fewer stamps are charged for entry of modern 'green' vehicles than for older models. Ecopoint stamps are stuck on an Eco card (from IRFO), one card being required for each leg of a transit journey through Austria.

Ecopoints   Points system for controlling transit of heavy lorries through Austria, replacing transit permits, and based on NOx emission* of vehicle – older vehicles needing more points than environmentally-friendly ('greener') newer vehicles.

ECR   Efficient customer/consumer response. Concept in logistics to minimize inventory and logistics costs and to optimize product availability.

ECSI   Export cargo shipping instruction. Shipping instructions from shipper to carrier.

ECU   European currency unit. Intended common currency of the Single European Market. Value of ECU against national currencies is quoted in daily financial papers. Now called by preferred name, the Euro.

EDC   Electronic diesel control. Key characteristic of so-called 'new generation' low-emission diesel engines designed to reduce fuel consumption and exhaust emissions.

'Eddie'   A heavy vehicle belonging to and painted in the colours of major UK road haulier Eddie Stobart seen by lorry spotters (the Eddie-watcher cult!) on journeys. *See also* 'Norbert' and Fleet names.

EDI   Electronic data interchange. System for the exchange of data/information/documents by electronic means (ie between computers). The transfer of structured data from one computer system to another.

EDIFACT   Electronic Data Interchange for Administration, Commerce and Transport. A United Nations standard for handling and actioning trading data.

EDP   Electronic data processing. *See also* EDI.

EEA   European Economic Area. A combination of all EU member states and Liechtenstein, Iceland and Norway (ie EFTA* countries).

EEBPP   Energy efficiency best practice programme. Project of DTLR* to promote energy conservation in industry (eg improved fuel efficiency in road transport). Studies carried out by such as ETSU*.

EEC   European Economic Community. Now the European Union (EU)*.

EEV   Enhanced environmental vehicle. A Euro-standard ultra-clean vehicle (ie low emission and low noise vehicle).

Effective stock   The sum of the physical stock of a particular product and the quantity of that product ordered for a particular period, but not yet received. *(Source: ILT Supply-Chain Inventory Management SIG)*

Efficient consumer response (ECR)   An initiative whereby elements of the supply-chain work together to fulfil consumer wishes better, faster and at less cost. *(Source: ILT Supply-Chain Inventory Management SIG)*

EFT Electronic funds transfer. System for making payments electronically. Has benefit of reducing payment times, loss of cheques in the post or theft, etc.

EFTA European Free Trade Area. A trading block of national states (ie Austria, Finland, Iceland, Norway, Sweden and Switzerland) that have agreed to have no barriers to trade between them.

EFTPOS Electronic fund transfer at the point of sale. New technology system which allows holders of 'switch' bank cards (plus Lloyds Bank Payment and Barclay's Connect cards) to pay for goods bought by direct transfer from the payee's bank account without the need to use cash or write a cheque.

EGR Exhaust gas re-circulation. System used to help reduce NOx emissions from vehicle exhausts.

EIA European Intermodal Association. European-wide association of intermodal transport operators, based in Brussels.

EIB European Investment Bank. Provides funds for, among other things, road developments in European countries.

Eight-wheeler Term for rigid vehicle with four axles (ie twin steering axles at front and tandem bogie comprising two axles at rear – one or both driven). Largest type of rigid vehicle currently permitted on UK roads – pmw (subject to design and plating) 32,000 kg. Ideally suited to tipper/tanker applications where stability is essential.

EIS Export Intelligence Service.

ELA European Logistics Association. Body representing national logistics organizations throughout Europe.

Elasticity of supply and demand Terms which indicate the extent to which demand will respond to changes in price and/or quality. Demand from commuters is generally inelastic (ie will not change much), but travel demand for pleasure purposes may be more elastic. There is also cross-elasticity of demand (eg as between car and train or bus, or between modes for distribution purposes). Elasticity of supply affects the extent to which operators can increase output in response to increased demand, thus it is easier for truck operators to do this than it is for shipping lines.

ELC European Logistics Centre.

Electric vehicles   Vehicles powered by electric storage battery. Normally used for short range/low speed operations (ie local deliveries – milk rounds). Such vehicles are exempt from VED.

Electronic data interchange (EDI)   The computer-to-computer exchange of structured data for automatic processing. *(Source: ILT Supply-Chain Inventory Management SIG)*

Electronic mailbox   Modern technology means by which correspondence can be passed between computers via telephone lines (ie land lines).

Electronic market place   In the transport context, where loads and available vehicle capacity are matched on the Internet. Used to be called clearing houses* and also known as freight exchanges*.

EMAS   European Union's Eco-Management and Audit Scheme. European equivalent of ISO 14001 international standard for environmental management.

Embargo   A term meaning prohibition. Usually used when cargos are embargoed (ie prohibited from moving or being shipped). Also applies on press notices that are embargoed for release at a certain time – often to coincide with a particular event.

Emergency   Under goods vehicle drivers' hours law, the circumstances when a driver can depart from the rules to deal with, or when he is delayed by, an emergency situation. Under EU law a driver may depart from the rules as necessary to reach a suitable stopping place when events arise requiring him to ensure the safety of persons, the vehicle or its load, providing road safety is not jeopardized. Details must be on his tachograph chart. In UK domestic operations, daily driving and duty limits may be suspended to deal with events which require immediate action to avoid danger to the life or health of one or more persons or animals, serious interruption in essential services (ie gas, water, electricity, drainage, telecommunications, postal services) or in the use of roads, railways, ports or airports, or damage to property. Details must be entered on the record sheet.

Emergency action code   Regarding the UK carriage of dangerous substances by road, the internationally recognized code indicated on vehicle (ie tanker) marking panels (ie Hazchem label). The code comprises a number (between 1 and 4) and a letter (plus sometimes the letter 'E') which together indicates to the emergency services the action they should take to deal with a spillage of the substance (eg '2YE' means apply water fog, wear breathing apparatus, contain substance and consider evacuation of area). This code is sometimes referred to as the Kemler code. Details in *The Carriage of Dangerous Goods by Road Regulations 1996 and related statutes.*

Employers' liability   Legal obligation on employers (under *Employers' Liability (Compulsory Insurance) Act 1969*) to carry insurance cover to protect their employees who may suffer injury or illness arising from their employment. Minimum cover required by law is £5 million in respect of any claim arising from a single occurrence – usually the cover provided is for an unlimited amount.

Employment Medical Advisory Service   Carries out periodic medical examination of workers in hazardous situations as required by regulations made under provisions of the *HSWA 1974* and the *Factories Act 1961.*

Employment Tribunal   Body appointed to resolve disputes between employees and employers on matters of employment rights and conditions, minimum wage issues, equal pay, certain health and safety matters, discrimination and some pension matters.

EMS   European Monetary System. A proposed system for European Community-wide monetary union including the establishment of a single currency and the concept of a central bank replacing national central banks (the Bank of England in the UK).

EMT   Extended mobility technology. A name given by Goodyear Tyres to its system for run-flat tyres which allow a car to be driven a reasonable distance to a place of safety where the wheel can be changed.

EMU (1)   European monetary union.

EMU (2)   Electric multiple unit. Train comprising electric or diesel-electric powered and non-powered coaches. *See also* DEMU and DMU.

Encapsulation   To enclose within. In transport, the enclosure of heavy vehicle engines to reduce noise for environmental purposes.

Endorsement   The adding of something to a document – eg a penalty added to a driving licence.

Enforcement/officer/authority   General term to mean the role of the DTLR* and its Vehicle Inspectorate Agency and its appointed certifying officers, vehicle examiners, etc who are authorized to examine vehicles, drivers records, etc. Certain such officers have powers to prohibit use of vehicles and to issue prosecutions. Would also include police.

Engine speed recording   Facility on certain models of tachograph instruments to record engine speed (ie revolutions per minute) on reverse side of chart in addition to standard recordings of time, speed and distance on face of the chart. Useful for determining how vehicles are treated by drivers (eg over-revving, coasting out of gear, etc).

Engineering plant   Legally defined in *RV (C&U) 1986*. May be generally described as motor vehicle/trailer which is movable plant or equipment specially designed and constructed for engineering operations and which cannot comply with the regulations. Also must not be designed to carry loads other than material that it has excavated (also includes mobile cranes).

Enterprise   Rail freight service of EWS* for lorry-sized consignments in single wagon loads or larger groups of wagons.

Enterprise requirement planning (ERP)   A further extension of MRP* whereby a single system embraces and integrates all aspects of business operations into a single database application. *(Source: ILT Supply-Chain Inventory Management SIG)*

Entitlement to drive   Under new system of driver licensing in UK (in compliance with EU requirements) licence holders have 'entitlement to drive' vehicles of the category for which they have passed the test (eg LGV/PCV entitlements).

Entry/exit visa   Authority given by a country (usually in advance) for an individual to enter or leave a country – indicated by a stamp or attachment of a document in the person's passport.

Environmental representation   *See* Representation.

Environmentally friendly vehicle   Vehicle with low exhaust emission of 'greenhouse' gases*.

ENXÒ   European Exchange Network. Global electronic communications network to facilitate the transfer of information between companies and generate transactions – initially a motor industry initiative to deliver cost savings through e-commerce.

E&OE   Errors and omissions excepted. Used on invoices to indicate that the issuer retains the right to make corrections or further charges to cover errors or omissions on the invoice.

EON   Enhanced other networks. Radio system, which automatically switches drivers from a BBC national radio channel, cassette or CD to a BBC local radio station to receive a current travel bulletin.

EOQ Economic order quantity. Logistics term to identify the minimum quantity of goods that can be supplied on an economic basis, anything less incurring a financial loss on the order.

EOS Electronic ordering system. Facilitates ordering via computer.

EPG Environmental Protection Group. Part of Department for Environment, Food and Rural Affairs (was formerly part of DTLR*/Ministry of Agriculture, Fisheries and Food). Produces research, newsletters, etc on various aspects of environmental strategy such as on air quality, water quality and waste.

EPOS Electronic point of sale. Logistics/retailing system for stock ordering, and replenishment triggered by till sales information.

EPS Electronic power shift (also electro-pneumatic shift). Gear change system – product of Mercedes-Benz.

EPU Entry processing unit. Customs term to describe one of its facilities/offices.

Equal pay It is illegal for employers to discriminate between men and women in respect of pay and other employment terms (*Equal Pay Act 1970*).

Equifax American insurance firm offering discounted premiums for clients dealing direct under insurance scheme called Comprehensive Loss Underwriting Exchange UK*.

ER Efficient replenishment. Another logistics buzzword for schemes to reduce distribution costs.

ERF British heavyweight truck manufacturer. Founded by Edwin Richard Foden of the famous Foden family of steam engine and lorry builders. Now owned by MAN*.

ERM Exchange rate mechanism. Artificial means by which the parity of respective currencies of individual EU member states (or any others) is retained (ie by permitting currencies to 'float' only within limited exchange rate ranges).

ERP Enterprise resource planning. Concept in manufacturing industry and logistics meaning to ensure greater co-ordination of business processes.

ERTMS European Rail Traffic Management System. Replacement system for ATP* (Automatic Train Protection) system on trains. Designed to prevent rail accidents.

ERTS   Enhanced remote transit shed. A Customs approved facility outside a port or airport where non-Community goods may be temporarily stored prior to Customs entry.

ES   Exponential smoothing. A weighted system for forecasting (usually of demand).

ESA   Employment Service Agency. Government employment service.

ESC   European National Shippers' Councils.

ESP   Events stock planning. More distribution industry jargon.

EST   Nationality symbol for Estonia – to be shown on the rear of vehicles from that country.

ESTA   European Association of Heavy Haulage Transport and Mobile Cranes. Trade association representing the interests of operators in these fields.

Establishment costs   Transport term for the costs of running the haulage 'establishment' (ie the premises/yard/office/workshop, etc). In general accounting these would be called overhead costs.

ETA   Estimated time of arrival.

ETC   Electronic trade credits. A system for making payments via the Internet.

ETCS   European train control system. Uses beacons beside track to electronically locate the train and, via a central control, automatically apply the brakes for red danger signals ahead. *See also* SPAD, ATP.

ETD (1)   Estimated time of departure.

ETD (2)   Electronic transfer of data (ie via computer).

ETF   European Transport Federation. Federation of European transport trades unions.

ETMC   European Transport Maintenance Council. A body of transport fleet engineers and others who meet to discuss common problems and developing trends in vehicle maintenance and technology.

ETSU   Energy Technology Support Unit. Part of Atomic Energy Authority plc Harwell concerned with developing and monitoring energy saving projects.

EU   European Union. New nomenclature for European Community following the 1993 Maastricht Treaty on economic union of the member states. Currently comprising 15 member states (UK, Austria, Belgium, Denmark, Finland, France, Germany, Greece, Irish Republic, Italy, Luxembourg, the Netherlands, Portugal, Spain and Sweden) with yet more wishing to join.

EUCARIS   European CAR Information System. A system developed largely to combat car crime which provides links between the national vehicle databases of participating countries enabling information on imported vehicles to be checked at the time of registration. It is helping to track down some of the 250,000 vehicles stolen annually in England and Wales that are not recovered.

EUR   Essential user rebate. A scheme proposed by the Road Haulage Association whereby essential road haulage services should be given a rebate on diesel prices to combat the government's annual road fuel duty escalator (started in 1993 to tackle the problem of pollution) under which fuel prices are increased by a percentage (currently 6 per cent) above the current rate of inflation.

Euro   Previously an ECU*. The single currency unit of the European Union.

Euro I   Also Euro II, III and IV. Emission standards for heavy diesel engines with maximum limits set for nitrous oxide (NOx), carbon monoxide (CO), unburned hydrocarbons (HC), non-methane hydrocarbons (NMHC) and particulate matter (PM). Euro I and II vehicles have been in operation for some time and the very stringent Euro III standard is due to come into force for new vehicles from 1 October 2001. Euro IV will apply from 1 October 2005.

Eurocrat   A bureaucrat (ie civil servant) of the European Union.

Euro-licence   Term for new type of European Union driving licence now being issued in Great Britain (ie single licence document showing all of a person's driving entitlements). Also called the pink licence but in fact it is pink and green.

Euro-Log   European Logistics Information System. A joint venture company specializing in creating and managing electronic links between all parties in a logistics chain.

EURO NCAP   European New Car Assessment Programme. Tests new vehicles (eg crash testing).

Euro-pallet   European standard pallet used in international freighting – 1200 mm x 800 mm and loaded up to 1,500 kg gross weight.

European Accident Statement   Document devised by insurance companies on which both (or all) parties to a road accident can enter and agree details of the occurrence irrespective of language difficulties. Saves disputes later as to what happened and who said what. Copies free from insurers, usually when issuing green cards for overseas travel with a vehicle.

European article numbering (EAN)   An international standard of product identification used in the grocery and retail areas of business. *(Source: ILT Supply-Chain Inventory Management SIG)*

Eurostar (1)   High-speed passenger rail service through the Channel Tunnel from London (Waterloo) to Brussels, Lille and Paris.

EuroStar (2)   Heavy-duty model in Iveco truck range.

Eurostat   Statistical office of the European Communities. Publisher of statistical information concerning the EU.

EuroTronic   Heavy vehicle semi-automatic gearbox. Joint venture product from Iveco and gearbox manufacturer ZF.

EURT   European Union of Road Transporters. A union of European transport unions with members from: France (UNOSTRA), Germany (BDF), Spain (FENADISMER), Italy (UNATRAS) and Belgium (UPTR and SAV).

EVA   Electric Vehicles Association. Trade association for manufacturers, repairers and suppliers of such vehicles.

EVB   Exhaust valve brake. Increases the braking generated by conventional exhaust brake – product of MAN Trucks.

EWS   English Welsh and Scottish Railway. Major American-owned UK rail freight operator formed from pre-privatization UK rail freight operations. Moves over 100 millions tones of freight annually throughout the UK and runs over 1,000 freight trains daily.

Exceptional hardship   Plea by convicted road traffic offender for the Court not to disqualify him from driving. Applicant may put forward reasons, but only of exceptional hardship, as to why he should not be disqualified. Same reasons cannot be used twice in under three years.

Excess fuel device Device on diesel-engined vehicles to provide additional fuel for starting purposes. Illegal to be located within reach of a person in the vehicle when it is moving. Produces illegal black smoke if used while the vehicle is on move. *See also* Cold start.

Excess stock Any quantity of inventory, either held or on order, which exceeds known or anticipated forward demand to such a degree that disposal action should be considered. *(Source: ILT Supply-Chain Inventory Management SIG)*

Exchange, Bill of Method of payment for exported goods – legally binding (ie unconditional) document in which issuer demands from recipient payment of agreed sum by agreed means. *See also* Bill of Exchange.

Exchange control Means by which national states control outflow of their own currency and inflows of other currencies. The UK abolished exchange controls in 1979 and all such controls within the EC have disappeared with the implementation of the Single European Market.

Exchange rate Price of one currency in comparison with another. Most European currency exchange rates are published in the daily press.

Exel Worldwide UK logistics operator. Exel plc was formed from merger of Exel Logistics and the Ocean Group (shipping specialists). Exel Logistics grew out of the National Freight Company (NFC), which in turn came from the old state-owned haulage operator British Road Services (BRS), part of which is now the truck rental division of Volvo trucks.

Exemptions In connection with legislation, specified exemptions to the provisions contained in statutes. In EU legislation. exemptions are referred to as derogations*.

Exhaust brake Form of brake on heavy vehicles whereby the back pressure through the exhaust system is used to operate a retarder applied to the propeller shaft between the gearbox and back axle.

Exhaust stack On some heavy goods vehicle the exhaust system is routed vertically at the back of the cab to emit the fumes high above ground level. The effect is to give the appearance of a smoke stack. On customized trucks* these are often chromed or made of stainless steel for effect.

Expedite To speed up. Expression used in express parcels and haulage operations meaning to get the consignment delivered as soon as possible.

Explosives (carriage of)   Strict legislation controlling the carriage of explosives by road – *The Carriage of Explosives by Road Regulations 1996*. Includes requirements for marking of vehicles; drivers to be given information about explosive substances carried and the steps to take in an emergency as well as being trained to understand the dangers of explosives.

Export licence   Government-issued document authorizing the export of specified restricted goods.

Extendible trailer   Articulated semi-trailer capable of being extended in length to accommodate loads of exceptional length. *See also* Trombone trailers.

Extranet   Network of computer systems accessed via the Internet using secure passwords. Used to transfer and share data.

EXW   An Incoterm* used where an exporter undertakes to make the goods available at specified premises, eg a factory or warehouse. The buyer (importer) bears the full cost and liability (eg accepting the insurance and freight charges) for the goods from the point of their acceptance at the specified premises until they reach their final destination.

Ex-works   A term used in preparing quotations to mean the price for the goods as they leave the place of production or packing.

Ff

F Nationality symbol for France – to be shown on the rear of vehicles from that country.

FAA Free of all average. Term used in shipping. *See* Average.

Factoring of invoices Scheme whereby a firm can 'sell' its invoices to a factoring house to gain quick payment. Factor is selective of invoices and deducts its commission which may substantially reduce the amount received. A useful source of funds when encountering cash flow problems.

Fail-safe braking System employed on heavy, air-braked vehicles whereby in the event of loss of air the brakes are automatically applied by springs. In effect the air holds the brakes in the off position, hence air pressure has to be built up when making a morning start so the brakes can be released.

Family group A group of related products for which demand can be aggregated in order to assess overall demand for the material or parts which make up the family group products. *(Source: ILT Supply-Chain Inventory Management SIG.)*

Fare A payment, usually for a person to travel by bus, train or aeroplane. *See also* Separate fares.

Farmer's goods vehicle Goods vehicle registered in the name of a person engaged in agriculture and used by him on public roads solely for carrying goods in connection with the agricultural land he occupies. Special rates of VED* apply.

FAS Free alongside ship. An Incoterm* used to describe shipping charges on a port-to-port basis only.

Fast Lane Customs system for rapid clearance of goods to or from EU destinations.

FCA Free carrier (named points). Combined transport Incoterm.

FCL   Full container load. Term for a full load in a shipping (ie ISO) or road-type container.

FCR   Forwarder's certificate of receipt.

FDR   Fuel duty rebate. Available to registered local bus services or, in London, a service run under a London local service licence or exempt from the need to have such a licence. Made under the *Fuel Duty Grant (Eligible Bus Services) Regulations 1985.*

Feeder   A term applying to a route or service with low traffic levels which feeds into a trunk operation (eg a local parcels collection service which feeds into a long-haul night trunk service or a railway branch line feeding passengers into the mainline station).

Feeder vessel   A short sea vessel used to fetch goods and containers to and from vessels operating on a hub-and-spoke basis.

FEM   *Federation Europeén de la Manutention.* EU body that researches and regulates the design of materials handling systems.

Fern Schnell Gute   German term, seen on heavy trucks, meaning literally, long distance, fast, good – a designation for the service offered.

Ferry ship/crossing   Generally means a roll-on/roll-off ship used for carrying wheeled traffic on short sea routes (as opposed to deep-sea shipping).

FEU   Forty feet equivalent unit. Refers to a 40-foot long ISO container. More generally such containers are referred to in 20-foot equivalent units (TEUs)

FFG   Freight facilities grant. Government grants to offset the costs of developing rail freight services (eg for terminal development and rolling stock).

FFI   For further instructions. Term commonly used in shipping.

FIATA   International Federation of Forwarding Agents Associations.

FIBC   Flexible intermediate bulk container. A flexible bulk container (ie packaging) used for dangerous goods carriage (if complying with relevant legislation), which has a capacity not exceeding three cubic metres and is designed for handling by mechanical equipment.

Fidelity guarantee   Regarding employment – a bond given by an insurance company after vetting an employee against the risk of theft of the employer's valuables/cash, etc. In the event the employee does steal, the insurers pay out.

FIDM   Foden Institute of Driveline Management. Training for heavy goods vehicle drivers, particularly on the use of electronically-managed engines and transmissions, provided by truck manufacturer Foden.

FIFO   First in first out. Method of stock rotation used where stock is turned over regularly. Issues are always made from the stock that has been held for the longest time.

Fifth-wheel (5th-wheel) coupling   Type of coupling used on articulated vehicles comprising fifth-wheel plate on tractive unit (on which at least 20 per cent of weight of load on trailer must rest) and kingpin on semi-trailer, which mate up, and lock into place. *See also* Sliding fifth-wheel.

FIG   Freight Interest Group. Sub-group of the Intelligent Transport Society (ITS is interested in IT issues relating to freight transport).

Fill rate   An item-based measurement that shows the percentage of demands that were met at the time they were placed. Fill rate only measures what happens when demands occur. *(Source: ILT Supply-Chain Inventory Management SIG)*

FIN   Nationality symbol for Finland – to be shown on the rear of vehicles from that country.

Financial justification   Process used to ensure that a particular project/purchase is financially justified (ie by resulting savings or operational benefits achieved).

Financial ratio   System used (mainly) in accounting and by bank managers to give a quick indication of the financial standing of a firm/client (eg current ratio which indicates the relationship of a firm's assets to its liabilities, or liquidity ratio – working capital to current liabilities – which indicates how quickly a firm could settle its debts).

Financial standing   Term used in operator licensing to indicate whether a licence applicant/holder has sufficient funds to be able to operate his vehicles both legally and safely. This is an essential requirement for licence holders under both UK and EC law.

Finished goods   Inventory to which the final increments of value have been added through manufacturing. *(Source: ILT Supply-Chain Inventory Management SIG)*

Finished goods stock   Stock that is available for supply to an external consumer, including items that have been supplied but not invoiced to an external consumer. *(Source: ILT Supply-Chain Inventory Management SIG)*

FIO   Free in and out. Term used where cargo is loaded and discharged at no cost to the ship owner.

First Aid (FA)   Legislation requires employers to advise employees about FA and provide training as necessary and FA boxes containing specified articles.

First-aider   Person trained in first aid procedures – usually nominated within a firm to be responsible for first aid matters in a department/section office.

First-in, first-out (FIFO)   Stock valuation – the method of valuing stocks which assumes that the oldest stock is consumed first and thus issues are valued at the oldest price. Stock rotation – the method whereby the goods which have been longest in stock are delivered (sold) and/or consumed first. *(Source: ILT Supply-Chain Inventory Management SIG)*

First pick ratio   During order picking, the percentage of orders or lines for which 100 per cent completion was achieved from the primary location or picking face. *(Source: ILT Supply-Chain Inventory Management SIG)*

First test   In connection with goods vehicle plating and annual testing, the first annual test for which a vehicle/trailer is submitted to goods vehicle testing station (ie in the anniversary month of original registration).

Fiscal charges   General term used to describe charges (ie taxes) raised by national governments on foreign vehicles entering their territory. Generally these fall into three categories: turnover taxes (ie for added value) such as VAT/IVA; fees for the issue of transport licences/documents; taxes or supplementary taxes such as on weight/number of axles/distance travelled in the country. Would also include fuel duties charged on excess fuel taken into a country in vehicle tanks – normal (ie free) limit is 200 litres.

Fiscal harmonization   Part of the plan for the Single European Market is to achieve harmonization (ie to bring into line) of duties and taxes charged by member states (on vehicle road tax/fuel, etc).

FIT Field impairment training. Element within police training programme for detecting drug drivers. *See also* DEC and DIRT.

Fit person Person who is considered by the Licensing Authorities to be 'fit' to hold a restricted 'O' licence*. Applicants for standard 'O' licences must be 'of good repute' for which basically similar requirements have to be met. In deciding 'fitness' the LAs take account of convictions recorded against the individual relating to goods vehicle operation (eg for overloading, unroadworthiness, driver's hours offences). In the case of LGV driver licensing, applicants must also be fit persons to hold entitlement to drive such vehicles.

Fixed assets Assets of a business which constitute part of the capital base and remain (relatively) permanent (eg land and buildings owned, plant, equipment, vehicles, etc, but not stock for resale).

Fixed costs The costs incurred in an operation which are fixed – as opposed to variable costs*. For example, VED, insurance costs, etc, which are paid annually and are therefore incurred whether the vehicle works or stands idle – hence reference to them in transport circles as standing costs*. *See also* TIDE.

Fixed order interval An inventory control system for which a maximum stock level has been calculated based on usage during the lead-time and order interval. Stock is reviewed at specified time periods and subsequent order size equates to the difference between the maximum stock level and the current inventory position. Thus, the order size will vary according to usage between reviews. *(Source: ILT Supply-Chain Inventory Management SIG)*

Fixed order quantity (fixed order size) An inventory control system where stock is reviewed continuously and, whenever the inventory falls to a predetermined point, an order for a fixed quantity of stock is generated. *(Source: ILT Supply-Chain Inventory Management SIG)*

Fixed penalty/notice (ticket) For certain road traffic offences a system of fixed penalties applies whereby the driver is given a notice (ie ticket) giving him the option of paying the fixed penalty (see below) or electing to have a Court hearing. The system operates on two levels: white tickets for non-endorseable offences (which may be left attached to the vehicle if the driver is not present) and yellow ticket for endorseable offences when the driver must be present and surrender his driving licence (then or within seven days at a police station).

Fixed penalty ticket office   The place where fixed penalties are paid within the statutory period of 28 days, or where application is made for a Court hearing, following receipt of a fixed penalty notice for a traffic offence. The address of the relevant office is given on the notice.

Fixture   Conclusion of shipbroker's negotiations to charter a ship.

Flag carrier   Term usually used to describe the national airline of a country (eg British Airways for the UK).

Flagging out   Concept whereby UK road haulage firms set up base in another EU member state from which to operate their vehicles to avoid the UK's exceptionally high rates of VED and duty on diesel fuel. In shipping, it is the practice of registering under a 'flag of convenience' (eg Panama or Liberia) largely to escape the high standards of safety, hygiene, etc imposed by the home country. *See* FOC.

Flat car   Rail terminology for a flatbed or flat platform type of wagon.

Flat rack   A type of ISO container with a flat platform and two ends but no sides, usually used for loading machinery and plant, etc.

Fleet names   Traditional practice in road haulage (and with airlines and ships) to name vehicles, usually with place names or female names. These are invariably signwritten on the front of the driver's cab. Practice popular with leading UK road haulier Eddie Stobart whose heavy trucks all carry female names – watched for and ticked off by its fan club supporters and others.

Flight path   The route or path followed by an aircraft.

Floating Vehicle Data   A scheme whereby vehicle tracking technology is used to provide information on traffic flows and build real-time data on moving vehicles.

Floppy disk   Computer term for small (ie portable) data storage disk. Usually in 5.25 or 3.5 inch standard sizes.

Flow chart   A diagrammatic representation of a sequence of planned events. Used in transport, for example, to plot when vehicles are due for service, safety inspection and annual test. Pinned on an office wall it acts as a constant reminder of due dates. Favoured by the Traffic Commissioners for this reason.

FLT   Fork-lift truck. Item of handling equipment capable of lifting and carrying by means of forks (or tines) which project from the front. Principally used for lifting and loading goods on pallets*.

Fly tipping   Illegal act of tipping spoil/rubbish/waste (particularly poisonous waste) on unauthorized sites (even on the public highway) to avoid costs/licence requirements for disposal in a proper manner on an authorized site.

FMCG   Fast moving consumer goods. Term used in distribution/logistics to describe products sold to the public through retail outlets, which move very quickly through warehousing systems thereby creating a need for special inventory control procedures and particularly efficient distribution.

FMU   Freight multiple unit. Self-propelled freight train typically formed of a small number of permanently-coupled rail vehicles with a driver's cab at each end. Faster and more flexible than conventional freight trains. *See also* Cargo-Sprinter.

FO   Free overside. Term used in quoting for shipping movements (ie price includes discharging from ship).

FOB   Free on board. Freighting term whereby the exporter's liability for goods ceases once they are delivered to the carrier.

FOC   Flag of convenience. Shipping practice where vessels are registered in states such as Liberia and Panama where taxes and duties are lower than in the ship owner's home state and where standards of safety and hygiene, for example, are not so strict. Hence the convenience factor and the ships fly the flag of the state in which they are registered rather than that of the owner's home state.

Focus groups   Groups of individuals, usually with specialist knowledge and/or experience who meet to debate, comment and lobby on specific issues (eg problems affecting a specific travel mode or matters of modal choice) and how they can be solved. Also (and perhaps more usually) groups of people recruited to give their opinions for use by government or by political parties. Psychologically-trained rapporteurs are usually employed in this role.

Fodex   Remote vehicle information retrieval system from Foden Trucks which removes the need for periodic downloading of diagnostic information with a laptop computer every time the truck returns home. An on-board data logger is 'polled' by Foden's mainframe computer in Sandwich via the gsm* cellular telephone network from wherever the truck is located anywhere in the world.

Footway/footpath   Right of way for persons on foot only.

FOR   Free on rail. Term used in quoting for the transport of goods (ie price includes free delivery onto rail system).

Force majeur   A legal term for an event that is outside the control of one or more parties to a contract and which may enable them to escape or avoid the contract conditions.

Forecast demand   The prediction, projection or estimation of expected demand over a specified future time period. *(Source: ILT Supply-Chain Inventory Management SIG)*

Forecasting   The imprecise science of trying to determine what will happen in the future. In trade/business circles, the task of predicting trends, demands, opportunities and potential for future income/profits.

Fork-lift truck (FLT)   Mechanical handling equipment with forks to lift and carry pallets. Used for stacking, etc in warehouses and for vehicle loading/unloading. Mainly electrically powered (by rechargeable battery) for warehouse operations but often gas or diesel powered for external operations.

Fork pockets   On containers and swap bodies, strengthened slots built in to the underside of the frame into which the forks (tines) of a heavy duty FLT* (or the grapple arms of an container crane) can be slotted for lifting purposes.

Forked tariff   The maximum and minimum prices which may be charged under a tariff system. For example, in European haulage, rates are controlled by a system of tariffs with a spread between maximum and minimum levels (currently 23 per cent of the maximum rate). Sometimes also called bracket tariffs.

Fortress Europe   A mythical situation (mainly created by the press) suggesting that members of the EU may progressively trade more within the Community than with outside nations thereby closing ranks on outside nations.

Forward projection   In transport terms, a load which projects beyond the front of a vehicle and which, subject to its length, may need an attendant and to carry markers (ie over 2 metres) and for the police to be notified in advance (over 3.05 metres).

Forwarder's bill of lading   A bill of lading* issued by a freight forwarder.

Forwarder's receipt   A document issued by a freight forwarder which provides evidence of receipt of the goods.

Forwarding agent   A firm acting on behalf of others (ie as an agent) in arranging the forward movement of cargo/freight. Usually in international trade where complex legal and documentary requirements must be met of which the forwarding agent has expert knowledge.

FOS   Fleet Organization System. Computerized system of vehicle fleet management. Product of Siemens VDO GmbH, Germany and marketed in the UK by VDO Kienzle (formerly Lucas Kienzle Instruments Limited).

Foster Report   Key report on road haulage operators' licensing by Professor Christopher Foster, published in 1978.

Four stroke   Workings of an internal combustion engine that operates on a four stroke cycle, namely induction, compression, ignition, exhaust.

Four-way pallet   A pallet designed to allow FLT* forks to be inserted from all four sides as opposed to the usual two-way entry.

Four-wheeler   Rigid vehicle with two axles. Pmw in UK (subject to design and plating) is currently 16,260 kg.

Fourth-party logistics   Concept whereby the fourth party logistics service provider acts as an interface between the client and a number of its individual logistics service providers. Andersen Consulting LLP claims the term to be its trademark, thus Fourth-party Logistics™, but the Hays Group also uses the term 'fourth party solutions' to describe their supply-chain business (also written 4PS).

Fourth stylus   In tachograph* instruments, an additional stylus for recording non-statutory functions (thermometer readings on fridge vehicles, door openings, etc).

FOW   First open water. Term relating to ship operating.

FPA   Free of particular average. Shipping term used to describe situation where the insurers are not responsible for partial loss claims (with certain exceptions).

FPN   Fixed penalty notice. A means of enforcing less serious traffic offences and reducing pressure on the Courts by imposing a fixed penalty payable immediately by post. Recipients can still elect for a Court hearing if they wish to contest the charge.

FQP   Freight quality partnership. Government initiative following publi-cation of its 'Sustainable Distribution Strategy' document in March 1999 in encouraging Local Authorities to get together with all interested parties, especially logistics operators, to find ways of achieving sustainable distribution systems reflected in greater efficiency, greater safety in road transport operations and reduced pollution from exhaust emissions and congestion. Such policies to be included in LTPs (Local Transport Plans).

FR   Final remuneration. A figure used in determining pension benefits.

Frameless trailer   Type of semi-trailer whereby coupling equipment and running gear* are mounted direct to the underside of the van body rather than, as conventionally, on a chassis frame. This design reduces weight and thereby increases payload potential.

Free circulation   Goods originating within the European Union or goods brought into the EU on which all duties and charges have been paid and all other formalities completed are classed for Customs purposes as being in free circulation.

Free stock   Stock available for immediate delivery (ie to meet immediate demand).

Freedoms of the air   General term referring to the basic concept on which bilateral and multilateral agreements on aviation between states are agreed; namely allowing the civil aircraft of foreign states to use each other's airspace either freely or with specified restriction. Specified in the *International Air Transport Agreement* made under the 1944 Chicago Conference, 'five freedoms' were established, namely:

1. The right to fly over the air space of any contracting state without landing.
2. The right to make a technical landing (eg for refuelling) in the territory of any contracting state.
3. The right to set down traffic in the territory of any contracting state, providing it originated in one's own country.
4. The right to pick up traffic in the territory of any contracting state, providing it was destined for one's own country.
5. The right to carry traffic between the territories of any two contracting states.

Freeport   Area where goods are stored prior to the payment of customs duties and taxes.

Freight   A consignment of goods, or the amount (ie charge) payable for the carriage of goods. An alternative term for goods transport (eg freight transport).

Freight container safety regulations   Regulations which control the standards of construction and conditions of use of freight (ie shipping – ISO-type) containers.

Freight exchange   Facility for matching loads and available vehicles (used to be called clearing houses*). Now much of the business is transacted electronically with many specialist e-commerce firms setting up for this purpose. Also referred to as the electronic market place.

Freight facilities grant   Government scheme to encourage switch of freight from road to rail. Provides funds to assist with capital investment in private rail facilities including equipment and locomotives provided for under *Railways Act*. To justify a grant the claimant company must show significant savings in lorry movements assessed as to their value by calculating the mileage saved on the basis of 20 pence per motorway mile saved, £1.00 per rural road mile saved and £1.50 per urban road mile saved. *See also* Track access grant, Section 8 grant and PACT.

Freight forwarder   Firm (ie agent) engaged in the business of arranging freight movements. Usually provides full service of organization, administration, documentation, insurance, etc to relieve the exporter/importer of these tasks.

Freight interchange   Depot/terminal where loads are assembled and loaded to or unloaded from vehicles. Road vehicles may also be loaded to or unloaded from rail.

Freight management   The function of efficiently managing freight movements by the most appropriate mode, or combination of modes, and including tracking goods through the movement cycle from initial collection to final delivery, the provision of transit data and proof of delivery.

Freight ton (or tonne)   Tonnage (imperial or metric) on which freight is charged.

Freighting   The function/task of moving freight by whatever mode (ie road, rail, sea, inland waterway, air or intermodal).

Freightliner   Currently the UK's second largest rail freight operator, principally concerned with moving containerized traffic between ports and inland depots.

Frequency   Meaning frequency of (bus, train or airplane) services. Fundamental to most service specifications since users (ie passengers) are concerned with how often services run within a given period of time, eg hourly, daily, weekly, etc. *See also* Headway.

FRES   Federation of Recruitment and Employment Services. Many driver employment agencies belong to this association. It publishes a Code of Practice for Agency Drivers*.

Front-end loader   Specialized vehicle with hydraulic loading arms allowing it to pick up skips/bins, etc from the front and hoist them over the cab to the load platform or to discharge into the body. Mainly used in refuse collection.

Front position lights   Under legislation the lights to be fitted to the front of vehicles and used between sunset and sunrise (commonly called sidelights).

Frontal impact (as in EU regulations)   Statutory requirement (EU) regarding the strength of heavy vehicle cabs to withstand specified force of frontal impact.

FSAVC   Free-standing additional voluntary contributions. A means by which a pensionable employee can set up a small personal pension fund. *See also* AVC.

FSR   Free of strikes and riots. Clause typically found in marine insurance policies.

FT   *Financial Times.* Leading UK financial and business newspaper, published daily on characteristic pink paper. Source of daily SDR* rate.

FTA   Freight Transport Association. Trade association for own-account goods vehicle fleet operators and users of transport services.

FTE   Full-time equivalent. Term used in assessing employment statistics.

FTP   File transfer protocol. A method of transferring files from one computer to another.

FTPA   Freight Trades Protection Association. Form of credit watchdog for members within the freighting industry.

FTZ   Free trade zone. Sites within or near ports where goods are free of customs examination and duty until they are removed for onward dispatch.

Fuel cell   An energy conversion device that electrochemically converts chemical energy into electrical energy. Revolutionary new form of vehicle propulsion using a combination of hydrogen and oxygen from the air that produces energy silently and without combustion. Electricity is produced with no emissions and no smog, the only by-product being water. Ford Motor Company is experimenting with fuel cell-powered vehicles.

Fuel consumption testing   New cars displayed for sale since 1978 must show official fuel consumption figures produced by official testing carried out in government approved laboratories/test tracks – *Energy Act 1976* and *Passenger Car Fuel Consumption Order 1977.*

Fuel duty escalator   The Government's annual road fuel duty escalator, started in 1993 and recently dropped, to tackle the problem of pollution, under which fuel prices were increased by a percentage above the current rate of inflation.

Fulfilment   Term used in logistics meaning to get the ordered goods to the customer quickly and at a convenient time (ie as requested or promised). Measured as a percentage based on accuracy (ie the right goods and the order complete) and on delivery within agreed/promised time scale. Latest use of the term is in e-fulfilment.

FWD (1)   Common abbreviation of the term forward (ie as in goods or charges forward).

FWD (2)   Four-wheel drive. Also written 4WD or 4 × 4.

FWD (3)   Front-wheel drive. Drive (ie transmission) system employed on most modern small and family-sized cars. Engines are usually mounted transversally with the gearbox built as an integral unit.

FYA   First year allowance. Accounting term referring to a tax allowance under which capital expenditure on fixed assets can be claimed in respect of the tax year in which the money was spent.

Gg

'G'   Circular plaque bearing white letter 'G' on green background to be seen displayed on the front of British and foreign registered heavy lorries – means vehicle complies with German requirements *(Geräuscharm)* for noise-reduced diesel engines.

G/A   General average. Relates to the apportionment of financial liability resulting from damage to or the loss of a ship or its cargo.

Galileo   EU Commission name for a civil and commercial global navigation satellite system (GNSS)* developed with EU funding. Similar in concept to the American GPS and Russian GLONASS systems.

Gantry crane   Form of mobile crane (usually operating on rails) with crane beam extending over a number of rail tracks or loading roads used in docks and container terminals, etc, for lifting containers*, swap-bodies*, etc.

Gas oil   Duty-rebated oil used for industrial purposes and to power contractor's plant, off-road vehicles and farm vehicles, etc. Coloured with a red dye for distinguishing purposes (hence common name of red diesel) and carries a lower rate of duty than diesel fuel for road vehicles and is therefore illegal for use in such.

Gas-powered vehicle   Vehicle powered by propane gas. Mainly such as forklift trucks but includes some cars and light vans converted to run on same, but retaining petrol system for starting.

Gatso   Brand name for roadside-mounted speed and monitoring cameras and mini radar. Takes its name from the inventor, ex-racing driver Maurice Gatsonides.

GATT   General Agreement on Tariffs and Trade. International agreement on trading conditions between nations throughout the world. Largely concluded in 1993. *See also* Globalization.

Gauge   Loading gauge* or rail gauge. The width of facilities to accommodate through trains carrying freight units (eg containers, swap-bodies, etc), also the width of the actual rail track (UK standard 4ft 8½ins). *See also* Static gauge and Kinematic envelope.

GB   Nationality symbol to be displayed on UK registered vehicles when travelling abroad. All vehicles should display their own nationality plates when travelling outside their own national territory.

GB Railfreight   New (2001) UK rail freight operator, initially contracted to move infrastructure material for Railtrack, but looking to expand into the general rail freight and rail logistics markets.

GBG   Nationality symbol for Guernsey (Channel Islands) – to be shown on the rear of vehicles from that country.

GBJ   Nationality symbol for Jersey (Channel Islands) – to be shown on the rear of vehicles from that country.

GBM   Nationality symbol for the Isle of Man – to be shown on the rear of vehicles from that country.

GBZ   Nationality symbol for Gibraltar – to be shown on the rear of vehicles from that country.

GCW   Gross combination weight. Combined weight of articulated tractive unit and semi-trailer including load/driver/passenger/fuel, etc.

GDP   Gross domestic product. The total value of goods produced and services provided within a country during a period of one year. Part of gross national product which also includes value of net income from foreign investments.

Gearbox (vehicle/tachograph drive)   Part of vehicle transmission system (see also drive line). Attached to rear of engine via clutch and provides facility for selecting alternative gear ratios depending on vehicle weight, road gradient and desired speed of travel. In case of tachographs*, small gear housing in which cog wheels adjust speed of rotation of tachograph drive cable to produce correct reading of speed/distance at instrument head.

Geartronic   Fully automated manual transmission with push button selection, for heavy trucks – product of Volvo.

General register   Under *Factories Act 1961* employers must provide a general register in which information is entered about the employment of young persons, certain painting and whitewashing of premises and other matters.

GHS   Globally harmonized system. For example, for the classification and labelling of chemicals. Concept devised at the 1992 UN so-called 'Earth Summit' in Brazil.

GiT   Goods in transit. Insurance to provide cover in the event of goods consigned for carriage being damaged or lost. Usually covers up to value of £1,000/£1,200 per tonne and needs to be extended if goods of greater value are carried.

GLO   Group Litigation Order. Usually employed when a number of claimants are suing a single defendant, but in the transport context this method of dealing with many individual cases at one court hearing has been used by the Home Office (in April 2001) to deal with the hundreds of road hauliers refusing to pay stowaway fines.

Global positioning system (GPS)   Satellite tracking system used for accurate positioning of vehicles', etc location.

Global warming   Adverse effect on the atmosphere from vehicle exhaust emissions and other pollutants – the so-called 'greenhouse' effect*.

Globalization   Phrase used in marketing jargon meaning the selling and servicing of products worldwide. Defined by the UK Department for International Development (DfID) as 'the growing interdependence and interconnectedness of the modern world through increased ease of movement of goods, services, capital, people and information'. It is a benefit to shipping and air transport because it means free trade and therefore increased traffic across the globe. Anti-capitalist protestors campaign against the consequences of the GATT* agreement expanding global trading.

Globetrotter   Volvo truck range particularly featuring high-roof sleeper cab (giving full standing room) primarily intended for long-haul and international haulage operations.

GLONASS   Global navigation satellite system. Russian satellite system equivalent to American GPS.

GLS   Gravity live storage. System whereby pallets or cartons are loaded on to a gravity roller conveyor which rolls the items down to the picking face.

GMC   General Motors Corporation. American builder of cars (automobiles in American speak) trucks and buses.

GMO   Genetically modified organism. Form of biological material, which may present particular dangers in handling and carriage.

GMPTA   Greater Manchester Passenger Transport Executive (PTE*).

GMT   Greenwich Mean Time. Standard time at the Greenwich meridian from which all other times are adjusted forward (eastwards) or backward (westwards).

GNER   Train operating company, Great North Eastern Railway. Operates services from London to the North and Scotland via the East Coast main line.

GNSS   Global navigational satellite systems. Use for location/positioning of vehicles, etc.

Gold franc (ie the Poincaré franc)   Theoretical gold franc originally used to provide a fixed (ie inflation proof) value for carrier's liability. With gold prices no longer stable it is replaced by the SDR*.

Good repute   A legal requirement for 'O' licence* applicants/holders and for professionally competent* persons nominated in support of a standard 'O' licence. Means they must have no relevant convictions against them (for overloading, illegal use or unroadworthiness of vehicles, drivers hours offences, etc) either in the UK or EU.

Goods Vehicle Centre   Swansea centre where goods vehicle plating and testing administration is carried out. Not to be confused with the Driver and Vehicle Licensing Centre* also at Swansea.

Goods Vehicle Tester's Manual   TSO* publication, which identifies all components on goods vehicle/trailers which require testing and specifies standard for such including reasons for failure in every case. Use by vehicle examiners at VI* goods vehicle testing stations and recommended for use by operators when examining vehicles for safety purposes (not to be confused with the *Tester's Manual,* which deals with cars and light goods vehicle within the MOT test).

GPS   Global positioning system. Satellite tracking system for accurate positioning of vehicle's, etc location.

GR   Nationality symbol for Greece – to be shown on the rear of vehicles from that country.

Gradient   The degree of slope of a road. Measured and indicated either as a factor against 1 (ie 1 in 6.25 gradient) or as a percentage (ie 16 per cent = 1 in 6.25; 12 per cent = 1 in 8.33). Relevant in transport terms as a standard against which vehicle handbrake efficiency is measured (ie the ability of the brake to hold the vehicle or vehicle/trailer combination on such gradient).

Grandfather rights   Term representing a situation where new legislation is applied (eg for professional competence and for large goods vehicle driver licensing) and it becomes necessary to include persons who were already qualified. These were said to be qualified under grandfather rights (ie they already satisfied the requirements and did not need to sit and pass an examination or pass a new test).

Gratuitous bailment   Legal term for situation where haulier carries goods free of charge. The haulier is the bailee and carries out his bailment duties 'gratuitously' (ie free of charge).

Green card   International motor insurance green card. Issued by insurance companies to cover vehicle travelling abroad. Ensures that motor vehicle policies provide full cover in the event of an accident abroad. Without the green card, motor insurance policies issued in the UK provide only the minimum cover required by law in the country in which the accident occurs.

Green logistics   Logistics operations conducted within a regime where environmental pressures, such as road congestion, air pollution, fuel efficiency and waste minimization are key determining factors in policy decisions.

Green Paper   Government document setting out preliminary ideas on a topic or topics for consultation with interested parties (usually the precursor to the publication of a White Paper followed by a Bill and subsequently an Act of Parliament*). *See also* White Paper.

Greenhouse gases   Vehicle exhaust emissions contributing to global warming – the so-called 'greenhouse' effect. Worst offenders are carbon monoxide (CO*), carbon dioxide (CO_2*), hydrocarbons (HC*) and nitrogen oxides (NOx*).

Gross weight (vehicle/axle)   The total weight of a vehicle/trailer or vehicle/trailer combination transmitted to the road by all the wheels. Includes load, driver/passenger, loose equipment and fuel. This should not exceed pmw* for the vehicle/combination.

Ground clearance   Minimum limit for goods-carrying trailers (ie 160 mm or 190 mm depending on axle interspace) built since 1 April 1984 specified in the C&U regulations.

Groupage   The business of accepting individual consignments to be combined with others to make up economic bulk loads for onward transportation. Also the business of dismantling full loads for individual consignment deliveries (see also break-bulk). Also known in modern parlance as shared user distribution*.

GSM   Global system for mobiles. Mobile phone system.

GRN   Goods received note.

GRT   Gross registered tonnage. Registered gross tonnage of a ship.

GTA   Group Training Association. Individual transport training groups set up under the auspices of the Road Transport Industry Training Board – mainly providing training for large goods vehicle driving but also for fork-lift truck driving, dangerous goods carriage, etc.

GTS   Green transport strategy. A strategy setting out the overall direction for an organization's environmentally friendly transport policy including clear aims and objectives for action.

GTW   The total weight of a vehicle/trailer combination transmitted to the road by all the wheels. Includes load, driver/passenger, loose equipment and fuel. This should not exceed permissible maximum train weight for the vehicle/trailer combination.

Guarantee vouchers   Used when moving export goods under the Community Transit scheme. A documentary guarantee (backed by insurance) that any customs duties, tariffs, etc payable will be met. Saves transporters having to pay duty or deposits against duties payable on individual consignments when crossing borders. Obtainable from FTA*/RHA* and Prudential Assurance Company.

Guard dogs   Legal restrictions on use of such in business premises under the *Guard Dogs Act 1975* (not applicable in NI*). Handler must be present or dog secured so not free to roam premises. An intruder injured by a loose dog has a right to sue for damages.

Guest workers   Skilled immigrant workers that the government is prepared to allow into the UK to fill vacancies where such skills are in short supply – but not truck drivers.

Guild of British Coach Operators   Association of coach operators dedicated to providing customers with first class coach travel services.

GUS classification   A classification of products into three categories for the benefit of goods flow control and stock control, based on a product's area of application within a product division. G = General products that may be required in several main article groups or operations centres and are administered centrally in the division. U = Unique products that are used uniquely in one main article group or operations centre but in several of its products, and administered locally in the division. S = Specific products that are used exclusively in one higher-level product, and whose procurement is effected per individual order. *(Source: ILT Supply-Chain Inventory Management SIG)*

GV   *Grande Vitesse.* A fast French rail service (ie as in TGV).

GV 9   Prohibition notice for unsafe/defective goods vehicle (now replaced by Form PG 9*).

GV 160   Prohibition notice (now re-numbered TE 160*) indicating that a vehicle is overloaded to the point of being unsafe. Issued by police and VI* enforcement officers. Vehicle must not be moved until excess weight is removed and clearance (Form TE 160C) is given. Prosecution may also follow.

GVC   Goods Vehicle Centre. Swansea-based department of the Vehicle Inspectorate* dealing with heavy goods vehicle plating and testing.

GVED   Graduated vehicle excise duty. Reduced rate of VED* payable by car owners whose vehicles are considered to be less polluting and therefore more environmentally friendly. It applies from 1 March 2001 to those vehicles not exceeding 1200 cc, but from 1 July 2001 vehicles up to 1549 cc engine capacity which fall into newly designated 'emissions bands' A, B, C and D and depending on the type of engine (eg petrol, diesel or alternative fuel).

GVM   Gross vehicle mass. Term frequently used instead of GVW – EU influence. *See also* MAM.

GVTS   Goods Vehicle Testing Station. Operated by the Vehicle Inspectorate, an agency of the DTLR*, and charged with conducting statutory vehicle testing for vehicles over 3.5 tonnes.

GVW   Gross vehicle weight. The total weight of a vehicle and its load.

Hh

H Nationality symbol for Hungary – to be shown on the rear of vehicles from that country.

HA The Highways Agency. DTLR* agency responsible for management of the UK's trunk road network.

Hackney carriage A licensed taxi permitted to ply for hire in the street and on a taxi rank, or to undertake pre-booked private hire journeys.

Hague Rules International convention of 1924 concerned with the carriage of goods by sea, particularly the liability of shippers and the bill of lading. Amended in 1968 and now known as the Hague-Visby Rules.

Hague-Visby Rules Relate to merchant shipping (sometimes referred to as Brussels Protocol – not to be confused with the Hague Protocol which deals with carriage by air) and are intended to avoid a conflict of law between shipping nations. Incorporated into English law and set out in a Schedule to the *Carriage of Goods by Sea Act 1971* and amended by the *Merchant Shipping Act 1981*.

Hail and ride Term for securing a hackney carriage* journey (ie 'calling a cab' in the street).

Hamburg Rules A revision of the Hague Rules (see above) in 1978 by UNCTAD*.

Handbrake Vehicle brake intended to secure the vehicle while parked. In law referred to as parking brake which most hold vehicle on specified gradient (ie 1 in 6.25 = 16 per cent).

Hard copy Computer term meaning the work shown on the VDU* screen printed onto paper for reference and retention.

Hard disk Computer term. Data storage disc built into or attached (as a peripheral*) to the computer – as opposed to floppy disks* which are portable.

Hard hat   Protective headwear worn on construction sites, in works, etc. Necessary for goods vehicle drivers in dock premises where there is danger of falling objects under *The Docks Regulations 1988. See also Safety in Docks*, from TSO*.

Hardship   Court consideration when convicted driver seeks to avoid disqualification of his licence. In practice the Court will consider only exceptional hardship* and then only once in three years for same reason.

Hardware   Computer term for the computer itself (ie the equipment including microprocessor*, VDU*, printer) as opposed to the software* (ie operating systems* and programs*).

Harmonization   In connection with the Single European Market – efforts by the EU* to achieve common rules, standards, taxes, duties, etc. In transport, for example, harmonization of vehicle weights and dimensions, road taxes on vehicles and fuel duty throughout the EU.

Haulage   The carriage of goods for hire or reward. Requires standard 'O' licence* if vehicle over 3.5 tonnes gvw are used – see also own account.

HAWB   House air waybill. *See* Waybill.

Hazard warning notice   Used in carriage of dangerous goods by road – correct name for label shown on tanker vehicles and tank containers carrying such in bulk. Specified in regulations *The Dangerous Substances (Conveyance by Road in Road Tankers and Tank Containers) Regulations 1981*. The notice shows the emergency action code* relevant to the substance, the internationally recognized identification number for the substance, by a symbol the nature of the risks (eg flammable, toxic, oxidizing, etc), a telephone number for emergency advice. *See also* Hazchem.

Hazardous substance   Common term for what are described in law as 'dangerous' substances (*see* HSE and Approved lists).

Hazchem (notice/label/board)   Common term for hazard warning notice described above.

Hazfreight   Common terminology for DTLR* approved training courses for goods vehicle drivers involved in the carriage of dangerous goods by road in bulk. Satisfies legal requirement for training/certification of such drivers for international dangerous goods transport under ADR*.

Hazpak   Common terminology for DTLR* approved training courses for goods vehicle drivers involved in the carriage of dangerous goods by road in packages. Satisfies legal requirement for training/certification of such drivers for international dangerous goods transport under ADR*.

HC   Hydrocarbon. Scientific designation for this product of vehicle exhaust emissions. A so-called 'greenhouse gas'* contributing to global warming. *See also* CO, CO_2, NOx and PM.

HCFC   Hydro-chlorofluorocarbon. An environmentally harmful ozone depleting substance (see ODP) used mainly as a refrigerant.

HD   Home delivery. System whereby retailers will deliver goods to the customer's home. Also includes delivery of goods ordered via the Internet for home delivery.

Headway   The time distance between successive vehicles operating a bus, train airplane service for example. Important to prospective passengers who want to know how long they have to wait for the next service. In theory these headway intervals should be as per the published timetable, but traffic congestion and other occurrences arise to interrupt the flow, thus on a three bus per hour schedule passengers may wait a long time and then see three buses arrive together. Clock-face headway is when services operate at regular and evenly-spaced time intervals, eg on the hour, 20 minutes past and 20 minutes to the hour.

Health and Safety at Work, etc Act of 1974   Intended to ensure the health and safety of persons at work. Sets out responsibilities and obligations of both employers and employees and gives powers to inspectors to issue prohibition notices to stop unsafe practices. Has resulted in considerable tightening of safety standards at work and many prosecutions of offending employers. Also spawned many relevant supporting statutes (COSHH*, First Aid*, RIDDOR*, Safety in Dock Premises*, etc).

Heavy goods vehicle   Legally defined as goods vehicle exceeding 7.5 tonnes pmw (including the weight of any trailer drawn). Relevant particularly to driver licensing requirements. Now replaced by term large goods vehicle – LGV* – due to implementation of EU unified driver licensing scheme*.

Heavy haulage   Common term for business of hauling exceptionally heavy or large items (ie abnormal loads* frequently outside scope of the C&U regulations* and within Special Types General Order*). Renowned industry sector for large, powerful and often specially built tractors and trailers.

Heavy lift An aircraft or ship designed and equipped specially for carrying exceptionally heavy items (eg machinery). In road haulage the equivalent would be an abnormal load or 'Special Types' vehicle.

Heavy locomotive Heavy vehicle legally defined as being one which is not constructed to carry a load and with an ulw exceeding 11,690 kg – namely, a pulling vehicle primarily used in heavy haulage (see above).

Heavy motor car Legal term for a lorry or bus being a vehicle constructed to carry goods or passenger and with an ulw* exceeding 2,540 kg. *See also* Motor car.

Heavy oil Correct term for describing diesel oil (as opposed to light oil – ie paraffin, etc). Diesel engines are correctly referred to as heavy oil engines.

Heavy rail Conventional rail services as opposed to tramway and light rail* (ie LRT*) systems.

Height marking Indication of overall travelling height* as per the C&U regulations. Legal requirement for marking of height where vehicles carry containers, skips*, engineering plant* or equipment. Actual height to within +/– 25 mm must be shown in cab when this exceeds 3.66 metres.

Heterogeneous cargo A term that describes a variety of cargoes.

HFC (1) Hydrofluorocarbons. Substance used as a refrigerant which is the least ozone harmful out of the range of CFCs* and HCFCs* used in such applications.

HFC (2) Hydrogen fuel cell. Environmentally friendly source of power for road vehicles.

HGV Heavy goods vehicle. Goods vehicle exceeding 7.5 tonnes gross weight. *See also* LGV.

Hi Viz Abbreviated terminology for high visibility. Usually referring to safety clothing* as particularly required to be worn under the *Docks Regulations 1988,* for example.

Hiab Well-known make of lorry-mounted cranes*. Now a generic term for lorry loaders.

HIDX High intensity discharge xenon (as in xenon discharge headlamps). New type of vehicle headlight, using iodine bulbs giving an intense bluish light, designed to give three times more light than conventional halogen headlamps and to cast a longer, wider beam of light, but causing less dazzle.

High bay   As in 'high bay warehouse' used for high density storage of palletized goods, up to 30 metres high.

High cube   (Also Hi-cube) Vehicle body providing high capacity for bulk/ light loads, usually mounted on small-wheeled chassis. *See also* Maxi Cube and Supercube.

High stowage factor   Cargo which has a high bulk to low weight relationship, eg polystyrene products or hay.

High street bank   Generally means big four clearing banks (Barclays, Lloyds TSB, National Westminster and HSBC) which offer cheque clearing accounts as well as full range of other banking services. Many other banks and financial institutions now compete with the provision of such services.

High visibility clothing   Fluorescent jackets, waistcoats, etc required by law for drivers in dock premises for safety reasons *(The Docks Regulations 1988)*.

Higher paid employee   For income tax purposes – an employee who earns (including any bonus, expenses, benefits in kind) £8,500 per annum or more.

Highway   Not defined as such in legislation, but term meaning 'road' which is defined as 'any highway or other road to which the public has access' (this includes bridges over which a road passes) – also means road maintained by highway authority. The *Oxford Companion to Law* defines a highway as 'a path over which all members of the public have liberty to pass or re-pass for business or pleasure'. It seems unlikely that this permits the parking of vehicles on roads.

Highway Code   DTLR* publication containing advice for all road users (ie on foot and on two/four wheels). Not law in itself but failure to follow guidance given could lead to prosecution for offences. It illustrates most road markings and signs, etc. All road users should have one. Copies available from TSO* and many other bookshops, etc.

Highways Agency   Agency of the DTLR* responsible for Britain's trunk road network.

Hire or reward (1)   In road haulage this means the carriage of goods for which payment is made – ie as opposed to the own-account* carriage of goods. Where the vehicles concerned exceed 3.5 tonnes gross weight a Standard 'O'* licence is required (unless otherwise exempt).

Hire or reward (2)   In the context of road passenger transport this means where any payment is made either directly or indirectly by the passengers, or on their behalf, for the purpose of travel or where the payment implies a 'right' to travel, even though the passenger may not actually travel. In this context, for example, payment of an inclusive price for bus or coach travel and entry to a theatre, sports event or other venue is classed as hire or reward. Similarly, where employees contribute towards the provision of works transport for travel to and from work by direct payment or by deductions from their pay packets, this is also hire or reward.

Hire purchase   Financial arrangement whereby a finance company pays for an asset (eg a vehicle) and the buyer repays the company the capital sum plus interest and administrative charges spread over a period of time (say two to three years). In law the asset remains the property of the finance company until the final transfer payment has been made when it becomes the property of the buyer. Contrasts with pure leasing where, in theory, the lessor never owns the asset.

H/L   Abbreviation for heavy lift. Term used in aviation for the movement of very heavy or large consignments by air.

HMC&E   Her Majesty's Customs and Excise. *See also* C&E.

HMRI   Her Majesty's Railway Inspectorate. Part of the Health and Safety Executive (HSE*) charged with controlling the health and safety risks to employees, passengers and others involved with railway operation.

HMSO   Her Majesty's Stationery Office, now The Stationery Office (TSO*). Publishers of all government publications, statutes, parliamentary reports (eg Hansard), etc plus those of many other 'public' organizations. Supplies direct and sells retail through its 'Government Bookshops' in main cities (ie London, Edinburgh, Cardiff, Manchester, Bristol, Birmingham, Belfast). Copies of its 'Daily Lists' of publications are available on subscription.

Holding company   A company which holds shares in other (subsidiary) companies (frequently all – ie wholly-owned). In goods vehicle operator licensing*, a holding company may have the vehicles of its subsidiary companies specified on its 'O' licence (and vice versa) but not those of associate companies*.

Holding cost   The cost associated with holding one unit of an item in stock for one period of time incorporating elements to cover: capital costs for stock; taxes; insurance; storage; handling; administration; shrinkage;

obsolescence; deterioration. *(Source: ILT Supply-Chain Inventory Management SIG)*

Home delivery Distribution sector providing deliveries to private addresses, mainly for mail order goods. Now expected to expand substantially to reflect growing trend towards e-shopping*.

Homologation To make or confirm the same. In vehicle manufacture, a specified number of a particular model has to be built to achieve homologation (eg with sports cars for racing, model only admitted to certain racing series after, say, 500 identical examples have been built).

Horsepower Unit of measurement of a rate of work (ie the power output of an engine). Engine power normally stated as bhp*, or in metric as kW* – ie 1 horsepower = 0.7457 kW.

HO/RT1 Home Office document used in connection with road traffic accidents (RTAs)*. Issued by police constable to drivers required to produce their documents (driving licence/certificate of insurance) at a police station within seven days.

HOV High occupancy vehicle lane. Traffic lanes reserved for vehicles (eg cars) carrying two or more passengers. Single-occupant vehicles are prohibited. A strategy used in some places in the UK and abroad to alleviate congestion by giving priority to those prepared to share cars, etc.

Hovercraft An air-cushion vehicle for carrying passengers and/or freight over land and water. Rides on a cushion of air and can move in all directions.

HP Horsepower*.

HR Nationality symbol for Croatia – to be shown on the rear of vehicles from that country.

HRO High risk offender. Person classed as such by DVLC* following drink-driving convictions or refusal to submit to a breath/blood test.

HSC Health and Safety Commission. Established under the *HSWA 1974** to administer and enforce the provisions of the Act through its operational organization, the HSE*.

HSE Heath and Safety Executive. The operational organization of the HSC. Its officers have powers to enter work premises and impose improvement and prohibition notices – effectively to stop work if dangerous practices or equipment are found – until matters are put right.

HSS High speed ship. Very large catamaran (ie twin-hulled) hydrofoil*
principally used for ferry services such as with Stena Line's HSS vessels
on the cross-Channel and North Sea routes and on Irish Sea routes between
Northern Ireland and mainland UK – said to be capable of 50 mph. P&O*
operates a similar vessel the 'Superstar Express' out of Larne to mainland
UK destinations.

HST High-speed train. Express train capable of running at sustained
speeds of 125 mph (ie HS125 InterCity services).

HSWA, 1974 Abbreviated title for the *Health and Safety at Work, etc
Act 1974* (see above).

Hub and spoke System in transport where all goods are brought into a
central point (ie the 'hub') for sorting and are distributed out from the
centre in all directions (ie the 'spoke'). A similar concept applies in air
transport where local services feed into a central hub where long-haul
connections may be made.

Hub reduction System of gearing in hub of heavy goods vehicle to
reduce stress on crown wheel and pinion in differential and on half (ie
drive)-shafts. Especially used on vehicles subjected to arduous conditions
(tippers on site work, etc).

Huckepak Like piggyback – specially built rail wagons for the transport
of road trailers by rail.

Human rights *Human Rights Act* came into effect in the UK in October
2000 introducing provisions giving rights to free elections; liberty and a
fair trial; respect for private and family life; freedom of thought, conscience
and religion, of expression and of assembly, association and to join a trade
union and prohibition against discrimination.

HUPAC Swiss combined (ie road-rail) transport operator.

Hybrid engines Vehicle engines powered by a combination of conventional fuels (eg petrol and diesel) and electric motor (thus diesel/electric
engines). Both Cummins Engine Co and General Motors in the US are
developing hybrid-powered trucks and buses principally to achieve lower
levels of fuel consumption and pollutant emissions.

Hydrofoil Fast craft propelled by water jet. Capable of operating at up
to 40 knots* in rough water providing a smooth ride for passengers.
Typically used for ferry crossings. *See also* Jetfoil.

Hypothecation   Means to pledge, usually money. In the transport context, it is the process whereby money secured from investment in transport measures (eg car parking fees, road charging/tolling, etc) is reinvested into the network, ideally to benefit public transport and other sustainable transport modes.

Ii

I Nationality symbol for Italy – to be shown on the rear of vehicles from that country.

IAM Institute of Advanced Motorists. Organization concerned with promoting advanced driving techniques for drivers of motorcars, heavy vehicles and motorcycles. Conducts driving tests for such with its own skilled examiners and awards coveted 'IAM' badges for display on vehicles.

IAN International Article Numbering. *See* EAN.

IATA International Air Transport Association. Worldwide body concerned with the air transport industry. Sets international conditions of carriage of passenger and goods by air (ie 'IATA Conditions').

IBC Intermediate bulk container. Term used in connection with dangerous goods carriage. Defined as rigid, semi-rigid or flexible portable packaging having a capacity not exceeding 3 cubic metres (or 1.5 cubic metres for carrying solids in packing group* 1).

IBM International Business Machines. One of the world's largest manufacturers of computers, etc. Sets system standard which other manufacturers match by making their machines compatible (ie IBM-compatible). IBM also renowned (revered even) as a company for its innovative management style.

IC (1) Internal combustion. System by which engines work on a two or four stroke cycle (by combusting fuel either by ignition or by compression inside the cylinder). *See also* CI.

IC (2) InterCity. Brand name for German railway's (DB*) InterCity rail services. *See also* ICE.

ICAO International Civil Aviation Organization. United Nations agency which promotes and coordinates the safety of air transport.

ICB International control book. Now almost defunct drivers' record book in diagrammatic form. At one time required by drivers on EU national and international transport operations but now replaced by use of tachograph. Current use for AETR* operations only if not using tachograph.

ICC   International Chamber of Commerce. Concerned with international trading.

ICD   Inland clearance depot. An inland terminal where customs clearance takes place.

ICE (1)   Institution of Civil Engineers. Educational and qualifying body for civil engineers with 75,000 members worldwide. Provides full range of publishing, training, recruitment and e-services through its subsidiary Thomas Telford.

ICE (2)   In car/cab entertainment. A vehicle radio/cassette/CD playing system by another name.

ICE (3)   German railway's (DB*) flagship InterCityExpress rail services.

ICHCA   International Cargo Handling Co-ordination Association. Trade body concerned with containerization and related shipping and transportation.

ICS   International Chamber of Shipping. Organization of national shipping organizations promoting the interests of its national members.

ICS Black Box   Commercially-manufactured on-board vehicle recording equipment (ie in effect an on-board computer).

IDP   International driving permit*. Required for driving in countries which do not accept European national driving licences (eg Bulgaria, Poland) – available from AA*, RAC*, RSAC*.

IDS   International Diesel Service. Diesel fuel supply service operated by Kuwait Petroleum (ie Q8 brand name).

IFW   International Freighting Weekly. Weekly newspaper covering the worldwide freight industry.

IGD   Institute of Grocery Distribution.

Igloo   Small, lightweight (ie aluminium), specially shaped freight container used in air transport. Basically, with sloped topsides to fit inside aircraft body holds.

IHT   The Institution of Highways and Transportation. Professional body for those engaged in highway design, traffic management and transportation planning, etc.

IJPDLM   *International Journal of Physical Distribution and Logistics Management.* Journal for logistics professionals.

ILB   Industry Lead Body. Another name for Industry Training Organization (ITO*) – which works with the National Council for Vocational Qualifications (NCVQs*).

Illegals   Euphemism for illegal immigrants (also called clandestine entrants*) – principally smuggled into Great Britain in the back of lorry trailers returning from Europe via the Channel ports, either with the (illegal) connivance of the driver/vehicle operator in response to bribes or, as in most cases, with no prior knowledge by the driver. Either way, offenders may be fined £2,000 per immigrant and the immigration authorities may impound the vehicle.

ILO   International Labour Organization. International body representing labour trade unions.

ILR   Independent local radio. Local radio stations supported by advertising. Useful in transport for regular local road/weather reports.

ILS   Instrument landing system. A system whereby aircraft follow instruments and air traffic control instructions to effect a safe landing.

ILT   Institute of Logistics and Transport, formed from the Institute of Logistics (IoL) and the Chartered Institute of Transport (CIT*) which merged in 1999. Professional body for those engaged in logistics and transport in all its modes. Promotes a range of educational courses, training seminars and conferences and awards Diploma in Logistics. Major annual convention in June – highlight of logistics and transport year. Information available from Web site www.iolt.org.uk.

IMCO   International Maritime Consultative Organization. United Nations sponsored body concerned with (among other things) the establishment of regulations for the safe shipping of dangerous goods, particularly in the form of a Code – see below.

IMDG   International Maritime Dangerous Goods. Code established by IMCO (see above) designed to ensure the safe carriage of such particularly where sea crossings (ie RO/RO* ferry services) are involved and incorporated into British law, ie the *Merchant Shipping (Dangerous Goods) Regulations 1981.*

IME   Institution of Mechanical Engineers. Professional body for qualified engineers.

IMF   International Monetary Fund.

IMI   Institute of the Motor Industry. Professional body for those engaged in the motor trade (mainly retail).

IMM   Institute of Materials Management. Professional body for those involved (mainly) in materials handling and related industries.

Immigration controls   Controls imposed by national governments to restrict the entry of non-national and other non-authorized persons into their territories. Mainly intended to stop illegal immigrants, terrorists and other unwanted/undesirable entrants. Such controls between EU states are to be abolished under SEM* liberalization concept.

Immobilizer clause   Found in goods-in-transit (GiT)* insurance policy conditions. Restrictive clause which requires vehicles to be fitted with anti-theft devices which must be set when the vehicle is left unattended.

IMO   International Maritime Organization. United Nations agency in international shipping concerned with governmental cooperation on technical matters, safety at sea and prevention of maritime pollution from ships.

Improvement notice   Issued by inspectors of the HSE* when they find work practices/equipment which do not fully meet *HSWA* * requirements. Employer is given a period of time in which to put matters right.

Inactive inventory   Stock of items that have not been used for a defined period. *(Source: ILT Supply-Chain Inventory Management SIG)*

Inbound logistics   The movement of goods inwards. The collection, receiving, handling and storing of goods moving inwards – returns for repair, replacement, claims assessment, redistribution, etc).

In-cab computer   Extension of modern communications technology to the vehicle cab. In-cab computers provide direct communication between driver and office/central computer for passing messages/relevant data. Some provide print out (ie hard copy*) facility for confirmation. Massive future trend predicted in this direction.

Incentives and restraints   Incentives are positive measures to encourage people to make less use of their motor cars and move towards greater use of sustainable transport (eg bus, tram and train services). Restraints are negative measures, which force car users to move to the use of alternative, more environmentally-friendly transport modes (eg by prohibiting or restricting car parking).

Inclusive tour   Travel package (usually holiday) supplied by a tour operator – generally including flights, coach transfer and accommodation, and the services of a company representative to assist during travelling and at the destination.

Incoterms   Guide to terminology used in international freighting. Issued by the International Chamber of Commerce (ICC*).

Indemnity   A word that means security or protection against loss or financial burden. Also the liability for payment of compensation for loss, damage or injury.

Independent demand   A classification used in inventory control systems where the demand for any one item has no relationship with the demand for any other item and variations in demand occur because of random influences from the market place. *(Source: ILT Supply-Chain Inventory Management SIG)*

Indictable offence   An offence which is sufficiently serious to be tried before a judge and jury in the Crown Court (ie enables heavier penalties to be imposed), for example causing death by reckless driving which could result in imprisonment on indictment. Most road traffic offences are tried summarily by a Magistrates Court with penalties imposed on conviction.

Indigenization   As in indigenization programme. A scheme (usually in developing countries) to restrict activities to the indigenous population. For example, in transport terms, South Africa had an indigenous diesel engine manufacturing policy – basically, no imports of such; all must be built in the Republic.

Indirect costs   Costs that are not directly attributable to an operation. For example, in road transport the costs of administering a vehicle, but not including the costs which relate directly to its operation (fuel, maintenance, etc).

Information Line   Highways Agency traffic information service available by ringing 0345 50 40 30.

Infrastructure   The fixed part of a transport system such as the road and the rail track, its environs (verges, footpaths and rail stations, etc), plus signs and signalling (traditional railway term for the infrastructure is 'track, terminals and signalling'). Also includes transport terminals, depots and interchanges, airports, seaports and canals.

In-house Term meaning operations conducted by the firm itself using its own staff and resources, facilities, etc as opposed to contracted-out operations, as in in-house transport operations, otherwise known as own account*.

In-line transversely Legal term (mainly in C&U regulations*) to describe 'across the vehicle' (ie as with wheels on an axle which are in line transversely). Transverse plane defined as: 'a vertical plane at right angles to the longitudinal axis of the vehicle').

Indivisible load Same as abnormal indivisible load*. One which cannot, without undue expense or risk of damage, be broken down into smaller loads for transport by road within the C&U regulations*.

Inflation accounting A system of accounting (especially in regard to depreciation calculations) which takes account of the effects of inflation. For example, calculating the likely replacement cost of a vehicle when the new price after five years may be, say, double the original price.

Information in writing Re the carriage of dangerous goods* by road, the information which the consignor must give to the haulier to enable him to comply with the law and to be aware of the risks to the health or safety of any person created by the substance being carried. Further, that which the employer must give to his driver indicating the identity of the substance, the dangers which may arise from the products being carried and the action to be taken in an emergency (ie spillage/accident) – usually accomplished by issuing a relevant TREMCARD*.

Inherent vice A defect in freight or its packaging which of itself may contribute to its deterioration, wastage and need for final destruction, without any negligent or other contributory causes on the part of the shipper or carrier.

Inland clearance depot Customs clearance depot for freight. *See also* ICD.

Inmarsat International satellite communications organization.

In-process goods Partially completed final products that are still in the production process either as an accumulation of partially completed work or the queue of material awaiting further processing. *(Source: ILT Supply-Chain Inventory Management SIG)*

Insolvent   A person/firm is insolvent when it cannot pay its debts. It is illegal for a firm to continue trading (ie accepting credit) when insolvent.

Inspector   Term for Vehicle Inspectorate (VI*) enforcement officers and vehicle examiners. Correctly, they are 'authorized examiners'* (which term also includes London taxi examiners, authorized police officers and persons appointed for the purpose by a chief police officer).

Insulated   Goods vehicle body lined with insulation for the carriage of cool products. Usually such also have refrigeration units for fully chilled/ frozen products carriage. *See also* ATP.

INTACT   Integrated Telematics for Advanced Communication in freight Transport. A European Commission funded project examining ways to combine telematics applications such as fleet management systems, route planning, tracking and tracing and two-way communication systems for road hauliers to advance efficiency and competitiveness.

Integral construction   A form of vehicle construction where the body and chassis form an integral unit as some buses and minibuses and in certain light goods vehicles such as panel vans*. Principally, the running units such as engine, transmission and suspension units are attached directly to the body shell.

Integrated carrier   Transport operator which has its own road vehicles and aircraft, usually offering Europe-wide or worldwide express deliveries. Provides the customer with, effectively, a 'one-stop' service.

Integrated systems   Computer term for multiple (micro) computer systems (eg desktop systems) which enable many units to be interconnected to each other and centrally to give free access and data exchange with central or remote data processing and printing. Also called integrated architectures.

Integrated transport   The key transport philosophy of the UK government in which not only bus and train services are integrated, but also where integration takes place in a wider scope. That is, between thinking and action, bus and train, passenger and freight, regional and national, public and private, services all working together as idealized in the government's White Paper on the Future of Transport: 'A New Deal for Transport – Better for Everyone' published in July 1998.

Intelligent transport systems   Use of modern computing technology and telecommunications to aid the development and implementation of more efficient and safer transport systems. *See also* Telematics.

Interchange In passenger transport, for example, a terminal where passengers can board, alight and change buses/services. In road freight and combined road-rail transport, where loading and unloading takes place and/or road vehicles are loaded on to or off rail wagons (eg freight interchange*).

InterCity A service between main centres such as a main line passenger rail service operating between say, London and Manchester, etc.

Interface Term (especially in relation to computers) for the matching of different units (ie VDU to micro-processor to printer to peripherals, etc) – the junction between two devices.

Interim licence In operator ('O') licensing*, the Traffic Commissioner* may grant (on request) an interim licence to enable an urgent operation to start pending his consideration of the full licence application. A vehicle windscreen disc is issued and the licence will remain valid until the TC's decision. The grant of an interim licence is no guarantee of a full licence.

Interline Service where passengers or freight can be transferred from one vehicle or aircraft to another, usually belonging to the same operator, for onward travel to the destination.

Intermediate product A product for which independent demand can exist and for which there is also demand as part of another higher-level product eg a single can and a multi-can pack or a subassembly spare and the major assembly of which it forms part. *(Source: ILT Supply-Chain Inventory Management SIG)*

Intermediate stock *See* Decoupling stock.

Intermodal Transport of goods using a number or variety of modes (ie road, rail sea, air). Mainly the combination of road/rail for which many systems are being developed in Europe and elsewhere. The future of EU transport appears to lie in this direction.

Intermodal vehicle In the UK a heavy vehicle (artic or drawbar combination) allowed to run at 44 tonnes gross weight provided it is engaged solely on intermodal operations to or from a rail terminal. Must be equipped with road-friendly suspension*.

International driving permit Form of driving 'licence' acceptable internationally but particularly where, for example, normal UK licence is not recognized. Available from RAC*/AA* to UK residents over 18 years of age and covers only vehicles which they are qualified to drive (ie on their normal licence).

International proof of compliance   In connection with ATP* operations, the certificate or more particularly the plate issued when the vehicle/container is tested to show that it complies fully with the requirements of the Accord.

International transport operations/journeys   Term referring to transport operations that cross national boundaries (eg UK, Europe, Northern Ireland, Irish Republic, etc). Particularly relevant to operator licensing*, professional competence qualifications* and exemptions to EU driving hours/tachograph regulations.

Internet   A global system that connects computers and allows users to access information across the world for the cost of a local telephone call.

Internet shopping   The business by which individual consumers (ie shoppers) order goods over the Internet for home delivery. *See also* e-shopping.

Interrupted rest period   Provision in EU hours law whereby drivers' normal daily rest period may be interrupted, once only and for not more than one hour, when journey involves travel in part on ship or rail. This must include Customs clearance and other formalities; the driver must have access to a bunk/couchette for both parts of rest and rest period must be increased by two hours.

Interspace   In C&U regulations, the area in which minimum ground clearance for trailers is measured (ie on single axle semi-trailers, between the point of support at forward end and the centre of axle on semi-trailer; on multi-axle semi-trailers, between point of support at forward end to midway between centres of the foremost and rearmost semi-trailer axles – in the case of other trailers measured from centre of front axle or midway between such axles and midway between rear axles).

Intranet   Computer network with restricted access eg to password holders or to permitted users within a firm.

Intrastat   Customs system for collecting statistics on the trade in goods between countries of the European Union.

Intrinsically safe tachograph   Tachograph* designed for and fitted to goods vehicle wired to meet special requirements for petroleum and other dangerous goods carrying vehicles (in common terms, to meet 'petroleum regulations'). Such vehicles have battery master cut-off switches which isolate current to avoid electrical discharge. Where tachographs are fitted a continuous current supply is necessary to operate the clock so a limited by-pass of the master switch is arranged via a barrier device in accordance with exacting standards imposed by BASEEFA*.

Invalidation of insurance cover   Likely if policy conditions are breached or vehicle is used for unauthorized purpose. Mainly occurs, for example, when vehicles are driven by non-licence holders, are not correctly 'O' licensed* or road taxed or are operated in unroadworthy condition (ie contrary to law).

Inventory   A detailed list of goods (ie in warehouse or on board a vehicle).

Inventory control   Management task of keeping check on inventory of goods to ensure none go missing and that stock levels are maintained so that supplies are available where and when required. Usually a function for computers which monitor outflows of orders (via order processing system) and inflows of new stock so are able to show automatically current stock level (in theory if no theft, etc).

Inventory management   The effective management of stock, materials, parts and finished products, including additions and deletions (ie control of movements in and out). Essential for determining capital investment returns and the viability of stock levels and for the avoidance of opportunity cost (ie money tied up in stock that could be better used).

Inventory modelling   The evaluation of alternative inventory design characteristics or inventory parameters using analytical or simulation processes to assist management decisions. *(Source: ILT Supply-Chain Inventory Management SIG)*

Inventory policy   A statement of a company's goals and approach to inventory management. *(Source: ILT Supply-Chain Inventory Management SIG)*

Inventory process   Any business process that involves inventory. Includes the receiving of parts, putting them away, and their storage, withdrawal, issue and movement through work in process, while simultaneously tracking their movement and maintaining records of those events and their effects. *(Source: ILT Supply-Chain Inventory Management SIG)*

Inventory records   Records that reflect how much and what kind of inventories a company has on hand, committed (allocated) to work in process, and on order. *(Source: ILT Supply-Chain Inventory Management SIG)*

Inventory shrinkage   Losses resulting from scrap, deterioration, pilferage, etc. *(Source: ILT Supply-Chain Inventory Management SIG)*

Inventory usage   The value of the number of units, or quantity, of an inventory item (stock usage) consumed over a period of time. *(Source: ILT Supply-Chain Inventory Management SIG)*

Inventory value   The value of inventory at either cost or market value. The value of the inventory is usually computed on a first in first out* (FIFO), last in first out* (LIFO) or average cost basis. *(Source: ILT Supply-Chain Inventory Management SIG)*

Investors in People   A National Standard setting a level of good practice for improving organizational performance through training and development of the workforce.

Invisible exports   Income from exports including banking, insurance, foreign investment, shipping and incoming tourism.

IoTA   Institute of Transport Administration. Professional body for those engaged in all forms of transport. Conducts examinations and awards various membership grades on results. Membership in UK and abroad. Membership in certain grades confers professional competence*.

IPPC   Integrated Pollution Prevention and Control. New regulatory package from the Environment Agency to control pollution.

IPS   Institute of Purchasing and Supply. Professional body for those engaged in purchasing and supply functions (includes a logistics/distribution element).

IR   Inland Revenue. UK tax collecting organization (ie the dreaded taxman).

IRL   Nationality symbol for the Republic of Ireland – to be shown on the rear of vehicles from that country.

IRFO   International Road Freight Office. Department of DoT* based at Newcastle upon Tyne which deals with international road freighting documentation (allocation of road haulage permits, etc). Provides general advice to international hauliers and publishes free booklet, *A Guide to Taking Your Lorry Abroad.*

IRTE   Institute of Road Transport Engineers. Professional body for road transport engineers. Membership in certain grades confers professional competence*. Now merged with the Institute of Plant Engineers to form the Society of Operations Engineers*.

IRU International Road Transport Union. International body (effectively international trade association to which national trade associations belong – eg RHA*/FTA*/CPT* in UK) based in Geneva and concerned with all aspects of road transport from goods/passenger vehicle operation to taxis. Involved with setting standards, campaigning to governments and the EC, etc for more liberal control of transport, on legislative measures and on free traffic flows, etc. Holds annual world congress, publishes handbook and other relevant road transport oriented literature (on transport in the environment, etc).

IRU Academy Sets international standards for the Certificate of Professional Competence (CPC*). Has a number of national training organizations accredited to it.

ISDN Integrated services digital networks. High-capacity telephone lines capable of transmitting substantial volumes of data at high speed.

ISI Information Society Initiative. Government and industry partnership designed to help small and medium-sized enterprises thrive in the information-based economy and improve their efficiency and profitability through the effective use of information technology*.

ISO International Standards Organization (or International Organization for Standardization). Body concerned with the establishment of international standards in many spheres, eg in transport connection, the dimensions for and corner fittings of shipping containers.

ISO 9000 The ISO series of standards for quality assurance – has superseded BS 5750* in UK.

ISO container Shipping container built to conform to the dimensions and specification of the ISO*.

ISP Internet service provider. Firm providing Internet and e-mail connection services to users, usually on subscription.

Issue list A document that states all the parts to be issued.

Issue tickets An authorization to withdraw allocated stock items from the stockroom. When presented to the stockroom, they can be exchanged for the parts designated. *(Source: ILT Supply-Chain Inventory Management SIG)*

Issuing documents The physical documents that communicate specifically how much of what needs to be issued to where. Issue lists, issue tickets and issue decks are all forms of issuing documents. *(Source: ILT Supply-Chain Inventory Management SIG)*

IT (1)   Information technology. Computer-based technology to provide information to business and private users; includes Internet access to the WWW and e-mail.

IT (2)   Intelligent transport, ie as in intelligent transport systems* (ITS).

IT (3)   Inclusive tour. A term used in passenger transport operations to describe journeys incorporating both travel and accommodation, plus meals, etc in some cases.

ITB   Industry Training Board. Now replaced by Industry Training Organizations (ITO*).

Item   *See* Stock keeping unit (SKU).

Item number   *See* Part number.

Itemized pay statement   A detailed statement of pay to which every employee is entitled showing the gross pay, any deductions, the net amount payable and where this is paid by alternate means (eg part cash/cheque, part by bank transfer), the different amounts so paid. Employees have a right to apply to a tribunal if pay statements are not provided or are not correct.

Iteration   Term basically meaning trial and error. A practice often used in connection with studies on alternative distribution/logistics strategies seeking to find 'best' solutions.

ITF   International Transport Workers Federation.

ITO   Industry Training Organizations. Department of Employment supported bodies that set training standards in most industries – they replace Industry Training Boards (ITBs*). Also known as Industry Lead Bodies (ILBs), which work with the National Council for Vocational Qualifications (NCQVs*).

ITS   Intelligent transport systems*.

ItT   Invitation to tender. Procedure involved in selecting third-party logistics contactors (ie inviting potential contractors to submit their proposals). The document is key to the process because it defines in a standard format and in precise detail the task to be undertaken. This facilitates objective comparison of competing quotations.

IVT   Infinitely variable transmission. Alternative to conventional multi-gear vehicle transmission system.

Jj

Jack-knife   Term for very dangerous accident situation where semi-trailer of articulated combination pushes rear axle of tractive unit out of line so whole combination forms a 'jack-knife', usually completely out of driver's control. Avoided by ensuring tractive unit and trailer are braked in a straight line and that rear wheels of tractive unit do not lock-up in heavy braking. *See also* Anti-jack knife.

JAGOLT   Joint Action Group on Lorry Theft. Group of transport industry experts led by the Metropolitan Police tackling lorry thefts via the Home Office Crime Prevention Agency.

Jake brake   Secondary engine braking system, operated by driver from switch on the dashboard. An engine compression brake which converts a heavy diesel engine into a compressor, popping the exhaust valve just before the piston hits TDC* to stop normal ignition phase. The forward motion of the vehicle forces piston back down on the next compression stroke.

JEDI   Joint Enforcement Database Initiative. Operator and vehicle database held by the VI* to aid its enforcement activities. Inspectors will carry laptop* computers so they can check relevant information while conducting checks on the roadside or in operators' premises.

Jetfoil   Fast craft propelled by water jet – advance version of the hydrofoil*. Rides on foils that lift the hull above the water thus producing a smoother ride for passengers. Capable of operating at up to 40 knots* in rough water. Typically used for ferry crossings (eg the Stena Line Seacat in use on some UK ferry routes).

JIC   Joint Industrial Council. Negotiating body between employers and employees on wages etc.

JiT   Just in time. Modern manufacturing/supply concept where, instead of holding stocks of materials/components etc, supplies are fed in only as immediately required. Has benefit of reducing stock levels and costs of inventory*, but requires efficient planning and execution (and relies on accurate, timely and reliable transport system) otherwise danger of 'stock-outs' and production stopping. *See also* TBL.

Joule   A measure of work done or energy expended when a force of one Newton* acts for a distance of one metre (ie 1 x Nm), equivalent to the lb/ ft measure in the metric system.

Journals   Trade, business and professional journals are a valuable source of information for those engaged in all forms of transport and the best means of keeping up-to-date with industry news. A wide variety of such journals are available and the ILT* maintains supplies of the following in its London Reading Room and the Corby Library: *Airline Business; Buses; Coach and Bus Week; Commercial Motor; Containerisation International; Distribution; Distribution Business; Economist; Fairplay & Fairplay Solutions; Flight International; Freight; Great Britain Bus Timetable; H&T (Formerly Highways and Transportation); IFW; Jane's Airport Review; Local Transport Today; Logistics Europe; Logistics Manager; Maritime Policy & Management; Modern Railways; Motor Transport; Parking Review; Passenger Rail Management; Planning; Public Transport International; Rail; Railway Gazette International; Surveyor; Traffic Engineering & Control (TEC); Tramways & Urban Transit; Transit.*

Journey permit   Re international road haulage, a permit authorizing a single return journey from the UK to the relevant country (eg Italy). Such permits are allocated by IRFO* at Newcastle upon Tyne on application. From 1992 (opening of SEM*) permit system within the EU is to be abolished to allow free operation across the whole of the EU area. Requirements may remain for travel to other mainland European nations (eg Austria, Hungary, Turkey, Yugoslavia).

JP   Justice of the Peace. An individual who sits as a magistrate (ie a lay judge) dealing mainly with minor offences or chairs preliminary hearings where cases are to be referred to a higher court (ie the Crown Courts). Can order the payment of fines on convicted offenders and driving licence endorsement or disqualification and impose custodial sentences of limited duration where appropriate.

JTC   Joint Training Committee. *See* NJTC.

Kk

K&N   Keuhn & Nagle. Major European forwarding, shipping and haulage group.

Kanban (1)   Japanese word for sign or card/ticket. Used to describe internationally recognized pictograms such as 'No Smoking' and many road traffic signs. Also used in motor manufacturing as part of the JiT* system.

Kanban (2)   A simple control system for coordinating the movement of material to feed the production line. The method uses standard containers or lot sizes with a single card attached to each. It is a pull system in which work centres signal with a card that they wish to withdraw parts from feeding operations or vendors. Loosely translated from Japanese, the word 'Kanban' means literally means 'billboard' or 'sign'. The term is often used synonymously for the specific scheduling system developed and used by Toyota Corporation in Japan. *(Source: ILT Supply-Chain Inventory Management SIG)*

Kangourou (or Kangaroo)   French system of rail transport whereby goods carrying trailers are carried by rail on specially built wagons.

Karolus Programme   EU* scheme for interchange of national civil servants involved in law enforcement of single market legislation (including drivers' hours, tachograph use, etc), leading in time to harmonized documentations (eg prohibition notices), harmonized spot checks on vehicles and legal documentation.

KD   Knocked down. Sometimes also CKD – completely knocked down. Usually refers to vehicles built for example in Europe and then disassembled for shipment to developing countries where they are re-assembled.

Keeper of vehicle   Person/firm named on vehicle registration document* as being the 'keeper' (ie the operator, not necessarily the owner – who may be a lessor/finance house, etc) and to whom owner liability* aspects of law apply (eg for failure by driver to respond to fixed penalty notices).

Kerb weight The weight of a vehicle in road-going condition, inclusive of oil, water and fuel but without a load or the driver or any passenger on board – not to be confused with unladen/tare/gvw.

Keyboard In computers, the means by which data is keyed in (ie input) to a computer. Most conform to QWERTY type as on typewriters (first six keys on top letter row) so enabling smooth transition from typist to word-processing operative.

Kienzle German firm (VDO Kienzle) which manufacturers tachographs* (also taxi/parking meters and computers). Long established and the original maker of such instruments, now world's largest. Tied up in UK with VDO Kienzle, now Siemens VDO (formerly Lucas Kienzle Instruments) which markets Kienzle products.

KiloNewton Unit of force (ie force acting for one second on a mass of one kilogramme to give it a velocity of one metre per second). In context of transport, a measurement of the force which sideguards on goods vehicle must be capable of withstanding (ie 2 kN over their length, apart from last 250 mm, under which they must not deflect more than 150 mm).

Kinematic envelope Additional clearance around static gauge of rail wagon to allow for lateral and vertical movement when travelling at speed. *See also* Gauge and Loading gauge.

Kingpin The pin fitted to articulated semi-trailers to connect with the fifth-wheel* coupling on tractive unit. The point from which certain measurements are taken (eg for determining whether sideguards are required – see sideguards). Some semi-trailers have twin kingpin positions to allow variation of imposed loads on rear axle of tractive unit, to adjust overall length of combination and to match fifth-wheel position on short or long wheelbase tractive units.

Kissing An expression used to describe the situation when the inner walls of a pair of tyres fitted to heavy vehicle twin wheel sets are seen to be touching (ie kissing). This is caused by reduced pressure in one or both of the tyres or excessive overloading. The result is increased fuel consumption, reduced tyre life and, potentially, an on-road blow-out (invariably at considerable cost for recovery and repair).

Kit A number of separate stock-keeping units that are supplied or used as one item under its own part number. *(Source: ILT Supply-Chain Inventory Management SIG)*

Kneeler/Kneeling buses   Buses capable (by means of compressed air system) of reducing the height of the floor at the front to allow low entry* for ease of boarding by elderly/infirm passengers, etc.

Knot   A measure of speed equivalent to one nautical mile per hour – ie 6,080 feet per hour. Typically used in the context of boat and ship speeds.

Kombi-trans   German rail system *(Kombiverkehr)* for carrying goods vehicle/trailers.

Kombiverkehr   German combined (ie road-rail) transport operator. Member of UIRR*.

KPI   Key performance indicator. Benchmark in a particular field/operation against which performance is measured (vehicle utilization, empty running, fuel economy, etc).

kW   Kilowatt = 1,000 watts. Unit measurement of energy – as in engine power output.

Ll

L   Nationality symbol for Luxembourg – to be shown on the rear of vehicles from that country.

'L'   Circular plaque bearing white letter 'L' on green background seen displayed on the front of foreign registered heavy lorries – means vehicle complies with Austrian requirements *(Lärmarm)* for noise-reduced diesel engines.

LA   Licensing Authority. Former issuing authority for passenger and goods vehicle operators' licensing (now called Traffic Commissioner*).

LAN   Local area network. A system for linking personal computers (PCs) together so they can share files, software, hard disks and peripherals such as printers.

Land bridge   An overland route for freight using road and/or rail transport as opposed to consigning it via a sea route (eg the Trans-Siberian Railway).

Land tractor   In effect an agricultural tractor not exceeding 7,370 kg ulw.

Land use planning   Assessment of the use of land for residential and industrial development and for road network development.

Landing legs   Retractable legs on articulated semi-trailer for support when detached from tractive unit. When loading/unloading in this condition a frontal support should be used for safety.

LAPC   Local Air Pollution Control. Another set of regulatory measures from the Environment Agency.

Laptop computer   Small personal computer conveniently sized for carrying around in a briefcase. Smaller and lighter than a desktop* model, but larger than a hand-held or palm-top unit. Usually has all the capabilities of a desk-top model.

LASH   Lighter aboard ship. A system where loaded barges (usually river barges) can be lifted aboard specially constructed ships for ocean crossing.

Last-in, first out (LIFO)   Stock valuation: the method of valuing stocks which assumes that all issues or sales are charged at the most current cost but stocks are valued at the oldest cost available. Stock rotation: the method whereby the newest goods in stock are delivered (sold) and/or consumed first. *(Source: ILT Supply-Chain Inventory Management SIG)*

Laydays   Period of days allowed in charter agreement for loading and discharging cargo.

LBTC   London Boroughs Transport Committee. Committee which took over old Greater London Council lorry ban. Its purpose is to control the use of roads within London to avoid environmental distress from heavy lorry noise, especially at night. Control is by permit issued to operators who show necessity to use the restricted routes during the restricted hours.

L/C   Letter of credit. A document setting out the terms of a documentary credit transaction.

LCA   Life-cycle analysis. Analysis of the penalties and benefits emanating over the life-cycle of a product. *See also* Terotechnology.

LCD   Liquid crystal display. Used in calculators, etc to display data.

LCL   Less than container load. Consignments that do not fully fill a shipping (ISO*) container.

LDC   Local distribution centre. A new breed of distribution centre designed to cater for inner-city delivery needs and home delivery fulfilment as envisioned in the UK government's 1999 *Sustainable Distribution* strategy document.

LDV   Leyland DAF Vehicles. Van production arm of Leyland vehicles taken over on its merger with Dutch-based truck manufacturer DAF* and subsequently bought out by the management.

Le Shuttle   Brand name for Eurotunnel's closed-circuit rail service for vehicles through the Channel Tunnel – using specially built freight and passenger vehicle wagons. System known in the trade as a 'rolling motorway*'.

Lead-time   The time between initiation and completion. In distribution, usually the time between receipt of an order and despatch for delivery or actual delivery.

Lease   A legal agreement/contract between two persons/firms, one to rent out, the other to hire assets/land/property, etc. In transport leasing is a common form of acquiring vehicles/plant (even office equipment – computers, etc). Lessee pays lessor regular amounts to cover capital cost of asset plus interest and admin costs, etc but never (normally, with pure lease) owns asset. Has advantage to lessee of providing assets without capital involvement – payment is made out of revenue. Forms of lease vary (ie balloon lease*/open-ended lease*).

LEC   Local export control. Customs procedure for export declaration whereby goods are cleared at exporter/consignor premises. Requires prior Customs approval and is dependent on volume of traffic.

LED   Light emitting diode. Form of 'bulb', which is often used for warning lights (eg as on Kienzle electronic tachographs to warn driver of fault in recording system).

Legal entity   A business organization that is given its own legal persona (ie separate to that of its owners) by being incorporated as a limited liability company (Ltd) – or a public limited company (plc) – under the Companies Acts. It can be prosecuted and sued as such.

Legal incapacity   Term used in 'O' licensing* when licence holder becomes incapable of managing his own affairs or becomes a patient under the *Mental Health Act.* In this event TC* may allow licence to continue in force for a period until a successor is found.

Legislation   Law, usually in written form. Common term for Acts of Parliament, regulations, orders (ie Statutory Instruments*), etc plus EC directives and regulations.

Les Routiers   French organization which vets and approves accommodation/ eating places (*Relais Routiers* – transport cafes) mainly on grounds of cleanliness and good value. Indicated by red/white blue *Les Routiers* sign. Frequently found on main routes and used by lorry drivers, always a sign of a good meal.

Lessee   Person or firm who obtains the use of equipment or vehicle under a lease* arrangement.

Lessor   Firm that provides equipment/vehicle, etc on lease (ie the leasing company).

Letter of credit   Used in export trading. Letter which authorizes payment for goods shipped, usually when specified pre-conditions are met. Not a guaranteed form of payment unless endorsed 'Irrevocable'.

Letter of hypothecation   Bank document outlining conditions under which international transactions will be executed on behalf of an exporter who has made specified pledges to the bank.

Letter of indemnity   A document that indemnifies a ship owner or agent from any consequences, risk or claims which may arise through 'clean' bills of lading being issued falsely.

LEV   Low emission vehicle. Road vehicle equipped with an environmentally friendly* diesel engine.

LEZ   Low emissions zone. Designated by local authorities as areas where only approved low-emission trucks and coaches (ie conforming to Euro 3 standard) are permitted to enter. Westminster Council in central London was the first council to impose such a restriction.

LGOC   London General Omnibus Company. Original London bus company, 'The General', founded in Paris in 1855.

LGV   Large goods vehicle. Term used since introduction of EU-style unified driving licences*. Replaces term heavy goods vehicle* (HGV*) but applies to same vehicles (ie exceeding 7.5 tonnes gvw).

Liability   Legal responsibility – eg of employer or user of a vehicle – to comply with the law or with the terms or provisions of a contract (eg an insurance policy). There is a risk of a person or firm being prosecuted if the law is broken.

Liberalization   Re transport, applies to steps taken towards SEM* in 1992 to remove barriers to trade between EU member states (eg by abolishing road haulage permit controls).

LIC   Local import control. A customs system for clearing imported loads at the importers' premises.

Licence curtailment   Penalty which Traffic Commissioner* can impose on goods (passenger) 'O' licence* when licence conditions are breached (eg by failing to maintain vehicles as required). Means that the number of vehicles authorized will be reduced for the remaining duration of the licence.

Licence disc   Disc issued when VED* is paid (or when exemption* is applied for) and when vehicles are added to 'O' licence*. Such discs must be displayed in vehicle windscreen – failure to do so is an offence.

Licence margin   In connection with goods vehicle 'O' licensing*, the difference between number of vehicles authorized on the licence and number currently specified. Vehicles can be added (ie either purchased or short-term hired) within margin without further application but TC* must be notified of registration number* within 28 days.

Licence revocation   Penalty which Traffic Commissioner* can impose on goods or passenger 'O' licence* when licence conditions are breached (eg by failing to maintain vehicles as required). Means that licence is cancelled and vehicles may no longer be operated until a new licence is obtained unless holder is disqualified by TC*.

Licence suspension   Penalty which Traffic Commissioner can impose on goods (passenger) 'O' licence* when licence conditions are breached (eg by failing to maintain vehicles as required). Means that licence is suspended for a specified period of time and vehicles may not be operated during that time.

Licence variation   In connection with goods vehicle 'O' licensing*, means an application made to vary the existing licence either by seeking authorization for more vehicles, by notifying change in the ownership of the business or seeking approval to use new/more operating centre(s). Variation applications involve newspaper advertising, etc and attract both environmental representations and statutory objections.

Licensing Authority   Former name for the issuing and controlling authority for goods vehicle licensing. Now called Traffic Commissioner (TC*).

Lien   A legal right to hold (eg goods) until charges are paid. In transport 'particular lien' is a standing right meaning a haulier can hold (but not sell or charge demurrage*) the load he is carrying until charges for that load (but not any other load) have been paid. General lien (ie the right to hold any load) exists only if provided for in the haulier's conditions of carriage – similarly with charging demurrage or disposal.

LIFE   London International Freight Exchange. Rail-connected terminal envisaged for Colnbrook, West London (near Heathrow Airport).

Life-cycle assessment   Assessment of the whole life of a product or business asset in terms of its development or its cost. In transport, the life-cycle cost of a vehicle is more important than its initial cost – eg the more expensive vehicle may be the cheapest in the long run. *See also* Tero-technology.

Lifed item   A consumable or repairable product for which the manu-facturer has specified a finite life in either some form of time period or in a number of cycles or activities. *(Source: ILT Supply-Chain Inventory Management SIG)*

Lifelong learning   Government initiative for 'cradle-to-grave' education and training.

LIFO   Last in, first out. Term used, for example, in employment – the newest employees go first if redundancies are necessary – and in stock control.

LIFT   London International Freight Terminal. Container storage and transfer terminal in Stratford, London.

Lifting axle   Axle on vehicle/trailer which is designed to be raised from the ground (usually by means of compressed air) to reduce tyre wear and scrub when running empty but to provide full gvw potential when lowered for running loaded.

Light locomotive   Legal term. Defined as a vehicle, not itself constructed to carry a load (apart from tools and loose equipment) and which has an ulw exceeding 7,370 kg. Effectively a towing vehicle only and used in heavy haulage*. *See also* Locomotive and Heavy locomotive.

Light rail   Modern terminology for tram-type transit system (LRT*). Usually operating within towns and cities or on short haul journeys (eg Croydon tramway and the Dockland Light Railway). *See* LRTA.

Lighter   Flat-bottomed craft (ie barge*) used to transfer freight (lighterage – see below) to and from ships in a harbour. Sometimes the lighters are actually lifted aboard and carried on the ships (ie a LASH*).

Lighterage   The procedure of transferring freight from ship to shore or vice versa by means of a lighter*.

Lighting-up time   Time when vehicle lights should be switched on (ie obligatory lights* must be on from sunset to sunrise). Normally, precise time is published in national daily press.

Limited (liability) company   Legal status for business, which has limited the liability of its members (ie shareholders). This means that in the event of collapse they are liable only to the extent of their shareholding (unless they have given personal guarantees for loans/ overdrafts, etc). Must comprise of at least two shareholders, one director and company secretary (who can be shareholders), must have registered office and display Certificate of Incorporation*. Annual accounts must be prepared by independent auditor (ie professional accountant) and copies together with annual return sent to Registrar of Companies* where they will be available for public scrutiny.

Line picking   System of picking orders from warehouse stock points.

Linear bar code   A method of automatic identification using a series of light spaces and dark bars of differing densities, in standard formats, to enable a computer to read data and letters accurately without keyboard entry. *See also* Bar code. *(Source: ILT Supply-Chain Inventory Management SIG)*

Linear motor   An electric induction motor producing straight line motion, used in certain transport applications (eg some monorail systems).

Liner   Ship plying a regular route in accordance with a published sailing schedule.

Liner terms   Sea freight charges that include the cost of loading into and discharging from the ship.

Lineside warehouse   A supplier warehouse positioned as close as possible to the production location to facilitate just-in-time* manufacture. *(Source: ILT Supply-Chain Inventory Management SIG)*

Linguistic skills   With the advent of the SEM*, now more than ever there is a need for people in transport (especially British) – managers/operatives/drivers, etc – to acquire 'linguistic skills' so they can converse with their opposite numbers in Europe.

Linkspan   The bridge between a quayside and a ferry ship over which vehicles are driven during the loading and unloading procedure. Such bridges are usually raised or lowered hydraulically to match the height of the ship.

Lion intoximeter   Machine used by police forces for determining the breath/alcohol levels of vehicle drivers suspected of drink/driving. Located in police stations, this machine supplements roadside breathalyser* test and provides a print-out of reading, one copy of which is given to the driver.

Liquidation   Means to pay off debts, etc and wind up. Action of business when no longer able to meet liabilities or closing for other reasons. Voluntary form of closure (ie voluntary liquidation) with no pressure from creditors whereby assets are disposed of, etc and debts paid. Contrasts with compulsory liquidation under pressure from creditors when return from disposal of assets may not cover debts and bankruptcy* may result.

Liquidity   A measure of a person/firm's ability to meet its liabilities from its current assets (cash in the bank, saleable stocks, etc).

Listeria   Bacterial disease in humans, mainly from food (ie food poisoning). In transport, is cause for concern in regard to carriage of chilled/ frozen food products where failure to maintain correct temperatures in vehicle bodies, etc can lead to disease (also salmonella*, etc).

LL   Load line (or loadline) – also called the 'Plimsoll line'. An internationally recognized marking on the external hull of a ship showing the lowest legal level at which it may sit in the water when fully laden (ie the line must not be submerged). The actual position of the line varies according to the waters in which the ship is sailing and the season of the year.

LLMC   International Convention on Limitation of Liability for Maritime Claims (1976). UK convention enacted by the *Merchant Shipping Act 1979*, which establishes limits of liability of carriers by sea.

Lloyd's Register   Annually published list of ships (by class). Also 'Lloyd's List' (daily shipping news). Both by Lloyds, incorporated society of underwriters based in City of London (established by Edward Lloyd 1688) – home of famous Lutine bell rung only when overdue ship arrives or one is lost.

LMC   Lloyd's machinery certification. Certification under Lloyds registration of the constructional quality of machinery related to shipping.

LNG   Liquefied natural gas. Low-emission fuel source for road vehicles. *See also* Natural gas and Compressed natural gas (CNG).

LOA   Length overall.

Local (bus) services   Defined for the purposes of registration under bus licensing rules as being, broadly, services operated with a public service vehicle (PSV*) on which passengers can make journeys of less than 15 miles in a straight line and are carried for hire at separate fares. Such services must be registered with the Traffic Commissioner (TC*) for the Traffic Area (TAO*) in which they are operated.

Load assembly   The function of bringing together individual orders or consignments to comprise a vehicle/container load. Usually in a loading bay*/loading dock*.

Load factor   A measure of the percentage by which the capacity of a vehicle is occupied or utilized (by the seats occupied on each journey or the tonnes carried on a goods vehicle, etc).

Load planning/scheduling   Technique for determining most efficient/ economic loads for vehicles according to route to be served/deliveries to be effected, etc. Can be done by computer for which a number of specialized software programs* are available. The essential aim is to achieve maximum utilization of load space and driver working time and most efficient sequence of deliveries (ie without unnecessary duplication of routes).

Load-sensing valve/device   Fitted to some goods vehicle to sense the weight on a wheel/axle for the purposes of adjusting braking effort to give maximum retardation without wheel locking.

Loadability   The ease with which the loadspace of a vehicle may be maximized.

Loadbase   Term used in theoretical calculation of vehicle axle weights. Loadbase is the distance from the centre line of the load to the centre of an axle (ie front loadbase allows calculation of rear axle weight and rear loadbase allows calculation of front loadbase using formula $(P \times D)/W$ where P = payload, D = loadbase distance and W = wheelbase).

Loading bay   Area within warehouse/transport depot reserved for loading/ unloading activities, load assembly, etc.

Loading broker   A person who acts on behalf of a liner company at a port.

Loading dock   Term used to describe loading area in warehouse/depot*, usually raised to approximate vehicle load floor height.

Loading gauge   A standard measure used to allow safe passage of rail wagons through bridges/tunnels, etc (ie the maximum height and width to which rail wagons must conform to avoid risk of collision with bridges, etc). There are some eight gauges in use in the UK and Europe varying between the smallest (BR W6) and the largest (Eurotunnel). *See also* Static gauge and Kinematic envelope.

Loading list   Term used in shipping to indicate all the items loaded on a vessel – also known as a manifest. In road transport it is called a consign- ment note.

Loan   Usually of money. In transport, by bank or finance house to purchase goods/assets, etc (eg vehicles). Repayable at one time or over period usually with interest added and sometimes a fixed administrative charge.

Local Plan　A statutory land use plan, usually prepared by a District council, setting out detailed, site-specific proposals for land use and transport, in accordance with the general policy of the County Structure Plan.

Location checking　The systematic physical checking of warehouse stock against location records to ensure location accuracy. *(Source: ILT Supply-Chain Inventory Management SIG)*

Lock　Structure at each end of a short stretch of canal* (inland waterway) comprising gates and sluices that are opened and closed to change water levels. Operated by boatmen to raise or lower the water level as required. (There are 1,549 locks on British waterways, the longest flight of narrow locks is at Tardebigge on the Worcester & Birmingham Canal, the longest flight of wide locks is at Devizes on the Kennet & Avon Canal). *See also* Staircase.

Locomotive　Heavy vehicle used for towing rather than carrying loads. Used in heavy haulage (ie Special Types* operations involving abnormal indivisible loads*). Defined in law. *See* Light locomotive.

Logger (1)　Vehicle or item of handling equipment used in timber loading and haulage.

Logger (2)　Abbreviation for data logger.

Logistics (1)　Total concept covering the planning and organizing of the supply and movement of materials/goods, etc from original source through stages of production, assembly, packing, storage, handling and distribution to final consumer. Distribution is but one element of whole logistics concept and transport a single element only of physical distribution. Logistics is an important function within firms requiring professional management (eg by those who are members of the Institute of Logistics and Transport – ILT*).

Logistics (2)　The time-related positioning of resources to meet user requirements. *(Source: ILT Supply-Chain Inventory Management SIG)*

Logistics service life-cycle　The period of time during which specialized logistics services go through the processes of conception, design, implementation, growth, maturity and then move towards decline, being subsequently replaced by more technologically-advanced concepts and systems.

Logistics suppliers   Industry term for road hauliers and third party* distribution firms that provide logistics services to manufacturers, retailers and other suppliers of goods.

Logo   A symbol or emblematic design adopted by organizations to identify the company or its products. In some cases the logo comprises the company name in a stylized format (eg the Freight Transport Association's initial letters within a circle of arrows). Most are trademarked to protect the owner against fraudulent passing off or copying of its products by competitors. Many such logos are instantly recognizable such as that of the EU, namely a circle of 12 gold stars on a blue background, and those used by, for example, Ford Motor Company (the blue oval), the Royal Lifeboat Institution (its flag) and by many other producers of household and food products.

LO/LO   Lift-on/lift-off. Loading method that involves lifting as opposed to rolling on wheels (ie RO/RO*).

London lorry ban   Ban on the use of certain London roads at certain times by heavy lorries (except those with LBTC* exemption permits) in the interests of environmental protection of London residents.

Lorry-mounted crane   Lifting device (ie crane) mounted on goods vehicle chassis to allow one-man loading and unloading of heavy items (palletized bricks, small machines, etc). Improves efficiency in handling, speeds vehicle turn-round, reduces labour costs and risks of injury in manual loading of such. Often referred to by generic term, Hiab*.

Lost sales   A customer demand for which no stock is available and where the customer is not prepared to wait for the item to arrive in stock but goes to another supplier. *(Source: ILT Supply-Chain Inventory Management SIG)*

Lot number   The allocation of a unique number to one or more of a product during manufacture or assembly, to provide traceability. *(Source: ILT Supply-Chain Inventory Management SIG)*

Low-energy vehicles   Vehicles that use fuels and technologies which reduce pollutant emissions and/or which have been manufactured using sustainable construction methods.

Low entry   Facility on buses whereby the floor can be hydraulically lowered (ie to effectively kneel – kneeler buses*) to allow ease of entry.

Low loader   Common term for articulated vehicle with drop-frame* or swan-neck* semi-trailer used in heavy haulage*.

Low stowage/factor   Cargo which has a low bulk to weight ratio (eg steel bars).

LPG   Liquefied petroleum gas. In transport used for the propulsion of, for example, fork-lift and works trucks. Also used to power some cars and light vans (in conjunction with petrol – mainly for starting) for economy reasons.

LRB   Licensing Review Board. One located at each Traffic Area Office* and responsible for reviewing the performance of licensed operators and for recommending follow-up investigations and disciplinary action by the Traffic Commissioner*.

LRP   Lead replacement petrol. A new type of lead-free four-star petrol for older vehicles unable to use normal unleaded petrol. It contains a proven anti-wear additive replacing the engine-protective lead content.

LRT (1)   Light rapid transit. Term used to describe tramways and metro systems (ie urban public transport systems) such as the Docklands Light Railway in London and the Manchester Metrolink tramway.

LRT (2)   London Regional Transport. Public authority responsible for London's transport, and for the privatized (but not deregulated) bus companies in the capital.

LRTA   Light Rail Transit Association. Organization representing light rail* transit operators of which there are a number in the UK (eg Bristol LRT; Croydon Tramlink; Dockland Light Railway; Manchester Metrolink, Midland Metro and Nottingham Express Transit). Produces international light rail magazine, *Tramways & Urban Transit*.

LSC   Learning and Skills Council. Statutory bodies replacing TECs*.

LSP   Logistics service provider. Contractor who provides logistics services.

LT (1)   Nationality symbol for Lithuania – to be shown on the rear of vehicles from that country.

LT (2)   Long ton. Measure of ships cargo tonnage. Long ton is English measure of 2,240 lb as opposed to American short ton (ST*) of 2,000 lb.

LTA (1)   Local Transport Authority (ie county councils, unitary authorities and PTEs*).

LTA (2)   Lost time accident. Industrial accident (ie accident to an employee at work) in which the injured person has to take time off work whether for an hour or two, or much longer. In calculating personal injury accident statistics, LTAs are recorded.

LTP   Local Transport Plan. Drawn up by local authorities as the basis for all local transport policy decisions (lorry bans, local road tolls, etc) and bidding for capital resources. The plans are devised at local level in partnership with the local community. *See also* FQPs (Freight Quality Partnerships).

Lump sum freight   Payment to a ship owner for the charter of a ship, or portion of it, irrespective of quantity of cargo loaded.

Luton   (Also known as Luton head). Closed vehicle body (ie van) where the load space is carried forward above the driving cab – as in pantechnicon* bodies for furniture removals.

LV   Nationality symbol for Latvia – to be shown on the rear of vehicles from that country.

LVRO   Local Vehicle Registration Office. Regional offices of the Driver and Vehicle Licensing Agency (DVLA*) where certain vehicle licensing functions are carried out (issue of trade licences, etc). Now called DVLA Local Offices.

LWB   Long wheelbase (ie the distance between the axles on goods vehicles). *See also* SWB.

Mm

M   Nationality symbol for Malta – to be shown on the rear of vehicles from that country.

MAA   Motor Agents' Association. Now known as Retail Motor Industry Federation*. Trade association for motor agents, vehicle dealers/distributors, etc.

Maastricht Treaty   The Treaty agreed by the EC member states, which came into effect on 1 November 1993 under which they formed themselves into an economic and monetary union – the European Union* (EU*).

MAC (1)   Minister's Approval Certificate. In connection with vehicle Type Approval, the certificate issued by the Secretary of State for Transport* (ie the Minister) in respect of a vehicle made outside the EU which has received UK Type Approval.

MAC (2)   Abbreviation for Macintosh as in Apple Macintosh. Popular computer system (on which the original manuscript for this book was written and revised).

MAFF   Ministry of Agriculture, Fisheries and Food (since the May 2001 government reorganization, the Department for the Environment, Food and Rural Affairs – DEFRA), with whom UK livestock hauliers must register under *The Welfare of Animals during Transit Order 1992* (enforcing in Britain the requirements of the EU directive, *The Protection of Animals During Transport* – EC Directive 628/1991) from 1 January 1993. This order also requires them to comply with strict rules to ensure that animals do not suffer distress or discomfort during transport by road and that the risk of the spread of disease is minimized.

Mafi trailer   A type of roll trailer (of German manufacture) used for moving containers onto roll-on/roll-off* ferries.

Magistrates' Court   A Court of summary jurisdiction where cases are tried summarily (eg most transport/road traffic offences) before a magistrate (Justice of the Peace – JP*) who has only limited powers to penalize. More serious cases requiring higher penalties are tried on indictment at the County Court before a judge and jury (eg causing death by reckless driving). Where a driver believes a driving test was not properly conducted, he can apply to the Magistrates' Court, which may order a free re-test. Large goods vehicle licence holder (ie LGV* entitlement), aggrieved by decision of TC* in regard to penalty against his licence, can appeal to Court but only after first appealing direct to TC, in writing, for reconsideration.

Magistrates' powers   Magistrates have powers to impose a free re-test where person believes their driving test was not conducted in accordance with regulations.

Maglev   Revolutionary railway system using magnetism created by a linear induction motor and magnetic levitation.

Magnum   Heavyweight model in Renault truck range.

Maintenance records   Under conditions on which an 'O' licence* is granted, must be made and kept available for inspection for at least 15 months. Normally include safety inspections* of vehicles/trailers, service records and driver defect reports*. Licence holder promises to keep such – licence in jeopardy otherwise.

Make to order   A manufacturing or assembly process established to satisfy customer demand only after an order has been placed. *(Source: ILT Supply-Chain Inventory Management SIG)*

MAM   Maximum authorized mass. Means the same as permissible maximum weight (pmw*) or maximum gross weight*.

MAN   Motorenwerke Augsburg Nürnberg. German manufacturer of heavy vehicles.

Managed transportation   System whereby logistics providers supply transport management solutions for clients thus allowing them to concentrate on their core business.

Mandatory disqualification   Disqualification of drivers licence by Court following conviction for offence carrying mandatory disqualification (eg for causing death, reckless driving, driving while unfit through drink/drugs, driving with more than permitted alcohol level, failure to provide a breath/ blood/urine sample, racing on the highway) or when penalty points added for present conviction combine with those already imposed to total 12 or more in three years (from date of first offence to date of current offence – not conviction) in which case mandatory disqualification must be imposed.

Manifest   Document listing all the goods or individual consignments making up a load on a ship or aircraft. In road transport, usually called a consignment note.

Manpower   Commercial staff agency – supplies goods vehicle drivers through its Overdrive* offshoot.

Manslaughter   *See* Corporate manslaughter.

Manual record   In connection with drivers' record keeping, when a tachograph* record cannot be made driver must make manual entry (record) on chart to show his activities for that time (ie driving, other work, break, rest period).

Manufacturer's plate   Plate fitted to goods vehicle/trailer by manufacturer to show maximum weights for individual axles and vehicle/vehicle-trailer combination at which it is designed to operate (ie design weights). These may be above current legal limits in GB in which case the lower legal limits may be shown.

Manufacturing resource planning (MRP2)   A method for the effective planning of all the resources of a manufacturing company. Ideally it addresses operational planning in units, financial planning in money, and has a simulation capability to answer 'what if' questions. It is made up of a variety of functions, each linked together: business planning, master (or production) planning, master production scheduling, material requirements planning, capacity requirements planning and the execution systems for capacity and priority. Outputs from these systems would be integrated with financial reports such as the business plan, purchase commitment report, shipping budget, stock projections in money, etc. Manufacturing resource planning is a direct out-growth and extension of material requirements planning* (MRP1). *(Source: ILT Supply-Chain Inventory Management SIG)*

Marginal costs   The costs of producing one further unit of output, or performing above the standard (ie when all fixed/overhead costs have been recovered). In transport, for example, the additional costs of adding an extra delivery when all fixed costs of the route have been covered by the other deliveries (ie leaving just the extra fuel, vehicle wear and driver time to be recovered). Where a driver is paid for a guaranteed day, his wage costs would not normally be taken into account when assessing the economics of making an additional journey.

Marker boards   Reflective marker boards (comprising red fluorescent and yellow reflective material) fitted to the rear of long vehicles in accordance with the *Road Vehicle Lighting Regulations 1989* as amended.

Market/market place   The area (or area of demand) in which a firm trades or plans to trade.

Market strategy   A plan for gaining a share of a defined market (see above).

Marshalling area   Assembly point for people/vehicle/goods to comprise a vehicle load. *See also* Load assembly.

Mass   Body of matter. In transport, modern term for the weight of a vehicle (ie gross mass = gvw).

Mass transit   Subway (ie underground) or surface heavy or light rail system for moving large numbers of people quickly over relatively short distances (eg commuter traffic).

Master cylinder   On a motor vehicle, the central reservoir where hydraulic fluid is held and distributed through a valve when opened to operate (ie brakes or clutch).

Master Driver   New (in 2000) driver training scheme developed by the RTITB* to boost skills and create a new class of 'master drivers'.

Material requirements planning (MRP1)   A system to support manufacturing and fabrication organizations by the timely release of production and purchase orders using the production plan for finished goods to determine the materials required to make the product. Orders for dependent demand items are phased over time to ensure that the flow of raw materials and in-process inventories matches the production schedules for finished products. The three key inputs are:

1. The master production schedule.
2. Inventory status records.
3. Product structure records. *(Source: ILT Supply-Chain Inventory Management SIG)*

Materials handling   The practice of planning and providing for the handling/movement of materials, usually in warehouses/works, etc and usually by fork-lift/works trucks but includes by conveyor, etc.

Materials management   The planning, organization and control of all aspects of inventory embracing procurement, warehousing, work-in-progress, shipping, and distribution of finished goods. *(Source: ILT Supply-Chain Inventory Management SIG)*

Matrix bar code   *See* Two-dimensional bar code.

MAV   Multi-activity vehicle. Car-speak for a high-roof variant of normal saloon or hatchback-type car.

MAWB   Master air waybill. *See also* Air waybill.

Maxi Cube   High capacity vehicle body for bulk/light loads. *See also* High Cube, Supercube and Pantechnicon.

Maximum stock   The upper limit, expressed in quantitative, financial or time-based terms, to which the stock of an item should normally be allowed to rise. *(Source: ILT Supply-Chain Inventory Management SIG)*

Maximum order quantity   An order quantity which, in principle, must not be exceeded. *(Source: ILT Supply-Chain Inventory Management SIG)*

MB or M-B   Mercedes-Benz. Renowned German manufacturer of commercial vehicles and quality motor cars. Now part of the giant German/American DaimlerChrysler vehicle manufacturing conglomerate.

MBO (1)   Management by objectives. Management system to achieve predetermined business objectives.

MBO (2)   Management buy out. Scheme whereby a firm's existing management and/or employees raise funds to buy their firm from its present owners.

MCA   Maritime and Coastguard Agency. Government agency responsible for developing, promoting and enforcing high standards of marine safety, minimizing loss of life among seafarers and coastal users and responding to maritime emergencies 24 hours a day. Also concerned with minimizing the risk of pollution of the marine environment from ships.

MDC   Mobil Diesel Club. Club card for obtaining diesel fuel and service on credit from Mobil Oil Co.

M'dise   Common abbreviation of the word 'merchandise' used in shipping documentation.

Measurement ton   The equivalent volumetric measure for one ton = one cubic metre.

MEBO   Management and employee buy out.

Medical certificate   In transport, mainly in connection with LGV* driver entitlement, form which has to be completed by doctor when driver is medically examined prior to applying for entitlement to be added to his licence. Also in connection with absence from work due to sickness, certificate which person obtains from doctor to give to employer.

Medical examination   In transport, mainly in connection with LGV* driver entitlement, examination of candidate by his own/company doctor prior to application for such entitlement. Doctor must complete Form DOT 20003 (available from main Post Offices, etc) and disclose all relevant medical facts which affect applicant's ability to drive.

Medical standards   In transport, mainly for large goods and passenger vehicle driver entitlements. Legally required medical standards that drivers must meet, particularly in regard to eyesight, heart condition, etc. Also set out in guidance notes from British Medical Association (BMA) to doctors.

Medium goods vehicle   Goods vehicle which exceeds 3.5 tonnes but does not exceed 7.5 tonnes gvw – may be driven by person with normal licence (ie category C1 under new EC licensing) aged 18 years and over.

Member states   Of European Union (ie Austria, Belgium, Denmark, Finland, France, Germany, Greece, Irish Republic, Italy, Luxemburg, Netherlands, Portugal, Spain, Sweden and the UK).

Mentoring   Scheme under which experienced people in industry act as mentors for younger and up-and-coming staff by providing advice, guidance and technical knowledge, etc.

MEP   Member of the European Parliament.

Merchant bank   Bank which specializes in providing funds for business development, major projects, business acquisition and merger (eg Hambros Bank Limited).

Meritor   Manufacturer of vehicle driveline equipment replacing the well-known Rockwell name for heavy vehicle axles.

Merry-go-round   Rail freight service where constantly linked trains of wagons travel on a circular, closed route often with automatic loading and discharge (eg carrying coal between a coal mine and a power station).

Merseytravel   Merseyside Passenger Transport Executive (PTE*).

METRO   West Yorkshire Passenger Transport Executive (PTE*).

Mezzanine   An intermediate floor between other floors, typically between the ground and first floors. Used to increase usable floor area for storage.

MHE   Materials/mechanical handling equipment.

MIB   Motor Insurers' Bureau. Body to which any insurance company offering motor insurance must belong (otherwise insurance not valid). Provides compensation (for personal injuries) to victims of accidents involving uninsured vehicles.

Michelin man   Well-known logo of the Michelin tyre company, known officially as Bibendum*.

Micro-processor   The working 'brain' of a micro-computer – processes data in accordance with operating systems and programs fed to it.

MIFT   Manchester International Freight Terminal. Container storage, handling and transhipment depot in Manchester.

Mile   A measure of distance – either a statute mile* (5,280 feet) or a nautical mile* (6,080 feet).

Minibus   A small bus or coach (ie a vehicle constructed or adapted to carry more than 8 but not more than 16 seated passengers – excluding the driver).

Mini freight train   Freight train system, currently under trials in the UK with Exel*, which uses small electro-diesel multiple (ie freight multiple units – FMUs*) rail units. More flexible than full-scale freight trains. It carries standard containers with loads up to 160 tonnes (ie five large lorry-load equivalents) at up to 75 mph. *See also* Cargo-Sprinter.

Minimum ground clearance   Minimum for goods-carrying trailers (ie 160 mm or 190 mm depending on axle interspace*) built since 1 April 1984. *See also* Ground clearance.

Minimum order   The smallest order quantity which, in principle, is allowed. *(Source: ILT Supply-Chain Inventory Management SIG)*

Minimum stock   A control limit within a stock control system which could indicate the point at which an order should be placed, or indicate if stocks are too low, for a specific item. *(Source: ILT Supply-Chain Inventory Management SIG)*

Minimum test vehicle   From 1 July 1996 the LGV* driving test requires vehicles of specified minimum weight and speed capability (known as minimum test vehicles – MTVs*) depending on the category of driving entitlement required.

Ministry plate Document (ie DTLR* plate) issued by Goods Vehicle Centre, Swansea indicating the pmw for goods vehicle/trailer in accordance with current legal limits. Must be securely fixed in cab/on chassis frame and weights shown (ie gross/train/axle) must not be exceeded in Great Britain.

Ministry man Term for DTLR* and Vehicle Inspectorate examiner*/ enforcement officer* employed by DTLR (now through Vehicle Inspectorate [VI*]). Visit from Ministry man has sinister connotations (if not definite prospect of enforcement action).

MIRA Motor Industry Research Association. Research organization and centre (with test track on the A5 at Nuneaton, Warwickshire) where vehicle/ component testing is carried out, etc.

MIS Management information systems. Systems which collate operational data and statistics, etc to provide management with relevant information on which to base decisions.

Mitigating circumstance Reason that driver would put forward in Court as excuse for committing offence, although accepting that he was guilty, in the hope that the Court will be lenient in sentencing.

Mixed driving Regarding drivers' hours law, where driver in a week drives within provisions of both EU and British domestic drivers hours law. He may conform fully to EC rules or follow more liberal domestic rules where appropriate.

MLW Maximum laden weight. Maximum gvw of vehicle allowed by law on the road. Used in vehicle speed limits to distinguish between classes of vehicle (eg not exceeding 7.5 tonnes mlw – exceeding 7.5 tonnes mlw).

MMO Multi-modal operator. Transport operator who consigns goods by a variety of modes or by combined modes (ie road-rail).

MNC Multinational corporation.

Mobile crane Defined in law as a crane used on roads either as a crane or to travel to places where it is to be used as such and which carries no load other than its own parts and equipment. Special duty rates apply.

Mobile engineering plant Defined in law as movable plant or equipment being a vehicle/trailer specially designed and constructed for engineering operations, which cannot comply with all aspects of C&U regulations and which carries no load other than its own parts and equipment – also includes mobile cranes (see above) which do not comply with the regulations.

Mobile phone   Modern technology communications where telephone can be fitted in vehicle or carried personally (eg in pocket/briefcase/handbag). Provides access to national telephone system permitting calls to any location and abroad (although, depending on location, reception is not always satisfactory).

Mobile storage   Powered racking on rails which opens up a gangway for access when required. Maximizes the use of floor space as there is only one gangway.

Mobile telephones   *See* Mobile phone.

Mobility   The ability to move. Frequently used in the context of the mobility allowance – a state benefit to help people with difficulties in moving about. Mobility is essential for people to get food, medical help and many other life essentials. A particular problem for people living in rural and remote areas and for the elderly and infirm. Lack of mobility can lead to reduced living standards (even deprivation) among these classes of people.

Modal   Alternative means of transport (ie road, rail, sea and air). *See also* Intermodal.

Modal split   Term used particularly in traffic forecasting to determine the percentage choice of modes (eg in passenger transport, what proportion of travellers use their car and what proportion use public transport for journeys).

Mode   Means manner in which things are done. In the transport context, means form used (ie road/rail/sea/air/pipeline, etc) or multi-modal (eg road-rail combined transport). In connection with tachographs*, means different modes which driver can select for recording.

Mode switch   On vehicle tachographs*, the switch which the driver uses to indicate his mode of work (ie driving/other work) or rest. Commonly drivers refer to this as the tachograph 'button' which they find hard to remember to turn as required – which is an offence.

Modelling   The concept whereby reality (especially future reality) is simply represented on paper to predict the likely consequences of particular strategies or policies. Invariably carried out on a computer with all relevant data (eg the variables and constraints) programmed into the equation and a number of 'what if?' scenarios developed to produce a 'best' solution.

Modem   Modulator/demodulator. A device which transmits computer signals via a telephone land line.

Modular system   A system comprising a number of (alternative/different) modules/sections/parts. In transport, for example, the different modules (ie A, B, C, D and E) in the CPC* examination syllabus.

Monopoly   The situation in which a single producer controls most or the whole of a given market. In the transport context, a situation where a single operator holds the largest share or the complete market thus making it difficult if not impossible for other operators to compete. NB: while British Rail held a monopoly of train services it had no monopoly of the movement of people or goods.

Monorail   Train system using a single rail either above, from which the train is suspended, or below, on which the train rides. Typically seen in amusement parks, etc (eg Disney World in Orlando, Florida, and in some cities).

Moped   Small-engined (not exceeding 50 cc) motorcycle which can be driven by 16-year-old person – must not exceed 250 kg kerb weight* or be capable of more than 30 mph.

MOT test   The annual test applied to motor cars and light vehicles (not exceeding 3,500 kg gvw) from the third anniversary of their date of original registration. Carried out at approved garages displaying the blue and white, triple-triangle sign. Test carried out in accordance with *Tester's Manual* (copies available from TSO*; not to be confused with *Goods Vehicle Tester's Manual*) and test certificate issued if condition is satisfactory.

MOTEC   Multi-Occupational Training and Educational Centre. Operated by Road Transport Industry Education and Training Board (RTIETB*) to provide skills training for transport, motor trade and related industries – at High Ercoll, Shropshire and Livingston, near Edinburgh.

Motor car   Legally defined as a vehicle constructed to carry goods or passengers and which has an ulw not exceeding 3,050 kg.

Motor contingency policy   Form of insurance taken out by firms to protect against situations which their normal motor insurance policy does not cover (eg where an employee used his own vehicle for business purposes but was found not to be correctly insured when a claim arose).

Motor tractor Heavy towing vehicle defined as one which is not constructed to carry a load other than tools and loose equipment and the ulw of which does not exceed 7,370 kg. Usually similar in construction and use to locomotives* (light and heavy) but at lower weight.

Motor Transport Weekly road transport newspaper.

Motorway fog code Code devised and recommended by DTLR* for use by drivers in fog on m-ways. To be found in the Highway Code*.

MOU Memoranda of Understanding. In the transport context, the agreement between the Customs Co-operation Council in Brussels and international trade bodies to encourage tightening of security to prevent drug smuggling and to assist Customs with detection of drug smuggling. FTA* and BIFA* are party to the agreement.

MOVA Micro-processor-optimized vehicle actuation. A computer-controlled traffic lights system, now largely superseded by the more up-to-date SCOOT* system.

Movement order Regarding the movement of abnormal indivisible loads: where such exceeds 5 metres width prior approval must be obtained from Secretary of State for Transport on Form VR1 – the movement order.

MP Mathematical programming. Means by which optimal solutions can be determined via alternative strategies using computer software packages.

MPP Maternity pay period. Statutory payment to employee following childbirth for up to 18 weeks.

MPV Multi-purpose vehicle. Car-speak for small minibus type of vehicle for families, etc.

MRP Material requirement planning. Logistics system to keep stock-holding to an economic minimum.

M/S Motor ship.

MSA (1) Motorway service area.

MSA (2) *Merchant Shipping Act 1988.*

MTV Minimum test vehicle*.

Multi-drop Form of distribution where vehicles/drivers are required to make many deliveries (usually to retail outlets and often in proximity to each other). As many as 30 to 60 such deliveries (or even more) may normally be accomplished in a day in some operations.

Multifret wagon   Low platform rail wagon used for carrying unit load traffic (eg containers and swap bodies) on intermodal rail services.

Multi-lateral agreement   Treaty between a number of national states (eg on road haulage movements).

Multi-lateral permit   Road haulage permit used in international transport for operations between any of the EU member states (but not outside EU). Permits allow haulier any number of journeys in year but for one vehicle only at a time. Allocated by IRFO* Newcastle upon Tyne but in limited supply and only issued annually prior to beginning of year.

Multi-load   Vehicle load comprising a number of units. Mainly used for carriage of dangerous goods in bulk tankers where different tank compartments contain different substances. In this case vehicle must display 'multi-load' label rather than specific substance label. *See also* Hazchem.

Multimedia   Computer terminology for systems which can reproduce text, graphics, sound and movement (ie video/film), usually via a compact disk (CD*).

Multi-modal transport   Where a number of modes are applied/used. In transport, for example, use of road and rail. *See also* Mode.

Multi-pull handbrake   System on (old) goods vehicle which had ratchet-type handbrake requiring a number of pulls to achieve braking effect but could be released in one movement – rarely seen on vehicles today (except preserved/historic examples).

Multimodal Transport Convention 1980   Major convention under auspices of United Nations to promote standard contractual provisions in multi-modal transport.

Multiple aspect signalling   Used on rail networks and signifying the following:

Red	Stop
Single yellow	Prepare to stop at next signal
Double yellow	Advance caution warning – next signal at yellow
Green	Line clear.

Multiplier   Term used regarding the need to determine (for driving licence purposes) the notional maximum gvw for vehicles/trailers which do not have plated weights. The multiplier is the factor by which the ulw must be multiplied to arrive at a notional gvw.

Multi-user distribution   A system where a number of clients share a distribution operation (ie as opposed to a dedicated operation).

MURLA   Motoring Uninsured Loss Recoveries Association. Formed by a group of 10 established legal expenses insurers which provide uninsured loss cover for transport fleet operators.

MV   Motor vessel. Usually prefixes the ship's name (eg mv Patricia).

Nn

N Nationality symbol for Norway – to be shown on the rear of vehicles from that country.

NA (1) Narrow aisle. Racking with an aisle width of 2.3 metres or less using specialized trucks for stacking. Can be specified up to 12 metres high giving high-density storage. *See also* VNA.

NA (2) Not available/applicable.

NAO National Audit Office. Independent auditor of government spending – on major road and rail infrastructure projects, for example.

Narrow boat Steel-hulled craft, usually long but narrow, designed specially for canals and other inland waterways and mainly used for leisure purposes, although some freight-carrying versions are still to be seen.

National Express Operator of long-distance coaches on express services, usually between large towns and cities (eg Norwich – London).

National Federation of Bus Users An independent group formed to give bus passengers a voice. Helps to develop good communication between bus companies and their passengers.

National identification plate White oval plate to be displayed on vehicles (a legal requirement) when travelling in national territories other than that in which they are registered and which shows by code letters (in black) the country from which they originate. Sometimes called nationality plate (ie the 'GB' plate).

National insurance (NI) State scheme whereby in return for compulsory contributions (rate depending on whether employed/self-employed, etc) benefits are paid by the state (unemployment/sickness/pensions, etc). Employer pays share for employees, self-employed pay their own at a basic rate plus extra based on profits of business.

National Power plc Constructs and operates electric power stations in the UK and worldwide. Successor to the previously state-owned UK electricity service.

National transport operations/journeys Term meaning transport activities carried out solely within the UK (ie without crossing national boundaries).

Nationalization When a state takes private enterprise activities into public ownership (eg as with much of the UK transport industry in 1947).

NATS National Air Traffic Service. The national service providing air traffic control services (ie the air-traffic control division of the Civil Aviation Authority – CAA*). To become partially privatized (as of 2001).

Natural gas Fuel now increasingly used to power commercial vehicles. Described as the cleanest of the fossil fuels and the least harmful to the environment under combustion. Proven to be a realistic alternative to diesel fuel for a wide range of applications. Available in either compressed form (CNG*) or liquefied form (LNG*).

Nautical mile A measure of distance at sea representing 6,080 ft travelled (but varies with altitude). Actually equates to one minute of the earth's circumference (ie one-sixtieth of a degree). *See also* Knot.

NAWDC National Association of Waste Disposal Contractors. Trade association for firms engaged in waste disposal.

NAWK National Association of Warehouse Keepers and Removers. Trade association for warehousing firms.

NBC National Bus Company. Acquired the bus and coach operations of the Transport Holding Company (THC) and British Electric Traction plc in 1968. These companies were sold under the provisions of the *Transport Act 1985,* and the NBC was wound up.

NBRC National Breakdown Recovery Club. Provides roadside breakdown assistance to its members.

NCEC National Chemical Emergency Centre. Organization dealing with emergency response to chemical incidents and accidents.

NCIS National Criminal Intelligence Service. Police agency which investigates such crime as drug dealing, football hooliganism and financial fraud.

NCVQ National Council for Vocational Qualifications. Body responsible for establishing (along with employers and others) a framework of National Vocational Qualifications (NVQs*).

NDC   National Distribution Centre. Centralized distribution warehouse/ depot serving the whole country.

NDSDTS   National (Dangerous Substances) Driver Training Scheme. A conglomerate of DTLR* approved dangerous goods training establishments for (mainly) goods vehicle drivers.

NEBOSH   NEBSS National General Certificate in Occupational Safety and Health.

NEBSS   National Examination Board for Supervisory Studies. A NEBSS certificate in the road haulage sector is one of the exempting qualifications for professional competence*.

Nederlandse Spoorwegen   Dutch Railways.

Negligence   Legal term for the tort (ie civil wrong – as opposed to crime which is a criminal wrong) of negligence which means a breach of duty of care by one person against another by which the other suffers damage. In transport, basically, hauliers have a duty to take care of goods consigned for carriage. If they do not and goods are lost or damaged this is negligence unless good reason otherwise can be proved (eg the goods were not properly packed by the sender or they perished of their own accord).

Negotiable bill   (ie of lading) A document (or bill) capable of being negotiated by transfer or endorsement. *See also* Bill of lading.

Net weight   The weight of goods or a load without the weight of the packing, or excluding the weight of the vehicle or unit load device into which they are loaded.

Network planning   Planning a system of interlinked activities. In distribution, planning a system of deliveries each of which comprises part of the network.

Networking   System whereby independent computer users are linked to each other and to central processing, information exchange and printing facilities.

Newton   A measure of the force necessary to give a mass of 1 kg an acceleration of 1 metre/sec^2 – named after Sir Isaac Newton of falling apple fame.

NEXUS   Tyne & Wear Passenger Transport Executive (PTE*).

NFC National Freight Consortium. Employee-owned successor to the state-owned transport company (which comprised at that time British Road Services, BRS Parcels, Pickfords, etc). Classic example of successful employee buy out. Now known solely as Exel with subsidiaries worldwide. *See* Exel.

NFDA National Franchised Dealers Association.

NG/NGV Natural gas/vehicle. Vehicle powered by natural gas.

NGVA Natural Gas Vehicle Association.

NI Northern Ireland. Province of six counties which, with Great Britain, forms the United Kingdom (UK). Has separate road freight operators' licence scheme (administered by DOE*, Belfast) but mainly transport legislation follows that of UK (ie EU law applies in full). Also NI is abbreviation for national insurance*.

NIC National insurance contribution. Compulsory payment by employers and most employees (and self-employed) to provide sickness/retirement benefits, etc (depending on class of contribution and payment record).

Night-out allowance Payment by hauliers to drivers when they have to stay away from home overnight. Agreements with Inland Revenue permit a certain amount of such allowance to be paid tax free, otherwise it is taxable pay (details from RHA* or local Revenue office).

Night risk clause Found in goods-in-transit* insurance policy conditions. Restrictive clause which requires loaded vehicles left overnight to be parked in premises (ie building/yard) which are locked or guarded.

NJTC National Joint Training Committee. Set up in 1974 under auspices of RTIETB* to run young driver training scheme for trainee heavy goods vehicle (now large goods vehicle) drivers.

NL Nationality symbol for the Netherlands – to be shown on the rear of vehicles from that country.

NLSC National Learning and Skills Council. New body launched in 2000, replacing TECs*, to be supported by local learning and skills councils.

NMCH Non-methane hydrocarbons. One of the constituents of exhaust gases.

NMW National minimum wage. Statutory minimum payment – set at £4.10 per hour for those over 21 and £3.50 for 18–21-year-olds, from October 2001.

Noise limit   Limits set in legislation for noise emitted by vehicles (especially heavies). Measured by noise meter on a 'drive-by' test basis. Noise levels are specified in decibels, ie dB(A), and vary according to engine power output and age of vehicle.

'Norbert'   A heavy vehicle belonging to and painted in the colours of major French road haulier Norbert Dentressangle as identified by lorry spotters on journeys. *See also* 'Eddie'.

North Report   Report commissioned by government on road traffic law (ie Road Traffic Law Review) under chairmanship of Dr Peter North. Many of the report's recommendations are now incorporated in legislation.

Notice of intended prosecution   Notice given/sent by police to offender to notify their intention of prosecuting. Not always necessary if offender was warned at the time of likely proceedings; or at that time or immediately after the offence an accident occurred; or a summons to appear in Court is sent within 14 days of the offence. Otherwise notice must (normally) be sent within 14 days but there are reasons when it may not be so.

Notifiable alteration   Under goods vehicle plating and testing requirements, when operator makes specified alterations to the structure or to the fixed equipment of a vehicle/trailer; to the steering, suspension, wheels and axles; or where a body of different design, construction or type is fitted, this must be notified to the Goods Vehicle Centre, Swansea on Form VTG 10.

Notification to highway and bridge authorities   Necessary notification when vehicles carrying heavy loads (ie exceeding 80,000 kg [five days' prior notice] or when weight on axles exceeds C&U regulations limit [two days' prior notice]) to authority for every district through which vehicle is to pass. *See also* Police notification.

Notify party   Shipping term referring to the party to whom the arrival notification form is sent.

Notional gross weight   When necessary to determine maximum gross weights for vehicles/trailers which do not have plated weights (for driving licence purposes) a multiplier* is used to convert the ulw to a notional gvw.

NOx   Emission of nitrogen oxide (NOx) from vehicle exhaust – contributor to the 'greenhouse' effect.

NPV Net present value. The outcome of discounted cash flow (DCF*) projections. Provides an accurate assessment of the whole life cost of an asset at today's prices/values.

NSSN National standard shipping note.

NTA National type approval. Euro-wide scheme to approve vehicles and components.

NtO Notice to owner. Notice sent to registered vehicle keeper (owner) requesting payment if a parking ticket has not been paid (ie by the driver).

NTO National Training Organization. Employer-led body that represents the interests of its particular industry sector in terms of training and education. Replaced Industry Training Organizations (ITOs*), Lead Bodies (LBs) and Occupational Standard Councils (OSCs). Concerned with identifying skill shortages and the training needs of the industry sector they represent and developing occupational standards and NVQs* and SVQs*.

NTDA National Tyre Distributors' Association. Trade association for tyre suppliers.

Nuisance Is an action (in legal terms) by a person/firm, etc which affects the 'reasonable comfort and convenience of life' of others. It is a crime if the nuisance is 'public' (ie where more than one or two persons, but not possible to say how many, are affected) or a civil wrong (ie tort) if the nuisance is 'private' (ie affecting only one or two persons).

NUR National Union of Railwaymen. Trade union for railwaymen but has statutory rights of objection* against goods vehicle 'O' licence* applications.

NVOC Non-vessel-owning/operating carrier – shipping term.

NVOCC Non-vessel-owning/operating common carrier. A shipping company issuing bills of lading for the carriage of goods on vessels which he neither owns nor operates.

NVQ National Vocational Qualification (in Scotland, SVQ – Scottish Vocational Qualification). A scheme of nationally recognized qualifications related to the workplace.

NVSR National Vehicle Security Register. A system for ensuring the security of vehicles used by major manufacturers – provides a security code to be etched into the vehicle windows.

Oo

'O' licence   Commonly used abbreviation for goods or passenger vehicle operator's licence. Needed by trade and business users of goods vehicle over 3.5 tonnes gvw (with certain exceptions), and by operators of passenger vehicles for hire or reward services (ie PSV* services). Issued by TC* when conditions of good repute*, financial standing* and professional competence* are met. Licence applicant/holder must also comply with declaration of intent*. Road haulage licences may be subject to environmental representation* and statutory objection*. 'O' licences can be penalized by TC when conditions are not met. Currently, approximately 400,000 vehicles are specified on 110,000 goods vehicle 'O' licences, while in the passenger sector some 85,000 vehicles are specified on approximately 7,500 'O' licences.

O/A   Overall (ie as in overall length/width, etc).

OAP   Old age pensioner. More appropriately called (eg in the US and Canada) 'senior citizens'. Body of people for whom special consideration is given in public/passenger transport matters.

OBD   On-board diagnostics. Equipment fitted in vehicles to monitor such as safety, security and emissions equipment and warn drivers of failure (eg when an exhaust emission-related component/system fails resulting in excess emissions above standard). Since 2000 new cars require OBD to control and monitor exhaust emissions.

Objection   In connection with 'O' licensing (see above), objections to applications/licence variations are permitted from list of specified bodies (mainly trade associations/trade unions plus police and local authorities, etc) on grounds that the conditions for 'O' licensing are not likely to be met. Objectors must send a copy of their objection to the applicant. They have a right of appeal to the Transport Tribunal* should the TC's* decision go against them.

Obligatory disqualification   Of driving licence. *See also* Mandatory disqualification.

Obligatory lights On motor vehicle/trailer, lights which must be illuminated between sunset and sunrise (ie front and rear position lights, rear number plate light, end-outline and side marker lights – where appropriate) when on the road.

OBO Oil or bulk ore carriers (ie multi-purpose bulk carriers/ships).

Obsolescent stock Parts which have been replaced by an alternative but which may still be used until stock is exhausted. *(Source: ILT Supply-Chain Inventory Management SIG)*

Obsolete stock Stock held within an organization where there is no longer any organizational reason for holding the stock. *(Source: ILT Supply-Chain Inventory Management SIG)*

Obstruction Offence caused by leaving a vehicle in a dangerous position, parking illegally or impeding the flow of traffic. Also by refusal to comply with request/direction of police constable to move vehicle.

Occupier liability Legal liability of occupier of premises to ensure that persons (including trespassers) who come onto his land are safe and that he gives warnings of, or protection against, potential dangers (by fencing off or covering open holes/trenches, by preventing access where dangerous work is carried out, etc).

Ocean Major UK-based shipping and logistics group, including Exel*.

OCR (1) Oxford, Cambridge and RSA Examinations Board. Successor to the Royal Society of Arts which conducts, among other things, the official road haulage professional competence examinations.

OCR (2) Optical character recognition. Term relating to a type of software used in scanning text.

Odometer Correct name for distance recording mechanism within vehicle speedometer/tachograph.

ODP Ozone depletion potential. Environmental description for substances that carry a high risk of depleting the ozone layer when they escape into the atmosphere.

OEC Overpaid entry certificate. Customs document.

OECD Organization for European Co-operation and Development. Found in export trading.

OEM   Original equipment manufacturer. Maker of components, etc (eg tyres/tachographs*) which are fitted to vehicles at the time of their manufacture.

Off the shelf satisfaction   *See* Fill rate.

Offence   In connection with transport, means an illegal act (to park where prohibited, for driver to exceed his driving hours, etc). Invariably, prosecution or issue of fixed penalty notice follows if detected.

Official receiver   Person appointed by a Court to administer the property (assets, etc) of a bankrupt person/firm (or insane person).

OFT   Office of Fair Trading. Official body concerned with protecting consumers and promoting their interests and with encouraging fair competition. In particular it deals with such issues as misleading advertisements and problem traders and keeps a watch on the consumer credit sector and licences those businesses that offer credit or money-lending services to consumers. It encourages competition, but strives to ensure this is fair by removing or limiting restrictions and by preventing or modifying anti-competitive agreements, rules or behaviour.

O/H   Overheight. A container or trailer with goods protruding above the unit profile.

Oiler   Old name for a diesel engine/vehicle.

OJ   Abbreviation for the *Official Journal**.

OJEC   *Official Journal of the European Communities.* Brussels-published document in which all EU legislation is published. Obtainable from TSO (but not over the counter).

Omnibus   Term for a passenger vehicle. First introduced in the French city of Nantes in the early 1820s, and brought to Paris by Stanislaus Baudry in 1828. George Shillibeer, a London carriage builder with interests in Paris, opened the first service in Britain, in London on 4 July 1829, where it was an immediate success.

OMO or O-M-O   One-man operation. Buses operating with a driver only (ie no conductor) who is also responsible for collecting fares and issuing tickets. Political correctness would suggest that this term should be replaced by OPO, one-person operation.

On-board computer   Alternative term for in-cab computer*.

On-hand balance   The quantity of an item shown in the inventory records as being physically in stock. *(Source: ILT Supply-Chain Inventory Management SIG)*

On-line   Computer term meaning that work is carried out (usually on a remote terminal) while directly connected to main/central processing unit (CPU*).

One-way rental   Form of short-term rental of car/truck/trailer on basis that it will be left at the other end of the journey (ie not brought back to point of original hire). Commonly used when hiring cars for airport trips.

OoG   Out of gauge. Refers to freight whose dimensions exceed those of the vehicle or container into which they are, or are to be, loaded.

OPEC   Organization of Petroleum Exporting Countries. Body that controls crude oil prices, etc.

Open access   EU directive that railway systems must be open to access by private (ie competing) operators.

Open account trading   Method of payment for exported goods whereby buyer settles in arrears, usually periodically – normally used only where satisfactory trading record exists or when dealing with reliable companies.

Open book costing   System of costing whereby the service provider makes all his costs visible to the client – ie transparency.

Open cover   A cargo insurance agreement covering all shipments made by the assured during a stated period of time. Usually subject to a cancellation clause and a limit on the value insured in any one ship.

Open-ended lease   Lease for hire of goods (usually vehicles) where date of termination is not specified leaving facility to negotiate when required. Normally pre-established termination charges are incorporated in lease document so lessee can determine most economical time to terminate depending on use of asset/market value, etc.

Opening stock   The stock of an item at the beginning of an inventory accounting period of time. *(Source: ILT Supply-Chain Inventory Management SIG)*

Operating centre   In connection with 'O' licensing*, the place (specified in the licence) which is approved for the parking of vehicles when not in use (ie where vehicles are 'kept'). It contravenes licence conditions to use any other place for parking without prior approval of LA* (ie by making variation application/placing newspaper adverts, etc).

Operating costs The costs incurred in operating vehicles or other transport modes. Usually includes both fixed and variable costs and overheads.

Operating system Term for basic system which allows a computer to function. On small computers (ie PCs*) this is commonly designated MS-DOS or Windows. Apple has its own MAC Operating System – OS. Important to ensure that programs (ie software) used are compatible with operating system.

OPRAF Office of Passenger Rail Franchising. Originally responsible for franchising of passenger rail services. Its duties are now subsumed by the Strategic Rail Authority (SRA*). *See also* ATOC.

OPS Occupational pension scheme. A pension for workers provided by their employer, normally with a contribution from the employee.

Optical analyser Regarding tachographs, equipment used to examine/analyse chart recordings under magnification.

Opti-cruise Electronically-controlled automatic gear change system. Product of Scania.

Optimal asset deployment Critical review of and efficient deployment of assets – crucial to the optimization of the total supply chain.

Order lead time (1) The time the customer waits between ordering and receiving a product, or the time it takes a distributor to receive and administer an order and make delivery of a product.

Order lead time (2) The total internal processing time necessary to transform a replenishment quantity into an order and for the transmission of that order to the recipient. *(Source: ILT Supply-Chain Inventory Management SIG)*

Order picker Person employed to 'pick' goods from stock in accordance with customer's order/picking list* ready for load assembly*. Also mechanical equipment designed to do the same job automatically when programmed.

Order picking The task of selecting goods/items from store to order (eg in accordance with a picking list).

Order point inventory system An inventory control system for independent demand items where a reorder requirement is generated and sent to a supplier when the on-hand inventory balance reaches a specified level. *(Source: ILT Supply-Chain Inventory Management SIG)*

Order processing Part of distribution function whereby customer orders are received, checked (to ensure goods available and customer has credit, etc) and assembled into vehicle loads/routes, etc ready for order picking and load assembly. Usually carried out by computer.

Organic growth In transport and logistics the means by which firms grow and achieve their strategic goals through development of their own business, as opposed to growth via the acquisition of other businesses or by forming trading partnerships/strategic alliances/joint ventures.

ORR Office of the Rail Regulator. The Rail Regulator is an independent statutory officer appointed by government under the *Railways Act 1933*. His focus is on the monopoly and dominant elements of Britain's railways, principally Railtrack*, and he regulates in the public interest, balancing these duties and functions. He is particularly concerned with regulating economic aspects of Railtrack's operation, especially its access charges.

OSD Open shelter deck. The sheltered deck on a ship is above the main deck and is used for carrying light cargo. The OSD is an open-type sheltered deck.

OTIF On time, in full. Distribution concept for delivery of orders as and when required.

OTS On-the-Spot. DTLR*/Highways Agency* joint project by the TRL* to visit road accidents while vehicles are still in situ in order to achieve greater understanding of accident causation and the development of effective counter measures.

Outbound logistics Activities connected with the movement of goods outwards as opposed to inwards. *See also* Logistics and Inbound logistics.

Outsourcing System whereby use is made of outside sources (eg transport/ warehousing or full-scale logistics service) replacing in-house facilities*. *See also* Third party.

Outstations Branches, depots or sub-depots of an organization situated some distance from the main operating centre. For example, as with bus and coach depots and haulage sub-depots. Airlines often refer to outstations in respect of facilities (eg for aircraft maintenance) located at the extremities of their long-haul routes.

Overbooking Ploy adopted by passenger airlines to ensure as many seats on flights are filled as possible, achieved by selling more tickets than the number of seats available on the basis that a number of ticket holders always fail to turn up (show) for the flight.

Overdraft   Financial arrangement whereby bank allows client to draw money which he does not have in his account (ie overdraw) to meet immediate needs on the expectation that funds will be forthcoming. Basically a short-term facility (for which security is needed) and not to be used for purchases of capital assets. Normally with a specified limit/ceiling and reviewable periodically.

Overdrive (1)   Component in vehicle gearbox to provide a high gear for economical cruising. Normally these days replaced by five/six speed gearbox.

Overdrive (2)   Commercial firm/agency supplying temporary goods vehicle and licensed large goods vehicle drivers on a daily/weekly or longer-term basis offshoot of Manpower* agency.

Overhang   The distance by which the body and other parts extend beyond the rear axle of a vehicle. This distance, measured from centre line of rear axle, must not exceed 60 per cent of wheelbase* and in the case of a tandem bogie (ie two axles) the measurement is taken from a point 110 mm behind the centre line between the two axles.

Overheads   The costs of a business which are not directly attributable to its operations (in the case of haulage, the costs of running the office/administration – telephones/postage/bank charges/legal and accounting fees, etc). In transport, often called establishment costs*. Usually the first (and best) place to look when seeking cost savings.

Overland   Term used to describe transport for the whole of a journey by land rather than by sea or air (eg road journeys to the Middle East and beyond).

Overlap recording   Regarding tachograph records where driver leaves chart in instrument over night/weekend and finds that more than 24 hours' recording has been made. For example, if he starts at 7 am one day and not until 8 am the next, a chart inserted on day one would show 25 hours' recording with an overlap from 7 am to 8 am on the second day. This is illegal.

Overloading   The illegal act of loading a vehicle/trailer in excess of its permitted maximum weight (ie gvw) or the weight permitted on its individual axles. Vehicles may be stopped for weighing purposes and prohibited from proceeding (by issue of Form GV 160) if they are unsafe due to excess weight. Heavy penalties are imposed on offenders.

Overrun brakes Brakes which are automatically applied on the overrun of a trailer (ie when the vehicle slows down, the trailer pushing on the coupling applies a spring operated brake). Not permitted on trailers exceeding 3,500 kg gvw.

Overvalued currency Currency whose rate of exchange is persistently below the parity rate.

O/W Overwidth. A vehicle or container with goods overhanging beyond the sides – and possibly beyond statutory limits.

Own account Term meaning operation by a firm of its own vehicle/s for carrying its 'own' goods – ie goods in connection with any trade or business carried on by the firm other than that of carriage for hire or reward (ie haulage*). In 'O' licensing* terms, requires a restricted licence unless goods are also carried for hire or reward.

Owner driver/operator Term for a one-man haulage business where the person both owns/operates the vehicle and drives it himself. Often abbreviated to o/d or (especially in USA) o/o. UK road haulage industry comprises great number of owner drivers most of whom provide good, personal service to their customers.

Pp

3PL *See* Third-party logistics.

4PL Fourth-party Logistics™*. A distribution system where a fourth party stands between the client and one or more of its third-party providers to manage the complete supply chain by assembling the resources, capabilities and technology of its own organization together with those of the third-party providers to supply a totally integrated supply chain system.

P Nationality symbol for Portugal – to be shown on the rear of vehicles from that country.

PACE (1) Acronym for *Police and Criminal Evidence Act 1984.*

PACE (2) Ports automated cargo environment.

P&D Pick up and deposit. Usually refers to a location at the end of a warehouse aisle or row where incoming and outgoing goods are held for pickup or deposit by aisle stacker trucks.

P&O Peninsular & Orient. Major UK-based shipping and haulage group.

P&R Park and ride*.

Packer Person employed in warehouse or furniture removals business to pack goods prior to transit, usually skilled.

Packing group United Nations designation for packaging requirements for dangerous goods to be carried by road in packages based on their degree of danger (ie group 1 – high, group 2 – medium, group 3 – low risk). *The Carriage of Dangerous Goods Classification, Packaging and Labelling and Use of Transportable Pressure Receptacles Regulations 1996* apply.

PACT Pilot Action for Combined Transport. EU* scheme providing funds to hauliers interested in setting up combined transport* operations – funds can be used to buy capital equipment including vehicle. *See also* Freight facilities grant, Section 8 grant and Track Access grant.

PACTS Parliamentary Advisory Council for Transport Safety.

Pallet   Flat, usually wooden, portable platform/base on which loads are stacked for moving/lifting – by pallet/fork-lift trucks. Usually built to standard dimension 1,200 × 1,000 mm and capable of carrying up to 1,500 kg. For use in storage systems (ie on pallet racking) and carried in road vehicles (ie loaded on floor or supported on hydraulic tracking systems – eg Joloda system).

Pallet racking   Warehouse shelving designed to accommodate standard pallets (eg 1,200 × 1,000 mm) up to five or more tiers high.

Pallet truck   Warehouse equipment for moving/loading pallets, usually pedestrian controlled and manually operated, or may be powered.

Pan-European   The whole of Europe – as in pan-European transport/ logistics which covers all of Europe.

Panel van   Term for integrally-built van in which chassis, body and driver's cab are built as one (eg as with Ford Transit*) unlike other goods vehicle (usually heavier ones) which have a separate chassis on which the engine, transmission and running gear, bodywork and cab are added.

Pantechnicon   High cubic capacity vehicle body used mainly in furniture removals trade, usually incorporating a Luton* head over the driver's cab. *See also* Highcube.

Pantograph   A hinged structure (frame) mounted on the roof of an electric rail locomotive to enable electric current to be drawn from the overhead wires/cable (catenary*). Also on trams* and trolleybuses*.

Paradigm   In the logistics context, a term that means a typical example or pattern of behaviour (doing things the way they have always been done rather than doing them in the way best suited to the situation in hand).

Parent part   Any finished goods, end item, or part that is mixed, fabricated, assembled, stirred, or blended from one or more other components. *(Source: ILT Supply-Chain Inventory Management SIG)*

Pareto chart/diagram   A chart/diagram which shows figures diagrammatically in order of magnitude (often in columns or blocks).

Pareto's law   Concept applicable in many circumstances where the largest bulk (eg of orders) is attributable to the smallest source (eg customers). Thus it can often be said that 80 per cent of orders come from just 20 per cent of customers or, conversely, 80 per cent of revenue comes from 20 per cent of orders. Often called the 80/20 rule and can be applied in many situations. *See also* Pareto principle.

Pareto principle   The heuristic rule which states that where there is a large number of contributors to a result, the majority of the result is due to a minority of the contributors. Sometimes known as the 80/20 rule which states that, in many cases, approximately 80 per cent of the turnover (stock, etc) can be ascribed to approximately 20 per cent of the customers, articles or orders. The actual ratio in a particular case can be determined by ranking the customers and products, etc in order of magnitude and then calculating what percentage of the turnover (stock, etc) corresponds to 10 per cent, 20 per cent, 30 per cent, etc of the customer and products, etc. The basis of ABC analysis*. *(Source: ILT Supply-Chain Inventory Management SIG)*

Park & Ride   System where car passengers drive to a designated parking location and then catch a bus into a town or city centre, for example. Same applies with some rail locations. Often a single fee covers both the car parking and the bus/rail journey. This concept is being heavily promoted as a means of reducing traffic congestion and pollution in central locations.

Parking brake   Vehicle brake (capable of being operated by independent means) intended to hold the vehicle secure when stationary (ie when parked). Must be capable of holding vehicle on gradient of at least 1 in 6.25 (ie 16 per cent), or 1 in 8.33 (ie 12 per cent) with a trailer attached, without the assistance of stored energy.

Parking meter zone   Designated area (ie in towns) where parking meters are used to control vehicle parking – indicated by a sign (blue circle with red border and diagonal stripe on white background) which states times when zone is in operation (ie when meters must be used). *See also* Highway Code.

Part I – V (MOT tests)   Various categories of annual test for goods vehicle as follows: Part 1 = first annual test; 2 = re-test when first test failed; 3 = periodical (normal) annual test; 4 = test following notifiable alteration*; 5 = re-test following appeal (ie to Area Mechanical Engineer* or Secretary of State for Transport*).

Part number   A unique identification number allocated to a specific part either by the manufacturer or user of the part.

Particular lien   *See* Lien.

Particulates   A harmful concoction of fine dust (soot) and black smoke emitted by diesel exhausts – said to be linked to lung and heart disease.

Passenger liability   In terms of motor vehicle insurance, mandatory cover for passenger (except employees of the vehicle owner/operator) under the *Road Traffic Act 1988*.

Passenger logistics   The logistics of providing passenger services.

Passenger miles   A factor of the number of passengers carried and the average length of their journey in miles.

Paternity leave   New social concept whereby fathers of new-born infants are entitled to two weeks paid leave (subsidized by the government).

Payback   Term used in financial calculations when determining the viability of a project/operation – how long it will take to recover the investment (ie payback period) and/or the return on the investment.

PAYE   Pay as you earn. Inland Revenue (IR*) scheme whereby employers deduct tax (under schedule E) and NI* contributions from employees' pay and submit amounts due to the IR.

Payload   Term for the load carried by a vehicle – in haulage the capacity of vehicle to carry a paying load (in terms of weight or volume – cubic capacity). A similar scenario applies in passenger transport where the payload is the number of seats available on any journey.

Pb   Lead, compounds of which are found in vehicle exhaust emissions.

PC   Personal computer. Small computer used by an individual as opposed to large, company-owned and operated machines. Often used by enthusiasts (ie computer buffs) as well as small businesses/schools, etc.

PCN   Penalty charge notice. Council-issued parking ticket for infringement of regulations – discount if paid promptly (usually within 14 days).

PCV   Passenger carrying vehicle. Term replacing public service vehicle (ie PSV*), introduced in connection with EC-style unified driver licensing*.

PDI   Pre-delivery inspection. System for checking new vehicles prior to delivery to customer.

PDM   Physical distribution management. The management concept/function of total distribution. *See also* Logistics.

P/E ratio   Price/earnings ratio. A term related to the share price for a firm and its profitability. A measure by which the financial viability of a firm is assessed.

Peak hours   The busy times of day for the transport network, particularly when people are travelling between home and work or vice versa. Usually measured in terms of the increased number of vehicle trips against the normal traffic flow.

Pedestrian-controlled vehicle   Motorized vehicle controlled by pedestrian (eg motor mower). Term found in legislation meaning vehicle not constructed to carry a passenger (C&U regulations) and regarding driver licensing (category K under new-style EU licences).

Pedestrian priority zone   An area (normally in a town or city centre) where space is reserved for pedestrians at the cost of other road users. Usually paved and with all vehicles prohibited except during specified times for delivery vehicle access.

Penalty points   Scheme for penalizing drivers convicted of road traffic offences (short of disqualification) whereby penalty points are added to the driving licence and when 12 such are accumulated in a three-year period the driver is automatically disqualified. Number of points added vary according to seriousness of offence (typically 3 for speeding conviction, 10 for reckless driving).

Peppercorn rental   In leasing, when primary period of lease has ended lessor (who has recovered his costs, etc) may allow lessee to continue renting at very low (ie peppercorn) annual rental.

Per pro   Term used in business/commercial correspondence meaning 'on behalf of' (ie where one person signs a letter on behalf of another.

PERA   Production Equipment Research Association. Transport/distribution connection is via relevant seminars/conferences run periodically.

Performance indicator   A predetermined factor of performance (standard) against which actual performance is measured to see whether the actual is above or below standard.

Period permit   Form of bi-lateral road haulage permit for international operations which permits unlimited journeys to a specified country during a specified period of time – as opposed to journey permits which cover only single journeys. Issued by IRFO* Newcastle upon Tyne. These were abolished for inter-EC transport under SEM*.

Periodic inspection   Legal requirement for employers to inspect driver's tachograph* charts to ensure the law has been complied with and if breaches are found to take appropriate steps to prevent repetition.

Periodic inventory   An inventory control system classification for independent demand items where the number of items held is reviewed at a fixed time interval and the size of any resultant order depends on the stock on hand at the time of the review. *(Source: ILT Supply-Chain Inventory Management SIG)*

Periodical test   Regarding goods vehicle testing, the part 3 test which is carried out annually after the first test. *See* Part I – V (MOT tests).

Peripheral   Regarding computers, term for parts added on/plugged in (additional storage capacity – ie hard disk; disk drive – to speed-up processing; printer, etc).

Peristaltic   As in peristaltic conveyor for example. Based on the science of peristalsis – the constriction and relation of muscles in a canal (eg the throat) creating wave-like movements which push the contents of the canal forward. A medical concept adopted for use in transport applications where the throat muscles are replaced by electric motors which provide a surging current to give the same effect.

Permit   *See* Road haulage permit.

Permitted tolerances   Regarding tachograph calibration, etc, the tolerances on speed, distance and time recording legally permitted at various stages (ie on test, on installation, in use).

Perpetual inventory system   An inventory control system where a running record is kept of the amount of stock held for each item. Whenever an issue is made, the withdrawal is logged and the result compared with the re-order point for any necessary reorder action. *(Source: ILT Supply-Chain Inventory Management SIG)*

Personal mobility   The availability of an individual's choice and freedom to move around by any particular mode.

PEST analysis   Political, economic, socio-cultural, technological. The concept of analysing the external PEST environment in which a company operates.

PFI   Private finance initiative. A strategy whereby government initiated projects are funded by private finance. *See also* PPP.

PFL   The Peoples' Fuel Lobby. UK-based protest and lobbying group formed to campaign against high fuel taxes.

PG 9   Vehicle Inspectorate* form used to denote prohibition of use of vehicle on the road. Issued by vehicle examiners* when vehicle found to be defective and unsafe to operate (also illegal and prosecution may follow). One of series of forms prefixed so (eg PG 9A/9B/9C) also PG 10, which clears prohibition.

PGR   Packaged Goods Regulations. Abbreviated term for the CDGCPL2* regulations.

PHARE   IRU* project to establish Vocational Training Centres in Central and Eastern European Countries (CEEC*) to bring standards into line with those of industry in the EU (ie Albania, Bosnia-Herzegovina, Bulgaria, Czech Republic, Estonia, former Yugoslav Republic of Macedonia, Hungary, Latvia, Poland, Romania, Slovakia and Slovenia).

PI (1)   Performance indicator.

PI (2)   Public Inquiry*. Hearing by Traffic Commissioner* of matters connected with 'O'* licences. Also part of the government's public consultation process on road building, route selection processes.

Pick face   The primary location in a warehouse at which order picking, of less than pallet loads, is undertaken. *(Source: ILT Supply-Chain Inventory Management SIG)*

Pick-up truck   Light goods vehicle with an integral open back/load space behind the driving compartment – sometimes called a backie/baccy (eg in South Africa). *See also* Car-derived van of which the pick-up is an open version.

Picker   Person employed to 'pick' goods from stocks on warehouse shelving in accordance with customer's order. *See also* Order picker and Picking list.

Picking   As in order picking – the task of selecting product items from stock. Carried out by order picker in accordance with a picking list.

Picking list   Term used in warehousing for the list used by order picker to make up order from stock. *See also* Order picking.

Piggyback (or Piggy-back)   System whereby purpose-built lorry semi-trailers are carried on specially-built rail wagons (pocket*, swing-bed* or spine* wagons) for the trunk leg of long-haul rail journeys.

Piggyback trailers   Specially strengthened road semi-trailers capable of being bottom lifted when fully loaded on to special rail wagons. Those with deflatable air suspension can be lowered to 3.58 metres for carriage on Railtrack W9 gauge routes. Trailers at normal 3.76 metres height can be carried on the enhanced Railtrack W10 gauge network.

PIKE   Police Intelligence Commercial Enquiry system, new since mid-1999. Infringement information is fed in from police forces in the UK and abroad for dissemination to all forces. Data is stored under driver and company name and vehicle registration number. The system is also said to be named after the Lincolnshire police constable who developed it – PC Pike.

Pilferage   Small-scale (petty) theft of goods from stock or from loads. Not easily detected until quantities mount up to a significant loss – or until the thief gets greedy.

Pipeline   A mode of transport used for moving large volumes of crude oil, petroleum gases. Typically over long distances as in Saudi Arabia and the trans-Alaska pipelines.

Pipeline stocks   The products which are currently being moved from one location to another. *(Source: ILT Supply-Chain Inventory Management SIG)*

PIRA   Packaging Industry Research Association. Trade association for firms in packaging industry.

PIW   Period of incapacity for work. Term used re statutory sick pay (SSP*) scheme. Means period following the first four days when an employee is absent from work after which he can claim statutory sick pay.

PL   Nationality symbol for Poland – to be shown on the rear of vehicles from that country.

P/L (1)   Partial loss. Referring to shipping claims where only part of the cargo vehicle or vessel is lost or damaged.

P/L (2)   Profit and loss account. Accountancy term referring to the account which compares total sales with total outgoings (ie expenditure). The balance shows gross profit or loss.

P/L (3)   Part load.

PLA   Port of London Authority. Statutory authority responsible for operation of the Port.

Plant   Items of equipment/machinery used in construction/engineering/ industry/factory processes, etc.

Plaque (calibration)   Regarding tachograph calibration, etc, small sticker (ie plaque) fixed inside body of instrument indicating date of calibration and technical details. Sealed with clear film and illegal to tamper with. Similar plaques added at two-year inspections and following minor repair work to installation.

Plating and testing   Term for annual goods vehicle test. Applies to goods vehicle over 3,500 kg gvw, all artics and trailers over 1,020 kg unladen (with certain exceptions). Plating (ie issue of DTLR plate* showing pmw.) takes place when vehicle first registered and verified at first annual test one year after registration. Subsequent tests follow annually at goods vehicle testing stations.

Play bus   Vehicle exempt from LGV* driver entitlement and plating and annual testing requirements. Defined as a vehicle originally constructed to carry more than 12 passengers but which has been adapted primarily for the carriage of play things for children.

plc (1)   Public limited company. Company whose shares are traded on the stock exchange and offered to the public at large and whose daily share priced is to be found in the financial columns of national newspapers.

PLC (2)   Product life-cycle. A concept whereby the life of a product from its original design and manufacture, through subsequent modifications, re-brandings, re-packagings, etc and its growth in the market place until its final decline and withdrawal are assessed.

PLE   Penske Logistics Europe. New name in pan-European logistics formed by US company Penske supported by GE Capital.

PLG   Private/light goods. Category of vehicle for excise licensing purposes – includes all privately used vehicles and goods vehicle up to 3,500 kg gvw.

PM   Particulate matter. An unhealthy, polluting discharge from diesel vehicle exhausts. One of the alleged sources for an increased incidence of asthma, especially among children.

PMR   Private mobile radio. *See also* Mobile radio.

PMW   Permissible maximum weight. Means maximum weight permitted for vehicle/trailer/combination on a road in Great Britain (ie weight which must not be exceeded otherwise offence committed). Indicated on DTLR plate* issued by Goods Vehicle Centre* which must be fitted to vehicle. This weight may differ from manufacturer's design weight but takes priority.

PNC   Police national computer. Contains, among other information, the VIN* given to vehicles and recorded on computerized DVLA* owner file. Allows the police 24-hour access to relevant details of all vehicles registered with the DVLA.

Pocket wagon   Purpose-built rail wagon with pockets into which the bogies of road vehicle semi-trailers slot to provide low-height transit for loading gauge clearance.

POA   Place of acceptance. The place where goods are received for transit and the place where the carrier's liability commences.

POD (1)   Proof of delivery. A signature by the recipient of goods confirming their delivery. Often used to substantiate haulage charges. Manual POD signatures are being replaced by hi-tech devices such as hand-held computers with signature capture systems from which delivery information can be down-loaded.

POD (2) Place of delivery. The place where goods are delivered and where carrier's liability ceases.

POE   Point of embarkation. Place where passengers board a ship or aircraft (or could be a bus/coach).

POI   Persistent Offenders' Index. System operated by DVLA* to identify persistent VED* offenders and check whether the rest of the operator's vehicles have been taxed.

Poids Lourd   French term meaning heavy lorry – usually seen as a label or plate on such vehicles.

Poincaré Franc (the gold franc)   Theoretical gold franc originally used to provide a fixed (ie inflation-proof) value for carrier's liability. With gold prices no longer stable it is replaced by the SDR*.

Poisonous waste   Term used in *Control of Pollution Act 1974*. It is an offence to deposit poisonous/noxious waste (whether liquid or solid) which may pollute land or cause environmental hazard.

Polarstream   Trade marked temperature control system by BOC (now jointly developed with Hubbard) which uses liquid nitrogen sprayed into the load space instead of using of a conventional refrigeration unit.

Police constable   Lowest rank of police officer – in law all policemen are constables irrespective of actual rank/title.

Police notification   Regarding the movement of abnormal or projecting loads (depending on dimensions), statutory requirement to notify police of every district through which it is to pass at least two days in advance.

187

Policy   A proposed course of action on a specific issue (for instance, a transport policy whereby a local authority determines its plans for traffic routes, parking restrictions, access times for loading and unloading, etc).

Portal   A door or gateway. In Internet terms it is a Web site that provides links to other sites.

POS   Point of sale. Where payment for goods is made (eg at the supermarket till/check-out).

Power to weight ratio   Relationship of vehicle gvw to engine power output. Minimum standard formerly set by law (4.4 kW* per 1,000 kg for post 1973 vehicles). Thus 38-tonner legally needed a minimum power output of 167.2 kW. In practice power outputs are generally much higher than this so the legal minimum standard has been abolished.

Power train   Vehicle engine/gearbox, etc. *See also* Drive line.

PPE   Personal protective equipment. Requirement under health and safety legislation that this must be provided by employers where appropriate.

PPG   Planning Policy Guidance. Government-issued guidelines for local authority and regional planners, eg PPG13 – Planning Policy Guidance Note 13: Transport, published in 1994.

PPK   Pence per kilometre. A method of calculating and expressing vehicle running costs*.

PPP (1)   Private pension plan. A private pension scheme arranged by, for example, a self-employed person with (usually) an insurance company.

PPP (2)   Public private partnerships. A strategy whereby government initiated projects (mainly large infrastructure developments – eg the forthcoming modernization of the London Underground) are jointly funded by private and public finance. *See also* PFI.

PPT   Powered pallet truck. The most popular battery powered truck used for picking, especially in distribution centres.

PPVA   *Public Passenger Vehicles Act 1981.* An act concerned with passenger vehicle licensing, etc. Established the Passenger vehicle operator's 'O' licensing system. *See also* 'O' licensing.

Pre-entry   In connection with Customs' procedures, standard system whereby exporter declares consignment to Customs prior to its clearance for export.

Preferential creditor   In event of business liquidation/bankruptcy, creditor who has preferential claim on assets ahead of ordinary trade creditors, etc (but not Inland Revenue for tax and NI*, Customs and Excise for VAT* and other taxes, etc). For example, employees are preferential creditors for any wage/salary due as are debenture* holders.

Premises   In connection with the *Health and Safety at Work Act,* legal requirements relating to premises/work places (especially in regard to their safety – of entrances/exits, etc) includes any vehicle which is the workplace of the driver.

Pressure sensitive   Regarding tachographs*, wax coated charts on which recordings are made are described as being pressure sensitive.

Primary distribution   Distribution of goods from the point of manufacture to a distribution centre (eg an RDC*). *See also* Secondary distribution.

Prime mover   The tractive unit of an articulated vehicle combination.

Principal carrier   A carrier who issues a Combined Transport document whether or not goods are carried on his own, a third party's or a consortium member's vehicle or vessel.

Private carrier   Legal term which means a carrier (ie haulier) who operates under conditions of carriage* (ie his own or as member, uses those of RHA*) – as opposed to common carrier* who does not.

Private hire taxi   A taxi that may only undertake pre-booked journeys (ie may not ply for hire in the street).

Privatization   When a government (state) hives off its publicly-owned assets to the private sector (eg as with British Rail in 1993). *See also* Nationalization.

PRN   Primary route network. The UK's trunk roads and other key routes.

Probabilistic (or stochastic) inventory control models   An inventory control system where all the variables and parameters used are treated as random variables. It is assumed that the average demand for items is approximately constant over time and that it is possible to state the probability distribution of the demand, particularly during the lead time for replenishment. *(Source: ILT Supply-Chain Inventory Management SIG)*

Procurement   Current term for what used to be known as purchasing or buying – ie the function in a firm of acquiring all the supplies needed for production and support. Concept is that all procurement is channelled through one source/department that ensures that appropriate discounts and bulk buying advantages are obtained and to keep all purchasing under budgetary control.

Product group   A group of related products. *See also* Family group.

Production lead time   The time taken to manufacture or produce an item after an external order has been received until the item is available for packing. *(Source: ILT Supply-Chain Inventory Management SIG)*

Production of documents   To police, usually driving licence(s), vehicle insurance, test/plating certificate as appropriate – on spot or at police station within seven days. Also to DTLR enforcement officer*/TC* – but 10 days allowed.

Professional competence   Legal requirement (UK and EU) whereby individuals who run/manage haulage vehicles (ie does not apply to own account*) must satisfy TC* that they are competent. This means that they hold a CPC* issued under Grandfather rights* scheme (ie prior to 1980), qualify by exemption (through membership of specified professional bodies), or have passed RSA* examination.

Profit and loss account   Accounting term which refers to the document (usually prepared annually) showing a firm's income and expenditure and thus its profit (ie gross) or loss. Also called the trading account. Neither to be confused with balance sheet* which shows assets and liabilities.

Pro-forma invoice   Accounting term for an invoice sent in advance to indicate to the buyer what the charges will be.

Program   Computer term for software* system which effectively 'tells' computer what to do. Wide range of programs available from standard (word processing, accounting, payroll, etc) to specialized (route planning, load scheduling, etc). Programs are purchased on floppy disk* or CD-ROM and are strictly copyright (ie must not be copied and passed on – they are licensed for use only by the purchaser).

Prohibition notice   Official notice (Form PG 9*) issued by VI* vehicle examiners* when vehicle found on road in defective (ie illegal) state. Notice prohibits its further use until rectified and cleared – prosecution may also follow. It is an offence to ignore such and too many will result in jeopardy of the 'O' licence*.

Prohibition on payments   Provision in EU law (ie *EC 3820/85* article 10) which prohibits payment of bonuses or wage supplements to drivers on basis of the amount of goods carried or distance travelled unless they do not endanger road safety.

Project Samovar   Part of the EU's Drive 2* initiative the aim of which is to study the effect that fitting journey data recorders (ie monitoring equipment) to vehicles has on driver behaviour – it is expected that driving standards will rise and accidents will fall.

Projecting load   Load which projects beyond the front or rear of a vehicle and which may (depending on the amount of projection) require marking, the carriage of an attendant*, and police notification*. Also may require additional lights in case of rear projection. Full details to be found in *RV (C&U) 1986* ss 81/82 and schedule 12.

Projection markers   Red and white diagonally striped markers (end and side) to be used on vehicles carrying wide or projecting loads in accordance with the provisions of Schedule 8 of the C&U* regulations. Must be indirectly illuminated at night. Illustrated in Highway Code*

Prometheus project   Programme for European Traffic with Highest Efficiency and Unprecedented Safety. European-wide project concerned with the development of 'intelligent' vehicles integrated into an intelligent road infrastructure.

Protection by privilege   Statements made in Court (and parliament) are protected by privilege so that if libellous/slanderous of another person there can be no action of redress. In case of public inquiry* before the TC* there is no such protection.

PS   *Pferdestarke.* German word for the metric equivalent of horsepower – a measure of engine output.

PSD   Purchasing strategy development. The process by which an organization defines its corporate objectives on purchasing (ie contractual agreements and business arrangements with its suppliers).

PSR   Passenger service requirements. Obligations imposed on train operating companies (TOCs*) to provide certain minimum passenger services.

PSV   Public service vehicle. Vehicle adapted to carry nine or more passengers and used for hire or reward (or, if less than eight passengers, is used for carrying such at separate fares in the course of a passenger-carrying business). *See* PCV.

Psychometric assessment/testing   A 'tool' used in the recruitment and selection of staff – ie the use of tests to determine an applicant's mental ability, aptitude and personality, etc.

PT   Particulate trap fitted to vehicle exhaust to reduce harmful emissions (ie a mix of pollutants). *See also* PM.

PTA   Passenger Transport Authority. Local government policy-making body in the UK's metropolitan areas (eg major conurbations such as Greater Manchester). Originally set up under the *1968 Transport Act* and *1972 Local Government Act* to plan, operate and co-ordinate public transport within their respective areas. Their influence on local bus operations was reduced by the *1985 Transport Act,* which removed their operating powers.

PTE   Passenger Transport Executive. Created under the *1968 Transport Act* and charged with establishing a coordinated and integrated public passenger transport system to meet the needs of the local area. The PTEs are controlled by the PTA*. PTEs are: CENTRO* (West Midlands PTE); GMPTE* (Greater Manchester PTE); Merseytravel* (Merseyside PTE); METRO* (West Yorkshire PTE); NEXUS* (Tyne & Wear PTE); SYPTE* (South Yorkshire PTE); and SPT* (Strathclyde PTE).

PTO   Power take off. Device mounted on and operating from vehicle gearbox to drive equipment via hydraulic pump (tipping body, refrigeration plant, lorry-mounted crane*, discharge blower on tankers, etc).

PTS   Patient transfer service. The provision of sitting ambulances by Health Trusts for day care patients, etc.

PTWs   Powered two wheelers. For example, mopeds, scooters and motorcycles.

Public inquiry (1)   In connection with 'O' licensing* and LGV/PCV driver entitlements, public hearing (at which press may also be present) at which Traffic Commissioner* 'interviews' licence applicant/holder on certain matters. This may be to give prior warning to new applicants about legal requirements, etc but also when existing holders are to be admonished/ penalized following breach of licence conditions, etc. At PI all statements made by subject/witnesses are recorded and taken to be statements/ declarations of intent* (ie legal promises) which must be fulfilled, also there is no protection by privilege* at such.

Public inquiry (2)   Part of the Government's consultation process on new road developments and route selection. Usually carried out by an independent inspector on behalf of the Secretary of State (eg for transport) who conducts the inquiry in an open, fair and impartial way, recording the facts and comments stated by witnesses both for and against the proposals (some of whom are experts, others being the lay public voicing objections on many relevant issues). The inspector makes a final report and his recommendations to the Secretary of State.

Public liability   Liability of a person/firm towards others if they suffer damage or injury at your hands (ie on your premises/by your vehicles). Insurance can be taken out to protect against public liability claims (eg when a customer visiting firm's premises slips on floor and is injured; when a passer-by is hit by a cab door or accidentally walks into a tail-lift. In everyday life, if a neighbour trips over your doorstep you are liable if they are injured and claim – normally this would be met under your household insurance).

Pull system   A system where orders for an end item are pulled through the facility to satisfy demand for the end item. An example of pull system is the JIT Kanban* process. *(Source: ILT Supply-Chain Inventory Management SIG)*

Purchase price   The price at which an item is marked for sale, or sold.

Purchasing lead time (PLT)   The total length of time between the decision to purchase an item and its availability for dispatch from the supplier concerned (that is, the sum of the order lead-time, the production lead time and any time necessary for packing or preparation for dispatch of a specific order). *(Source: ILT Supply-Chain Inventory Management SIG)*

Push system   A system where orders are issued for completion by specified due dates, based on estimated lead-times, or where the flow of material in a product structure is controlled and determined by the lower levels. *(Source: ILT Supply-Chain Inventory Management SIG)*

Put away rules   The internal rules and procedures for positioning stock in a warehouse or store after goods inward processing. *(Source: ILT Supply-Chain Inventory Management SIG)*

PVC   Polyvinyl chloride. Flexible plastic-like material.

Qq

QA   Quality assurance. A mark of distinction (eg ISO 9000*) indicating that a product or service meets established quality standards.

QC   Quality control. A management system to ensure that established quality standards are met on a continuous basis.

QCA   Qualifications and Curriculum Authority. Body that establishes training qualifications.

QFD   Quality function deployment. A benchmarking system based on customer requirements to perform to established quality standards.

QFF   Quick-frozen food regulations. Common industry terminology for *The Quick-Frozen Foodstuffs Regulations 1990* (as amended) – also EU Directive of similar title (ie the QFF Directive).

QR   Quick Response*. Faster than JiT*, QR aims to respond ultra-quickly to customer demand by reducing the time element between order and delivery.

Quadricycle   In motor vehicle terms, defined as a vehicle having four wheels and engine power not exceeding 15 kilowatts and an unladen mass (ie weight), including the weight of batteries in the case of electrically-powered versions, not exceeding 550 kg in the case of goods carrying models and 400 kg in any other case.

Quality licensing   System of governmental control (ie licensing) of goods vehicle operations based on 'quality' concept – namely, where primary concern is for safe and legal operation rather than any other criteria (see quantity licensing below). In practice, in the UK (and supposedly the rest of the EU), it specifically means the licence applicant/holder being a fit person to run goods vehicles (ie of good repute*), financially capable of operating the vehicles legally and safely (ie of appropriate financial standing*) and having sufficient knowledge of legal/business/operational matters to comply with the law, etc (ie being professionally competent). This form of licensing is sometimes looked upon as 'deregulation' and is frowned upon in some quarters (including USA, South Africa and Canada where there have been mass protests) because it does not provide the protection of a closed industry – basically any Tom, Dick or Harry can start up with a lorry if he has a little money and can pass a simple examination.

Quality management   The concept of ensuring that services supplied meet pre-determined quality standards (ie as with BS 5750*/ISO 9000*/ EN 29000) and as confirmed by assessment and approval by a qualified third-party assessor. This is a relatively new concept in transport but hauliers face increasing pressure from major customers to gain approval. In the competitive environs of EU (particularly) trading it is likely that quality approved hauliers will benefit over those which are not so approved.

Quantity licensing   System of governmental control (ie licensing) of goods vehicle operations based on 'quantity' concept – namely, where primary concern is to restrict the volume of freight capacity on the roads. Britain's old A & B carriers' licensing system was of this type until replaced by quality licensing (ie 'O' licensing*) under the provisions of the *Transport Act 1968*. The road service licence system introduced for bus and coach services by the *Road Traffic Act 1930* and replaced by registration of local bus services* under the *Transport Act 1985,* was a classic example of quantity licensing, giving the favoured operator or operators a monopoly of services along the stated route.

Quarantine stock   On-hand stock which has been segregated and is not available to meet customer requirements. *(Source: ILT Supply-Chain Inventory Management SIG)*

Quick response (QR*)   Term used primarily in connection with stock replenishment. Now largely replaced by efficient consumer response* (ECR).

Quoin   A timber wedge used to prevent drums from rolling.

Quota   A system of control by numbers. In international road haulage, scarce permits are issued under a quota (or restricted allocation) system.

Rr

R&D   Research and development. The system by which firms arrive at new products – ie by researching the market, and other competing products (and services) and developing new products. This may range, for example, from simple products such as stationery items to complex engineering, medical and pharmaceutical products.

RAC   Royal Automobile Club (and RSAC – Royal Scottish Automobile Club). Motoring organization providing (among other things) roadside assistance/ international travel service/Bail Bonds*/International Driving Permits*, etc.

Radial (ply) tyre   Vehicle tyre legally defined as being one structured with the ply cords extending to the bead at (substantially) 90 degrees to the peripheral line of the tread and with the ply cord 'stabilized' with a 'substantially inextensible circumferential belt'.

Radio frequency identification (RFID)   The attachment of transponders (which may be read only or read/write) to products, as an alternative to linear bar codes, to enable product identification some distance from the scanner or when out of line of sight. *(Source: ILT Supply-Chain Inventory Management SIG)*

Radio paging   System of communications whereby individual is contacted via personal pager (small, pocket-size, device which bleeps or vibrates alerting the wearer to contact the message centre/base, etc). Usually restricted to limited range and no voice contact possible.

Rail freight   Freight traffic carried by rail, booked either by container, wagonload or trainload.

Rail loading gauge   The profile of bridges and tunnels, etc above rail lines which determines the size of wagons that can pass through. Generally, gauges are known by name – eg A, B, B+, C, W6, Berne, UIC and Channel Tunnel.

Railhead   Rail depot*/terminal where loading/unloading and tranship-ment of loads/swap bodies* (eg to and from road vehicle) takes place. Key location in intermodal*/combined transport* operations.

Railtrack plc   Owner and operator of UK rail infrastructure* (ie track, signalling and stations, etc) – train operators pay track access charges for its use.

RAM   Random access memory. Computer terminology.

Random sample cycle counting   A method in which the particular parts to be counted are selected from the population of part numbers in a manner that has no inherent bias. In this selection process, each part number has an equal chance of being selected. *(Source: ILT Supply-Chain Inventory Management SIG)*

Range-change   Form of gearbox used on heavy goods vehicle. Four/five main gears are ranged down to provide double the number of ratios (ie 8/10) – necessary when trying to match narrow bands of engine speed to wide range of road speed/load/gradient capability. *See also* Splitter gearbox.

Rapid acquisition of manufactured parts (RAMP)   A make to order process to reduce the purchasing lead time for long lead time manufactured parts whereby product data is held in STEP (the international standard for exchange of manufacturing product data) by the customer and exchanged, in electronic format, when an order is placed. *(Source: ILT Supply-Chain Inventory Management SIG)*

Rapid intervention vehicle   Fast vehicle used by fire brigades to get quickly to a fire/emergency to start fire fighting/rescue pending arrival of main (usually slower) vehicle units.

Rapid Service Pass   Eurotunnel pass to allow regular Channel Tunnel (ie Le Shuttle*) users to travel on an account basis without having to stop and make payment on arrival at the Tunnel toll.

Rapid transit   Passenger transport system (usually rail) designed to provide quick journeys. Normally segregated from other traffic.

Rapporteur   A person appointed by an organization to report on its meetings. Also found taking part in focus groups*.

Raw material   Stock or items purchased from suppliers, to be input to a production process, and which will subsequently modified or transformed into finished goods. *(Source: ILT Supply-Chain Inventory Management SIG)*

RCT   Royal Corps of Transport. Military regiment concerned with providing transport/logistics support to the British army. Merged with other regiments in 1993 to form the Royal Logistics Corps (RLC).

RCV   Refuse collection vehicle. In the vernacular, a rubbish lorry.

RDA   Regional Development Agency. Concerned with regional economic development, including local proposals for transport and infrastructure.

RDC (1)   Regional Distribution Centre. Warehouse/transport depot from which goods are distributed regionally.

RDC (2)   Routiers Drivers' Club. Club for lorry drivers.

RDC (3)   Radio data communication. A means of data communications by radio between locations (eg in and between warehouses).

RDC (4)   Rural Development Commission. Administers the Rural Transport Development Fund (set up under the *Transport Act 1985*) on behalf of the DTLR*.

RDS   Regional Development Strategy. A strategy at regional level for the development of land, infrastructure and transport systems, etc.

RDS-TMC   Radio data system – traffic message channel*. Radio system and exclusive channel for up-to-the-minute road traffic information.

RDT   Radio data terminal. Used, for example, in warehouses to provide communication between static and mobile workstations (eg fork-lift trucks) and the main warehouse computer.

Reach truck   Fork-lift truck capable of reaching forward to withdraw pallets from racking or from high stacks.

Rear position light   Vehicle red rear light. Two required and must be switched on when vehicle on road between sunset and sunrise.

Rear reflective marker   System of fluorescent and reflective rear marking required on goods vehicles over 7,500 kg and trailers over 3,500 kg gvw*. Type of marker (ie diagonal stripes or 'Long Vehicle') to be used depends on length of vehicle/trailer.

Rear steer   Vehicle/plant where the steering axle is at the rear rather than the front. Also applies to certain long articulated semi-trailers where the rearmost axle is steerable (via connections from tractive unit) to give greater manoeuvrability and avoid excessive tyre wear through scrubbing when tight turning.

Rear underrun protection Legal term for rear bumpers on heavy vehicles/trailers. Required on vehicles over 3,500 kg gvw and trailers over 1020 kg unladen weight. Intended to reduce damage/injury to small vehicles, cyclists and motor cyclists, etc which may run into rear.

Rearward projection Load which projects to rear of vehicle/trailer. *See also* Projecting loads.

Rebated heavy oil Diesel (ie heavy) oil on which a reduced rate of duty is payable and illegal for use in road vehicles (with certain limited exceptions such as farm vehicles and construction plant) – but can be used to fuel separate 'fridge motors' (ie refrigeration units), etc. Coloured with red dye for distinguishing purposes and regularly tested for by HM Customs and Excise with road fuel testing units. Commonly called red diesel or gas oil.

REC Recruitment & Employment Confederation. Association of recruitment consultants. Together with RHA* and FTA* produced *Joint Code of Good Practice for Agency Drivers.*

Re-calibration In connection with tachographs, the re-calibration of an installation either following repair or, in any case, as required by law no later than six years after a previous calibration* (date indicated on plaque* in instrument).

Receiver *See* Official receiver.

Receiving date Date from which cargo is accepted by the shipping company for shipment on a specified sailing.

Recorder Instrument that records data.

Recording equipment Legal term for tachograph*.

Recovery vehicle Legally defined as vehicle constructed or permanently adapted primarily for the purpose of lifting, towing and transporting a disabled vehicle (max. two at any time) and used for recovery and removal of such. Now in separate VED* class and may not be used on trade plates.

Re-cut tyre Vehicle tyre in which all or part of the original (or a different) tread pattern has been cut or burnt deeper. Such tyres may only be re-cut in accordance with the manufacturer's re-cut tread pattern and used on vehicles exceeding 2,540 kg unladen and with wheels at least 405 mm diameter. They should not be used if the ply or cord has been exposed in the re-cutting process.

Recycling   The process of turning old/used/scrap/waste material into new products. The recycling process usually involves crushing and/or heating (melting down) the material first. A major element in protection of the environment – ie reusing scare resources. In the transport context, glass is recycled and used as a constituent of road surfacing material.

Red diesel   *See* Rebated heavy oil.

Reduced visibility   *See* Seriously reduced visibility – when vehicle dipped headlights must be used.

Redundancy   Situation when employee is dismissed for reason that (mainly) his job ceases to exist or business closes (but only applies where employment was for at least two years after reaching 18 years). An employee is not redundant if his job continues and he is replaced by another person. Redundant employee entitled to specified payments according to age, length of service and current rate of pay.

Redundant stock   Parts used in manufacture which have been removed from a bill of material by technical change or modification action. Redundant parts may also be obsolete if they are no longer used for any other application in the inventory concerned. *(Source: ILT Supply-Chain Inventory Management SIG)*

Reefer   Alternative term to describe a refrigerated vehicle/plant/ship.

Re-engineering   Term use to describe the process of re-organizing the internal workings of a business (eg what management consultants often advise their clients about at great cost; *see* BPR).

Refrigerated vehicle   Goods vehicle/trailer designed to carry goods (mainly foodstuffs) at controlled temperature*. *See also* ATP (1).

Refusal to test   Regarding goods vehicle testing, the right of the testing station to refuse to test a vehicle submitted in contravention of the stated requirements (eg late arrival, no documents, dirty, unsafe, insufficient fuel/ oil). Form VTG 12 is issued, stating reason.

Registrar of Companies   Official to whom all applications for limited company registrations are made, also annual returns of companies made under provisions of the Companies Acts. On registration companies are given registration number, etc and add word 'limited' to their name. As such they are strictly controlled as to conduct, etc by the law.

Registration document   Form V 5 issued by DVLC* when motor vehicle is registered – see below. Indicates details of vehicle, registration number and name of registered keeper (not necessarily the owner). When vehicle is sold, tear-off slip is used to notify DVLC of new owner, etc.

Registration mark/number   Provided for all registered motor vehicles – and registration document (see above). Must be displayed on plate (see below) mounted front and rear (with exceptions – eg motorcycles) and on rear of any trailer drawn. Rear plate must be indirectly illuminated when other obligatory lights* of vehicle are on. On vehicle first registered since 1973 plates must be of reflex reflecting material (except where goods vehicles have rear reflective markers*) black letters on white for front, black letters on yellow for rear.

Registration plate   Plate mounted on vehicle displaying its registration mark/number* on a retro-reflecting background.

Rehabilitation of offenders   Legal provision under which past offenders are no longer required to disclose such in response to official request (eg when completing application forms – for driver licensing/'O' licensing*). Period of rehabilitation depends on age of offender at time and penalty for offence.

Relevant axle spacing   Legal term used in connection with determining the permissible weights for articulated vehicle combinations, namely distance between rearmost axle of drawing vehicle and rearmost axle on semi-trailer.

Remould   Used tyre casing remoulded (ie with new tread, etc) to provide further operational life. *See also* Re-tread.

Removal note   Note confirming that goods are clear of customs.

Rental (car/truck/trailer/fork-lift truck)   Business of renting out (usually on relatively short-term basis) vehicles, etc. Such vehicles used by firms needing extra capacity for short periods or cover for their own vehicles which are temporarily out of service. Over 3.5 tonne vehicles may only be hired by a firm/business within the margin* on its 'O' licence*.

Re-order costs   The total cost of placing a repeat order for an item either externally with a supplier or for internal manufacture. The costs may include elements to cover: order preparation, administration, IT overheads, correspondence, telephone, transportation, goods inward processing, inspection and for manufacture, batch set up costs and other production overheads. *(Source: ILT Supply-Chain Inventory Management SIG)*

Re-order level (ROL) (or re-order point – ROP)   The calculated level of stock within an inventory control system to which the quantity of a specific item is allowed to fall before replenishment order action is generated. *(Source: ILT Supply-Chain Inventory Management SIG)*

Re-order quantity (ROQ) (or replenishment order quantity)   The calculated order quantity necessary to replenish stocks at a given point in time. The method of calculation, and the timing of the order, will vary depending on the type of inventory control system in use. Quantity-based systems are checked continually to determine if an order should be placed; time based systems only have a count of stock at predetermined intervals and orders placed as required; a distribution system plans orders to meet distribution needs; and production-based systems only order stock to meet manufacturing requirements. *(Source: ILT Supply-Chain Inventory Management SIG)*

Repair period (RP)   The total out of service time, including transit time, from when a repairable component becomes unfit for use until the time it is returned to stock and is available for further use. *(Source: ILT Supply-Chain Inventory Management SIG)*

Repairable item   An inventory item that is not normally consumed in use but one which will be repaired and re-used as part of the normal stock policy for that item. Such items have a repair lead-time as well as a procurement lead-time. *(Source: ILT Supply-Chain Inventory Management SIG)*

Replacement decision   Management decision as to when vehicles, etc should be replaced by new ones based on combination of economic and operational factors (eg rising maintenance costs, falling residual value*). Also, availability of new vehicles and market for second-hand has a bearing.

Replacement vehicle   In connection with 'O' licensing*, replacement of one vehicle by another and the need to notify the TC* on Form GV 80 within one month.

Replenishment system   The function of replenishing stocks as they are used/consumed to ensure that a process or supply does not run out.

Reportable accident   An industrial accident required to be reported to the Health and Safety Executive (HSE) under RIDDOR*.

Representation   In connection with goods vehicle (but not passenger) 'O' licensing*, owners/occupiers of land in the vicinity* of vehicle operating centres* have right of representation against 'O' licence applicants on grounds that the use of such places will affect their enjoyment of their land (ie environmentally only). They have no right of appeal (as with objectors*) should the application go against them.

Res ipsa loquitur   Legal term meaning that the facts speak for themselves.

Residual value   The value of a vehicle when its useful life for the owner has expired. A (theoretical) figure used in depreciation calculations to indicate the value likely to be obtained (or necessary to obtain) when the vehicle is eventually disposed of.

Responsibility for maintenance   Regarding 'O' licensing*, the fact that no matter who carries out maintenance work (or under what contractual terms), it is the user (ie 'O' licence holder) who remains responsible in law for the mechanical condition of vehicles/trailers. The same applies when vehicles are hired (unless complete with driver), borrowed or a driver hitches your tractive unit to somebody else's semi-trailer – the driver's employer (ie the user) remains responsible.

Rest period   Requirement under regulation *EC 3820/85* for driver to take a rest period between driving days and once each week when he has driven. Rest is period of time when driver is free to dispose of his time as he wishes. Daily rest is normally 11 hours but may be reduced to nine hours three times in week (with the reduction made up by end of next following week) and weekly rest is normally 45 hours which may be reduced to 36 when drivers is at base and 24 when away (reduced time must be made up en bloc by end of third following week).

Restraints and incentives   Restraints are negative measures, such as those which force car users to move to the use of alternative, more environmentally-friendly transport modes (eg by prohibiting or restricting car parking). Incentives are positive measures to encourage people to make less use of their motor cars and move towards greater use of sustainable transport (eg bus, tram and train services).

Restricted HGV driving licence   Heavy goods vehicle drivers' licence which restricted holder to driving vehicles of 10 tonnes maximum gvw – this restriction disappears with the introduction of new EU unified driving licence* system.

Restricted 'O' licence   Operator's licence available to transporters of their own goods (ie own account*) where the carriage is not for hire or reward. Conditions of fitness (ie fit person*) and financial standing* have to be met but no requirement for professional competence*. Vehicles under such licence may carry goods in UK or internationally. Restricted passenger vehicle 'O' licences* are available to operators of PSVs* which carry no more than 8 passengers, or not more than 16 passengers when used for purposes not connected with a passenger-carrying business or when used by an operator whose main business is not that of operating PSVs with more than eight seats.

Restricted road   Road on which 30 mph speed limit applies (ie one with street lamps positioned not more than 200 yards (in Scotland 185 metres) apart. Possible for some such roads to be designated as non-restricted and other roads without street lamps designated as restricted roads.

Resuscitation   A word that means to revive from near death. Useful first aid skill but otherwise best not attempted at scene of accident unless absolutely vital – more harm than good may be done.

Retarder   Device on vehicle to help reduce its speed by means other than conventional wheel brakes (eg as with 'Jake Brake'* which operates on engine overrun to produce compression effect). Engine also has retardation effect in low gear.

Retread   Vehicle tyre which has had a new tread moulded on to give the casing a further period of life.

Retro reflex reflector   Vehicle reflector facing to the rear or side which reflects light back from whence it came. Such reflectors are required by law to indicate the presence and width of a vehicle when seen from the rear. Most vehicles require two red reflectors at rear and long vehicles/ trailers at least two amber reflectors on each side (possibly more on account of length).

Return load database   Computer file (ie database) containing information on the availability of return loads. Accessible by licensed users of system.

Return on capital   Term meaning the financial benefit (ie return) gained from the use of capital (eg the return from an investment in a business). Usually calculated by dividing the net profit by the capital invested (eg £10,000 net profit on £100,000 investment means a 10 per cent return on capital).

Returnable transit packaging (RTP)   Packaging that can be returned and re-used. Also known as re-usable secondary packaging (RSP).

Revenue A word that means income. In the transport context, it is income from passenger fares, on-vehicle advertising, haulage and shipping rates, the sales of airline tickets, etc. Total revenue/income must be declared for tax purposes, although expenses incurred in achieving that revenue may be declared (ie it is not compulsory!).

Revenue weight The gross plated or plated train weight of a vehicle being the maximum weight that it may legally operate in Great Britain and which determines the amount of VED* payable.

Reverse logistics Distribution terminology for collecting returns (eg surplus, damaged or recalled goods) and bringing them back to the depot/warehouse and integrating them back into the system (ie for scrap, repair or replacement, etc).

Reverse trading The practice of trading part-finished goods/components for raw materials.

Reversing Causing a motor vehicle to travel backwards – illegal if distance reversed is greater than necessary for safety or reasonable convenience of the occupants or other traffic (except road rollers).

Reversing accidents Too many for comfort, and cause of concern to safety organizations and government.

Reversing alarm Fitted to vehicles to warn (especially pedestrians) that vehicle is reversing. Sometimes called bleeper – legally called audible warning instrument. May be fitted voluntarily to goods vehicles over 2 tonnes (and certain others) but not to cars/light vehicles. Sound must not be confused with that of pedestrian crossing signal.

Review interval The time between assessing order requirements in a fixed order interval system. *(Source: ILT Supply-Chain Inventory Management SIG)*

Revocation Action of TC* when he cancels an 'O' licence* for disciplinary reasons. This means vehicles may no longer be operated until new licence gained. Offender may also be disqualified from holding another licence.

RF Radio frequency. In logistics typically used to report movement or location of goods to a control system – an RF reader can read bar codes and/or electronic tags.

RfD Railfreight Distribution. Former British Rail freight operation providing conventional freight and intermodal services. Now privatized and owned by the EWS (English, Welsh and Scottish) Railway company which bought all of British Rail's freight operations when they were privatized.

RFG (1) Rail freight grant. Government grants designed to encourage the switch from road to rail transport by helping to fund feasibility studies and infrastructure developments.

RFG (2) Rail Freight Group. Pressure/lobby group representing the interests of suppliers, manufacturers, operators and customers concerned with promoting the growth of rail freight in the UK.

RFOL Road Freight Operator's Licence. Northern Ireland version of 'O' licence*. Basically same as GB system but issued by DOE* Belfast.

RfS/RFS (1) Road-friendly suspension. On heavy goods vehicles, a system where conventional steel leaf springs on drive axles are replaced by air suspension (or a system equivalent to air suspension) providing at least 75 per cent of the spring effort to reduce road damage.

RFS (2) Received for shipment. Receipt issued by carrier, shipping company, etc on receipt of goods for shipment/transport.

RHA Road Haulage Association. Trade association for professional haulage industry.

RHDTC The Road Haulage and Distribution Training Council. The 'lead body' responsible for setting the occupational standards and evolving the framework of National Voluntary Qualifications (NVQs*) in the industry to meet government targets.

RHIF Road Haulage Industry Forum. Joint body comprising members of the road haulage industry and representatives of government (most particularly the Minister for Transport) formed to discuss key industry issues. Originally established to discuss high levels of fuel duty and VED on trucks.

RHITSC The Road Haulage Industry Training Standards Council. Body set up to establish a career structure in the industry.

RID Regulations concerning the international carriage of dangerous goods by rail.

RIDDOR *The Reporting of Injuries, Diseases and Dangerous Occurrences Regulations 1995.* Legislation that requires among other things the need to report certain specified accidents/diseases to HSE* and keep records of reportable accidents, etc. *See also* Accident book.

Rigid vehicle Vehicle on which the drivers cab and the load-carrying body are mounted on a rigid chassis (may have two, three or four axles). In law defined (under the C&U regulations) as a vehicle not constructed or adapted to form part of an articulated vehicle.

Ring fencing Term used in connection with financing (usually public financing) to mean that certain funds are reserved for a specific purpose (eg vehicle taxes being reserved for funding road building and repairs, or speeding fines being reserved to fund more enforcement, rather than going into a general fund). *See* Hypothecation.

Risk assessment An employer's legal responsibility to assess the risks to the heath and safety of his workforce and others from the activities of his business or within his premises.

Risk Prevention Officer Proposed in UK that transporters of dangerous goods should employ or appoint a suitably qualified person as RPO*. *See also* DGA – Dangerous Goods Advisor.

RITC Rail Industry Training Council. Examining and awarding body for qualifications in the rail industry.

RJC Regional Joint Council. Body comprising trade unions (TGWU* and URTU*) and RHA* established to negotiate wages and conditions; but its decisions are not binding on operators.

RLC Royal Logistics Corps. British Army regiment formed in 1993 from a merger of former regiments, namely the RCT*, the Royal Army Ordnance Corps, the Royal Catering Corps and the Royal Pioneer Corps. Provides total logistics support for the British army in peacetime and in war situations.

RMIF Retail Motor Industry Federation (was MAA*). Trade association for motor vehicle retailers.

RMT The Rail, Maritime and Transport Union, formerly the National Union of Railwaymen (NUR) and the National Union of Seamen (NUS).

RN Release note. A receipt signed by the consignee acknowledging delivery (ie receipt) of goods.

RO   Nationality symbol for Romania – to be shown on the rear of vehicles from that country.

Road   Defined in law as any highway* or any other road to which the public has access – including bridges carrying the road.

Road charging   *See* Road pricing.

Road construction vehicle   Defined for legal purposes as one constructed or adapted for conveying built-in road construction machinery and not for carrying any other load except its own articles and material used for road construction – *V(E)A 1971* s4(2).

Road friendly suspension   Suspension system for heavy vehicles which meets legal conditions for causing minimum road damage – mainly achieved through the use of air suspension*.

Road Haulage Forum   A discussion body comprising the road haulage industry (RHA*, FTA*, etc) and DLTR* Ministers, initially on fuel and vehicle licence costs, but other relevant matters also covered.

Road haulage permit   Road haulage permit needed to transit/enter countries with which UK has negotiated agreement. Available in many forms from IRFO* (under allocation system). Illegal to travel without valid permit, to transfer permit or use one in another name, etc – heavy penalties imposed on offenders. To be abolished for inter-EU transport under provisions of SEM*. *See also* Bi-lateral and Multi-lateral permit.

Road network database   Computer file (ie database) on which the whole road system (UK and Europe) is logged by grid reference and which can provide (on access) so-called 'best' route between any two points depending on criteria selected (ie shortest distance, fastest travel, mainly motorways, avoiding certain obstacles/bridges/town centres, etc).

Road pricing   Scheme whereby road users are required to pay more directly for their use of the road, either on a general basis or for use of specific stretches/areas. This is done by licensing or by electronic means whereby use is specifically measured (via electronic signals and receivers which provide recording of a vehicle being on a particular road at a particularly time, etc).

Road speed limiter   Device fitted to goods vehicles and coaches to limit road speed. Currently plans to require such by law on goods vehicles.

Road traffic accident   Accident involving motor vehicle on road in which damage to another vehicle or roadside property occurs or other persons are injured. In the event of such, driver must stop, give his name and address, that of the vehicle owner and the vehicle registration number and report to police as soon as reasonably possible but in any case within 24 hours.

Road transport offence   An offence taken into account when determining the 'good repute'* of an 'O' licence* applicant or holder. Conviction for one such offence (based on the Traffic Commissioner's* assessment of its seriousness) is sufficient to rule against good repute and thus the right to hold a licence.

Road train   Term (particularly in Europe) for lorry and trailer (ie drawbar*) combination.

Roadnet   Computerized road network database (see above) available from Synergy Distribution Systems Limited.

Road-rail systems   Transport systems designed to permit a combination of road and rail travel (usually by mounting vehicle on special rail wagons – *see* Piggy-back and Kangourou).

RoadRailer   Form of road-going semi-trailer, emanating from North America, which can be converted, by switching bogies, to run on rail for intermodal transport operations.

Roadwatch   Computerized road network database from AA*.

Robotics   Science of designing and building robots (ie machines that operate as though human) following instructions from computer (ie the brain) to perform multiple and intricate functions. Mainly used in manu-facturing (especially motor industry).

RoCE   Return on capital employed. A financial measure of the return – sometimes called the yield (eg often profit, but not always) – from a business enterprise measured against the capital invested.

RoL   Re-order level. A pre-established stock level at which point re-ordering takes place or is automatically initiated.

Roll cage   Metal cage on trolley wheels used for picking and assembling orders and loading goods onto vehicles. Can be disassembled for convenient storage.

Roll-on/roll-off   Also written as RO/RO. Form of ferry ship (mainly used on short-sea crossings) which accommodates wheeled freight (and other) traffic.

Roll trailer   A low, flatbed trailer used in dockside operations for moving containers onto and off roll-on/roll-off* ferry ships.

Roller-bed floor   Floor accommodating many rollers (ie like large ball bearings) which can be raised hydraulically to allow easy manual movement of pallets, etc in any direction to achieve maximum space utilization, and then lowered to leave flat, solid floor on which pallets will not move. Found mainly in aircraft freight holds and in some goods vehicles.

Rolling motorway   Intermodal transport system where complete road vehicles are carried on special drive-on/drive-off low-height rail wagons (eg Eurotunnel's freight shuttle through the Channel Tunnel).

Rolling road   Equipment used in vehicle workshops and test stations, etc to provide facility for testing brakes. Also used in connection with calibrating tachographs.

Rolling stock   Term to describe rail wagons and carriages, etc. Also occasionally used in respect of goods vehicles, trailers, buses and coaches.

ROM   Read only memory. Computer terminology.

RO/RO   Roll-on/roll-off. Loading method for ships whereby wheeled freight (eg road vehicles and trailers) is driven or shunted on to specially-built RO/RO ferry ships.

ROSCO (1)   Road Operators' Safety Council. Promotes road safety principally in the bus and coach industry, but also includes road haulage interests. Founded 1955. Administers annual safe driving awards scheme.

ROSCOs (2)   Rolling stock companies. A constituent of the privatized railway system providing passenger coaches under lease to the train operating companies (TOCs*).

RoSPA   Royal Society for the Prevention of Accidents. Body concerned very much with road accidents and very active in accident prevention. Awards accident-free driving medals.

Roster   List showing turns of duty (or leave) for people at work (eg bus drivers).

Rota   List showing names of people and times at which they must undertake given duties (eg of bus drivers' working patterns). *See also* Roster.

Rotable   An repairable inventory item that can be repeatedly restored to a fully serviceable condition and re-used over the normal life cycle of the parent equipment to which it is related. Such items have a repair lead time as well as a procurement lead time and normally have a serial number that is retained throughout the rotable life regardless of the extent of replacement of its component parts. *(Source: ILT Supply-Chain Inventory Management SIG)*

Rotating lamps   Term for lamps legally defined as beacons – those which rotate to give a flashing effect. Blue permitted on emergency service and certain other special vehicles (eg those transporting human tissue for transplant, bomb disposal, mines rescue, mountain rescue), amber permitted on range of breakdown, Special Types*, highway service vehicles, etc and green on doctors' cars (*see* Doctor's beacons).

Rounding order quantity   That element of an order that has been added to the basic order quantity to meet a constraint imposed by the manufacturer or to optimize overall supply chain costs. *(Source: ILT Supply-Chain Inventory Management SIG)*

Routeing   The practice of planning routes for vehicles to achieve most economic or efficient delivery (usually) to multiple delivery addresses. Spelling 'routeing' preferred to 'routing'.

RPC   Reduced pollution certificate. Certificate confirming vehicle has been built, or modified by the fitment of additional equipment, to more stringent emission standards.

RPE   Respiratory protective equipment. Requirement of health and safety legislation that this must be provided by employer where necessary.

RPG   Regional Planning Guidance. *See* LTP and PPG.

RPI   Retail price index. National scale of price indexes relating the current price to a base of 100 in 1987. For example, the RPI at the end of 1999 was 166.7 against a base of 100 in January 1987 but would be 539.5 against the 100 base of January1974.

RPO   Risk Prevention Officer. Proposed in UK that transporters of dangerous goods should employ or appoint suitably qualified person as such. *See also* DGA – Dangerous Goods Adviser.

RRP   Resource requirements planning. A planning concept used in manufacturing or distribution to ensure that all the necessary resources are brought together at the point of production or distribution as and when required to complete the process.

RRRA   Road Rescue Recovery Association. Trade association for vehicle roadside recovery operators.

R&RTHC   Roads and Road Transport History Conference. Organization concerned with the history of and research into road transport and the preservation of transport archives, etc.

RSA   Royal Society of Arts. National examining body in many fields including transport. Also responsible for conducting professional competence* examination scheme on behalf of DLTR*. Now part of OCR – ie Oxford, Cambridge and RSA.

RSAC   Royal Scottish Automobile Club. Motoring organization offering (among other services) roadside assistance. Also issues Bail Bonds* and International Driving Permits*.

RSP   Rapid service passenger – Eurotunnel system to allow regular Channel Tunnel (ie Le Shuttle) users to use the service without payment and pre-booking delays.

RTA (1)   Road Traffic Acts. Common abbreviation used in reference to these Acts.

RTA (2)   Road traffic accident. Police nomenclature.

RTA (3)   Road Traffic Adviser. Telematics (the use of advanced technology to provide remotely controlled information) research project jointly funded by government and private industry designed to make more efficient use and improve safety of the existing road network by giving drivers the information they need to make decisions about their driving and routes via vehicle-mounted transponders and receiving equipment.

RTCC   Regional Traffic Control Centre – of the Highways Agency*.

RTDF   Rural Transport Development Fund.

RTI   Returnable transport item. For example, pallets, roll-cages.

RTIETB   Road Transport Industry Education and Training Board. Training body established under *Industrial Training Act 1964*. Now privatized and known as CENTREX*.

RTITB   Road Transport Industry Training Board.

RTP (1)   Returnable transit packaging. Packaging designed to meet producer/supplier legal obligations under regulations to eliminate packaging waste.

RTP (2)   Regional transport plan. *See also* RTS.

RTPI   Royal Town Planning Institute. Body representing the interests of professional planners.

RTS   Regional transport strategy. A framework in which local transport plans (LTPs*) are drawn up by local councils and on which such councils base all transport policy decisions (lorry bans, local road tolls, etc).

RTSO   Range-change, twin countershaft, splitter, overdrive transmission. Heavy truck transmission system from manufacturer Eaton.

RUC   Royal Ulster Constabulary. Civilian police force in Northern Ireland. Responsible for law enforcement in regard to transport in NI as with police in GB.

RUCC   Rail User Consultative Committees. Bodies representing rail users (ie campaigning for better rail services, etc). Act in a consumer protectionist role.

Run-flat tyre   Vehicle tyre designed specially to be capable of running when flat or under-inflated but at restricted speed and for a limited distance (commonly referred to as such or as get-you-home spare). Legally referred to as 'temporary use spare tyre'.

Running costs   The (variable*) costs of running a vehicle (eg fuel, tyre costs and maintenance) as opposed to the fixed costs* of ownership.

Running gear   On a vehicle, the wheels, axles and suspension units which may be built as a unit for direct attachment to chassis or to chassis-less (ie monocoque) body, as with panel van* or frameless* semi-trailer.

Rural Bus Challenge   Fund provided by Government for which local authorities and other agencies can bid for improving public transport provision in these areas. *See also* Urban Bus Challenge.

Rural Bus Services Grant   Budget (from the government) intended to fund means of encouraging the use of public transport.

Rural Transport Development Fund   Fund from DTLR* intended for developing innovative rural transport services such as car-sharing, taxi-buses and dial-a-bus services. Administered by the RDC; *see* RDC (4).

RUS   Nationality symbol for the Russian Federation (ie of independent states) – to be shown on the rear of vehicles from that country.

RVI   *Renault Vehicules Industriels*. Renault Trucks, French manufacturer of heavy vehicles.

Ss

S   Nationality symbol for Sweden – to be shown on the rear of vehicles from that country.

SACTRA   Standing Advisory Committee on Trunk Road Assessment. DTLR* committee (quango).

SAD   Single administrative document. Standardized single customs document (Form C88*) used for declaring export/import consignments to Customs. Replaced many individual documents and designed for ease of understanding irrespective of language, etc.

SAE   Society of Automotive Engineers. US standards organization for testing all things automotive including, particularly, vehicle engine oils which are given an SAE rating – eg 5W/40 SAE.

Safe containers   Under the *Freight Containers (Safety Convention) Regulations 1984*, owners, lessees and others must ensure that containers supplied or used comply with conditions of safety specified in the *International Convention for Safe Containers 1972*.

Safe to cross   Audible (as well as light) signal on pelican crossing indicating that it is safe to cross. Intended to aid poorly sighted people and the blind, etc.

Safety committee   Under *Health and Safety at Work, etc Act 1974* provisions, where requested by two or more safety representatives* firm must establish safety committee to review safety policy, etc.

Safety glass   Glass constructed or treated so that if fractured it does not fly into fragments likely to cause severe cuts. Legally required for motor vehicle windows (ie in case of goods vehicles, windscreen and all windows in front of and on either side of driver's seat).

Safety in docks   Legislation concerned with safety in dock premises – *The Docks Regulations 1988*. Requires lorry drivers to wear high visibility clothing* and hard hats*. Also HSC* approved code of practice for same *Safety in Docks* (available from TSO*).

Safety inspections Regarding 'O' licensing*, regular inspections of vehicles/trailers for safety purposes which licence applicant/holder promises to carry out. Failure to comply could result in jeopardy of the licence.

Safety of loads on vehicles DTLR* code of practice on this subject (copies available from TSO*). Shows how to safely load and secure many different types of goods, etc.

Safety policy Employers are required to state their policy (in writing) in regard to the health and safety at work of their employees (if more than five) under the *Health and Safety at Work, etc Act 1974*.

Safety representative Under the *Health and Safety at Work, etc Act 1974* (and the *Safety Representatives and Safety Committee Regulations 1977*) safety representatives may be appointed by recognized trade union. Normally such must have been employed with firm for at least two years or had two years' similar experience.

Safety signs Regulations (ie *Safety Signs Regulations 1980*) requiring that all safety signs comply with specifications laid down (ie warning, prohibition, mandatory and safe condition signs).

Safety stock The stock held to protect against the differences between forecast and actual consumption, and between expected and actual delivery times of procurement orders, to protect against stockouts during the replenishment cycle. In calculating safety stock, account is taken of such factors as service level, expected fluctuations of demand and likely variations in lead time. *(Source: ILT Supply-Chain Inventory Management SIG)*

Sale and leaseback Scheme whereby firm sells its assets (ie property/ vehicles, etc) and leases same back from finance house. Means of releasing capital for other purposes yet still providing exclusive use of assets.

Sales forecast The prediction, projection or estimation of expected sales over a specified future time period. *(Source: ILT Supply-Chain Inventory Management SIG)*

Salmonella Bacterial disease in humans mainly arising from food. As with Listeria*, cause of concern to transporters of chilled and frozen foods because of dangers of such arising if temperatures are not properly maintained.

Samovar *See* Project Samovar.

Sample stability   If a sample produces a particular result, and by increasing the sample size it continues to produce the same result, the sample has stability and can be assumed to be representative of the population. This is an important characteristic when the population size is unknown or extremely large. *(Source: ILT Supply-Chain Inventory Management SIG)*

SAMT   Semi-automatic manual transmission. A form of heavy vehicle gearbox from manufacturer Eaton.

Satellite tracking system   System whereby vehicles can be located by means of signals transmitted from the vehicle to a base via a satellite. Provides accurate, live, location details. Useful in tracing stolen vehicles. See also global positioning system (GPS).

Scania Alert   Safety device developed by Scania Trucks to help drivers to keep awake while at the wheel. It bleeps at varying intervals and pitch.

Schedule D   Income tax payable by person carrying on profession or business in UK (ie based on profits from such).

Schedule E   Income tax payable by employee via PAYE* system (ie deducted by employer from wage/salary). Based on amount of earnings with certain deductions.

Scheduling   The planning and organizing of vehicle loads and journeys to achieve most economic/efficient deliveries. Computer programs available for same. In passenger transport operations, the planning of timetables and services, etc.

SCM   Supply chain management*.

SCOOT   Split cycle and offset optimization technique. Highly sophisticated computer which controls traffic flows in congested town/city centres which has largely superseded the MOVA* system. Operated by the Highways Agency of the DTLR*.

SCOR   Supply-chain operations reference model developed and endorsed by the Supply-Chain Council of USA. A standard reference model for supply-chain operations.

SCP   Simplified clearance procedure. Customs procedure for declaration of goods for export alternative to pre-entry and used where goods are not restricted or dutiable. Requires exporter to have CRN*.

SDR Special drawing rights. Special measure of value used in connection with the assessment of carrier's liability under CMR* whereby compensation must not exceed 8.33 units of account per kg of gross weight (ie of the load). Current rate can be found daily in the *Financial Times*. *See also* Gold franc and Poincaré franc.

SDS Safety data sheet. Documents containing relevant information on chemical substances and emergency procedures for dealing with incidents/accidents involving such substances.

Sealing Regarding tachograph installation, the sealing of connecting points in system to avoid (or indicate) illegal interference. Seals are of lead (ie Customs type) squeezed onto wire and impressed with code number registered with DTLR*. Unauthorized tampering is illegal.

Search engine Computer software that searches the World Wide Web for information/Web sites as directed by the user (ie by inputting key words or a URL for the site).

Seasonal stock Stock held to meet seasonal or fluctuating demands.

Seat factor A measure of the proportion of seats (on a bus or an aeroplane) sold or occupied out of the total number available.

Seat mile Productivity factor representing one seat available for one mile.

Secondary brake Vehicle braking system provided by secondary means of operation either independently of service braking system* or by means of split system*. Must provide 25 per cent efficiency on post-1968 vehicle.

Secondary distribution Distribution of goods from a distribution centre to the final customer. *See also* Primary distribution.

Secretary of State (SoS) Government minister with seat in cabinet. Transport is currently a cabinet post but has not always been so. Within DTLR* SoS has a number of departmental Ministers (eg roads and traffic/aviation, etc) reporting to him.

Section 8 grant A government grant payable in connection with the removal of freight traffic from road to rail under the provisions of Section 8 of the *Railways Act 1974*. *See also* Freight Facilities Grant and Track Access Grant, also PACT.

Section 69 public inquiry Regarding 'O' licensing*, the legal provision (*TA 1968* [as amended] s 69) which gives TCs* powers to call a licence holder to public inquiry for disciplinary purposes and administer penalties (eg curtailment*, suspension* or revocation*).

Selective inventory control   The application of varying levels of control to the total inventory to enable managers to concentrate on significant matters (see ABC analysis and ABC classification). *(Source: ILT Supply-Chain Inventory Management SIG)*

Self-employment   Means working for one's self or running one's own business. Important to ensure that Inland Revenue (IR*) requirements are fully met otherwise such work will be counted as employment and customer will have to meet employer's share of national insurance (NI*) contributions, etc and pay tax for self-employed person. Self-employed must pay own NI contributions and declare earnings to IR.

Seller's interest   Form of insurance taken out by exporter (without the knowledge of the buyer) when goods are sold C&F* or FOB* only leaving insurance to the buyer, in case any claims on the foreign insurance are not honoured.

SEM   Single European Market. Concept of Treaty of Rome whereby EU member states (currently 15) formed a single market with no barriers to trade (ie free movement of goods, services, people and capital). Some provisions in force earlier but took effect fully from 1 January 1993 (publicity geared to '1992').

SEMA   Storage and Equipment Manufacturers Association. Sets minimum standards for the construction and erection of storage equipment. Also attempts to promote standardization.

Semi-trailer   Trailer which forms part of an articulated vehicle* and is coupled in such a way that a minimum of 20 per cent of the weight of the load is borne by the drawing vehicle (ie the tractive unit*).

Separate fares   Separate fares in the context of PSV* operation are those:

- paid directly to the bus or coach company by the passenger either on the vehicle or in advance;
- paid indirectly through a booking agency, ticket office or via any other organization; and
- where the payment for travel is included in an overall package price, as in the case of holiday and tour bookings, sports and leisure outings.

Where an organization makes a lump sum payment to an operator for the hire of a bus or coach but the passengers are not required to make any contribution towards the cost of travel and the coach operator was not responsible for arranging the outing or assembling the passengers, this is not counted as separate fares for these purposes.

Sequencing   Logistics term used in supply-chain solutions in connection with the sequencing (ie timed delivery) of components into a production line.

Seriously reduced visibility   Not legally defined, but generally accepted to be when a driver cannot see for more than 100 metres (328 feet) ahead and must switch on dipped headlights for safety reasons. *See* Highway Code s201.

SERPS   State earnings related pension scheme. A government pension scheme for all employees based on earnings – additional to the 'old age pension' – unless contracted out by employer offering an approved personal pension scheme (APPS*) with benefits equal to SERPS.

Service   Regarding legal proceedings, the serving on a person/firm of a summons or writ (ie answerable in Court).

Service brake   Main part of vehicle braking system intended to meet normal braking requirements and providing the highest efficiency of any part of the vehicle braking system (ie 50 per cent efficiency on post-1968 goods vehicles).

Service level (1)   Distribution term meaning the level (ie frequency, accuracy and speed) of delivery service given to customers (normally refers to standard level rather than exceptional).

Service level (2)   The desired probability that a demand can be met from stock (for an individual item, group of items or a system) which can be expressed in a number of ways:

- Percentage of orders completely satisfied from stock.
- Percentage of units demanded which are met from stock.
- Percentage of units demanded which are delivered on time.
- Percentage of time there is stock available.
- Percentage of stock cycles without shortages.
- Percentage of item-months for which there is stock available. *(Source: ILT Supply-Chain Inventory Management SIG)*

SETA   Sectoral Education and Training Authority. New concept in training provision with a SETA to be established for an industry (eg transport) and for chambers within the SETA to accommodate the interests of individual sectors (eg road, rail, passenger and shipping).

Shared user (distribution)   A term used in distribution operations to indicate a system whereby the products of a number of clients are consolidated into economic vehicle loads for particular destinations. In effect, the opposite of dedicated contract distribution*. May also be called groupage*.

Shared user solution   *See* Shared user (distribution). Used to be called general haulage.

Shelf life   The maximum time an item may be stored before use.

SHInc   Abbreviated term used in shipping meaning that Sundays and holidays are included.

Shipper   Industry term for person/firm who consigns (ie sends/despatches) goods for transport – namely, the consignor*.

Shipping invoice   Document relating to goods shipped. It usually shows all relevant details of consignee and consignor, the nature and amount of the goods and their loading point and final destination.

Shortage (or Stockout) costs   The economic consequences of an external or internal inability to meet a demand from stock. External impacts can include backorder costs, present profit loss from lost sales and future profit loss from loss of goodwill and reputation. Internal impacts can include lost production, production rescheduling and delays in completion dates. *(Source: ILT Supply-Chain Inventory Management SIG)*

Showmen's goods vehicle   Goods vehicle registered in name of travelling showman and subject to special rates of VED.

Shrink wrap   Plastic film covering used to contain goods on a pallet.

Shrinkage   Loss of goods due to evaporation, leakage, deterioration, theft, etc. Often an allowance in weight is made for shrinkage – eg when loading bulk products.

Shunter   Term describing a vehicle (or the driver of a vehicle) used for moving trailers around in a transport yard or on a dockside. Also rail locomotive used for shunting and marshalling wagons and passenger coaches.

Shunting   The task of moving road trailers or rail wagons around with a shunter*.

Shut out   Cargo refused shipment because it arrived after the specified closing date for receiving cargo.

Shuttle service   A service that operates over (relatively) short distances backwards and forwards providing a fast link between two points with limited waiting time (eg with bus services or Le Shuttle service through the Channel Tunnel).

SI   Statutory Instrument*.

Side marker lamp   Lamps fitted to vehicles/trailers and loads to make them more visible to other road users. Normally two required on each side plus others according to length.

Side-facing reflector   Retro reflectors* fitted to side of vehicle/trailer or load to make them more visible from the side. Normally two required on each side plus others according to length.

Sideguard   Safety device fitted to side of vehicle/trailer to prevent persons being carried/swept underneath. Required on goods vehicles over 3.5 tonnes gross and trailers over 1,020 kg unladen (with exceptions).

Sidelifter   Form of heavy fork-lift truck designed to lift and carry long loads sideways (timber/pipes, etc).

Sidewall   Part of vehicle tyre forming wall between tread and wheel (see below).

Sidewall marking   Markings on tyre sidewall (see above) to indicate (among other things) make/model, size, pressure and load/maximum speed capability (by indices), etc. Also each has individual number (see tyre company literature for full details).

Silo   A large drum-like storage facility for liquid, powder or granular (ie free flowing) materials.

Simplified record book   Record (ie log) book for use by drivers operating within British domestic driving hours' rules (ie when exempt from EC rules). Comprises weekly sheet with columns for daily entries.

Simulation modelling   The process of determining a clear understanding of a project, the objectives to be achieved and the likely costs/results, in advance, by means of computer simulation. Such programs allow the use of a variety of 'what if' scenarios to find the 'best' result.

Sine die   Latin term used in shipping meaning 'with no appointed day' (ie indefinitely).

Single European Act   Act of 1985 designed to implement the requirements of the Treaty of Rome* and ratified by EC (now EU) member states who adopted measures 'with the aim of progressively establishing the internal market over a period expiring on 31 December 1992'. The internal market is defined as 'an area without internal frontiers in which the free movement of goods, persons, services and capital is ensured'.

Single European market Comprises 15 EU member states (Austria, Belgium, Denmark, Finland, France, Germany, Greece, Irish Republic, Italy, Luxembourg, Netherlands, Portugal, Spain, Sweden and the UK) with no trade barriers between them.

SITC Standard International Trade Classifications. Term relevant to export trade for the purposes of determining precise trade classifications for goods.

SITL *Semaine Internationale du Transport et de la Logistique.* Annual week-long transport and logistics conference and exhibition held, usually in March, at the Parc des Expositions, Paris-Nord Villepinte, France.

SITPRO Simplification of International Trade Procedures. Committee set up in 1968 by National Economic Development Council to study and improve trade procedures, simplify documents, etc (eg as with SAD*).

Six-mile exemption In connection with VED*, provision whereby exemption applies (on application) to vehicles which travel on the road between premises owned by person/firm in whose name they are registered but not exceeding six miles in week.

Six-wheeler Term for three-axle rigid vehicle. *NB:* paired (ie twin) wheels count as one.

SK Nationality symbol for Slovakia – to be shown on the rear of vehicles from that country.

Skeletal trailer Trailer with 'skeleton-type' frame specially designed, and with twist-lock fittings, to carry containers. Idea is to reduce unladen weight by excluding platform structure.

Skidchek Product of Grau-Girling. Claimed undisputed leader in vehicle anti-lock* braking systems. Especially fitted to trailers.

Skip Also called builder's skip. Defined as container for carriage on vehicle and which can be placed on roads (but only with prior approval of highway authority) for storage of builder's materials/rubble/waste/soil, etc and household rubbish. Carried on special vehicle (*see* Skip loader).

Skip changing The practice of missing intermediate gears when changing up or down through the gearbox of a heavy vehicle. *See also* Block changing.

Skip loader   Vehicle specially designed and constructed to carry skips (see skip) with hydraulic arms for lifting and placing on road/ground.

Sleeper cab   Vehicle cab with provision of driver's bunk (may be two such), usually behind seats, for sleeping. Opposite of day cab*. *See also* Sleeper pod.

SKU   Stock keeping unit. Unit used for stock accounting and control records: pallet, tonne, drum, item, carton, bag, etc.

Sleeper pod   Relatively new term referring to the attachment on top of a heavy vehicle cab of a 'pod' (usually made of fibreglass) in which driver sleeps. Favoured in certain operations (eg with maximum length drawbar combinations*) because requires no additional chassis length as with conventional sleeper cabs but frowned upon by governments/unions because of limited accommodation provided.

Sliding fifth-wheel   Fifth-wheel coupling* on articulated tractive unit which can be moved forwards or backwards to accommodate longer/shorter semi-trailers or adjust weight imposed on tractive unit drive axle/rear bogie.

Slot   In aviation, an allocated time slot for aircraft take-off. In shipping, space on board a vessel occupied by a container, or a sailing schedule allocation.

Small goods vehicle   In 'O' licensing*, goods vehicle defined as not exceeding 3.5 tonnes pmw* (ie which is exempt from such). Also, exempt from EU drivers' hours law, tachograph fitment and can be driven by person age 17 years.

Smart card   Plastic card containing magnetic information (or incorp-orating a micro-chip) as with credit cards and capable of accepting and storing data. To be used with new-style digital tachographs from 2003 for electronically recording driving time and driver's working activities, etc. *See also* DIC. 'Incremental smart cards' can be charged with a cash value by a bank machine, and can then be 'decremented' by a given amount when presented to an automatic machine in return for a bus trip, replenish-ment of fuel, or a seat at the cinema, etc.

Smart words   Term referring to the use of industry jargon or buzzwords; but they don't always lead to slick logistics solutions.

SME   Small and medium-sized enterprise. Small and medium-sized firms have been identified by government as being in need of its initiative (ie UK online for business) to get online.

SMMT   Society of Motor Manufacturers and Traders. Main trade association in UK for such. Organizer of principal UK annual commercial vehicle exhibition (ie the CV show).

Smoke emission   It is an offence to allow a vehicle to emit smoke, also visible vapour, grit, sparks, ashes, cinders or oily substances. Smoke emissions are checked at goods vehicle testing stations and sometimes in roadside tests with smoke meters or visually by examiners. Smoking diesel vehicles can be prohibited from use (*see* PG 9) and prosecution can follow. Cause is usually poor maintenance (especially of fuel system – ie pump and injectors) and may also be from illegal use of excess fuel device*.

Smoke opacity   Re above, description for the density of smoke – ie how well you (or more particularly a vehicle examiner) can see through it. If he cannot, it's an offence.

SMP   Statutory maternity pay. Payment made to employee following childbirth.

SNCF   Société national des chemins de fer Francais. French national railway system. Operates Kangourou* system for carrying road freight trailers. SNCF Fret is the freight division of SNCF.

SO$_2$ Sulphur dioxide. A constituent of vehicle exhaust emissions.

SOB (1)   Son of a bitch. Derogatory Americanism (ie a curse).

SOB (2)   Shipped on board. Endorsement shown on a bill of lading confirming that goods have been loaded on a vessel.

Social (or socio-) cost-benefit analysis   A system used in decision making, in particular for determining whether a particular project should go ahead, by comparing different projects, by comparing present and future time periods and by taking the viewpoint of society rather than that of the individual or companies.

Social regulation   EU drivers' hours rules (ie regulation *EC 3820/85*) are termed the social regulation because they relate to the social conditions of work for goods vehicle drivers.

Society of Operations Engineers   New professional body formed by a merger of the former Institute of Road Transport Engineers (IRTE) and the Institute of Plant Engineers.

Software   Computer term for programs which provide instructions for the computer (without which it can serve no purpose). Vast range available either standard (eg word processing/ accounting/payroll) or special (route planning, etc). Normally purchased on floppy disk*.

SORN   Statutory off-road notice. Requirement of DVLA* that vehicle owners/operators declare that their vehicle/s is off the road (ie not in use and not left parked on the public highway) if VED is not renewed. Scheme to clamp down on tax dodgers.

Sortation   In an express parcels operation – ParcelForce, Lynx or TNT for example – the process of sorting individual consignments/parcels, etc for dispatch to their correct destination.

Space cab   High-roof sleeper cab on DAF* heavy vehicles primarily intended for long-haul and international haulage operations.

SPAD   Signal passed at danger. Phenomenon associated with rail operations where the train driver (for whatever reason) passes a signal set at red for danger. Alleged to be the cause of a number of recent serious rail accidents. *See also* ATP, ETCS and TPWS.

SPAM   Not tinned luncheon meat (ie Specially Prepared American Meat)! Formally described as 'Unsolicited commercial messages' sent over the Internet via e-mail (electronic 'junk mail'). Mainly unwanted advertising material.

Spares (or spare parts)   Components or parts, either consumable or repairable, from the associated bill of material used to maintain or repair machinery or equipment. *(Source: ILT Supply-Chain Inventory Management SIG)*

Spatial awareness   An awareness of space or distance. People frequently fail to walk because they are under the misconception that the distance between locations is greater than it actually is. Especially relevant when the London Underground system comes to a standstill.

SPD   Short period disqualification. A driving disqualification not exceeding 56 days where driving licence is not actually impounded, only marked by the Court.

Special order   In connection with the carriage of abnormal loads*, special order needed from Secretary of State for Transport* when moving loads which exceed five metres wide.

Special reason   When driver convicted for motoring offences and faces disqualification of his licence, he may request non-disqualification for special reasons (ie grounds of exceptional hardship*).

Special Types plate   Plate fitted to Special Types vehicle* which indicates the manufacturer's recommended maximum operational weight at specified speeds for Special Types use.

Special Types vehicle   Heavy vehicle designed to carry abnormal indivisible loads* and which because of its size and weight cannot operate within the C&U regulations. Operates under *The Motor Vehicles (Authorization of Special Types) General Order 1979* as amended.

Specified vehicles   In connection with 'O' licensing*, the vehicles which are actually specified on the licence by registration number/type/maximum gvw.

SPECS   A type of speed camera that measures vehicles travelling over a defined distance and calculates the average speed of the vehicle over that distance.

Speed limiter   *See* Road speed limiter.

Speed recording   Regarding tachographs*, the recording of speed on charts (ie in 20 kph steps). Equates to what driver sees indicated by speedometer needle.

Speed transducer   Regarding electronic tachographs*, the device that converts the rotational speed of gearbox to indicate/record correct road speed at instrument head.

Speed warning light   Regarding tachographs*, a warning light in the face which can be set to come on at a pre-determined speed to warn driver that he is exceeding pre-set limit.

Spent convictions   Under provisions of *The Rehabilitation of Offenders Act 1974*, convictions sustained in the past which no longer have to be declared (eg on 'O' licence*, driving licence applications, etc), thus described as spent.

Spine wagon   Rail wagon designed for piggyback operations, designed round a central spine and carrying outrigger platforms on which road semi-trailer bogies are carried. Has advantage of being narrower and lighter than conventional pocket piggyback wagons*.

Split rest period   Under provisions of regulation *EC 3820/85*, driver may split daily rest period* into two/three separate periods so long as one is a minimum of eight hours, the others are at least one hour each and total rest for day is increased to 12 hours.

Splitter   Form of gearbox on heavy goods vehicle. Additional set of gears 'splits' main ratios to provide number of intermediate ratios (at about 18 per cent variation on the next up/down gear) to allow more efficient engine/road speed matching. May be added to range-change* gearbox to provide as many as 12 to 16 ratios. *See also* Twin-splitter.

Spoke system   Distribution system where deliveries to regional distribution centres or direct to customer are made from a central hub. *See* Hub and Spoke.

Spot hire   The hire of a vehicle on a casual (ie one-off or daily) basis rather than on a longer-term contract.

Spray suppressant material   Material used for making goods vehicle anti-spray devices. Designed to absorb or dissipate the energy of water thrown from the tyre to reduce the degree to which it shatters into fine droplets on hitting the surface (as with Monsanto Clear-Pass, etc).

Spreader   A steel beam used to spread the lifting cables/chains, etc to each end of a container/swap body, etc being lifted for transfer from road to rail or vice versa.

Spring brakes   Form of vehicle brake designed to provide fail-safe system in event of air loss (ie basically, air holds spring compressed and brakes off, but in failure springs expand and apply brakes – thus fail-safe).

SPTE   Strathclyde Passenger Transport Executive (PTE*).

SQA   Scottish Qualifications Authority. Body appointed by DTLR* to establish and conduct examination system for Dangerous Goods Safety Adviser (DGSA) qualification.

SQRS   Safety, quality, reliability systems. A variation on the quality management theme but in this case indicating the ability of firms to react seriously to safety issues through structured risk assessments.

SRA   Strategic Rail Authority. Created under the 1998 White Paper on Transport to provide a clear, coherent and strategic programme for the development of the railways. It absorbed the functions of OPRAF – the Office of the Passenger Rail Franchising Director.

S/S   Sailing ship.

SSAP scheme   Statement of accounting practice. Basis on which auditors prepare company annual accounts. In case of new SSAP 21, leased vehicle/plant, etc are shown as assets unlike previously where they were not shown (hence the term 'off balance sheet financing').

SSN Standard shipping note. A six-part SITPRO* aligned document (ie a type of consignment note).

SSP Statutory sick pay. Pay to which employee is entitled after being off work sick for at least 4 days (ie PIW*) – *Social Security and Housing Benefits Act 1982.*

ST Short ton. American measure equal to 2,000 lb.

Stacker truck Type of fork-lift truck* used to stack pallets to a height or recover same.

Stage A section of a passenger vehicle service/journey, usually between points at which a change in the fare occurs.

Staircase A series (flight) of locks* on a canal* where the top gates of one lock are also the lower gates of the next (ie as at Bingley on the Leeds & Liverpool Canal, and Foxton on the Grand Union Canal).

Standard lists In connection with goods vehicle plating and testing, lists produced by vehicle manufacturers of the relevant data for every model/ variant they produce. Used by Goods Vehicle Centre*, as basis for determining plated weights, etc. Copies available from TSO*.

Standard 'O' licence Form of operators' licence needed for carriage of goods for hire or reward on over 3.5 tonne pmw* vehicles – covering national (ie UK) operations only or both national and international operations. Applicants must be of good repute*, of appropriate financial standing* and professionally competent*. Also required for hire or reward passenger vehicle operations other than those covered by a restricted* PSV 'O' licence.

Standing costs Transport industry term for the fixed costs* of vehicle ownership (eg VED*, insurance, driver wages, etc). *See also* TIDE.

STARLS State-of-the-art logistical solutions. Industry jargon for pro-posals put forward to clients by third-party* distribution firms/consultants in connection with efficiency/cost improvements.

Statement of ownership In connection with the fixed penalty offence scheme, when driver of vehicle does not respond to notice within 28 days allowed, registered keeper* of vehicle is contacted and may pay the penalty or is required to provide a statement of ownership. He must state whether he owned the vehicle at the time of the alleged offence, if not give name of person who owned it at the time (if known).

Static gauge   Physical dimensions of a railway vehicle at rest (see also kinematic envelope, gauge and loading gauge).

Stationery Office   *See* HMSO and TSO.

Statutory attendant   An attendant as required by law to accompany a vehicle carrying abnormal* or projecting load (depending on dimensions, etc). Required only on first and last vehicles if three or more travel in convoy. Such must be in addition to the driver and his role is to warn the driver and any other person of any danger that may arise from the use of the vehicle.

Statutory break   Break of 45 minutes (minimum) required by law when driver within EU rules (ie regulation *EC 3820/85*) has driven for 4½ hours. Alternatively he may take shorter breaks spread throughout and after the driving period so long as they total 45 minutes and the driving does not exceed 4½ hours.

Statutory Instrument   Document containing statutory regulations/orders, etc. Has designated number SI... and year (eg C&U regulations are SI 1078/86). Copies available from TSO*. Listed as published in TSO daily list of publications available on subscription.

STC   Said to contain. Term used on transport documentation – usually by a recipient signing for parcels/cartons, etc the contents of which he cannot see.

STD   Socialist Truck Drivers. A movement intent on demonstrating against industry shortcomings (eg the lack of adequate truck parking facilities across Europe).

STEP   International standard for exchange of manufacturing product data.

Stevedore   Dockside worker (or firm of such) engaged on loading and unloading ships.

STGO   Abbreviation for *The Motor Vehicles (Authorization of Special Types) General Order 1979* as amended. Legislation which permits the use of vehicles operating outside the provisions of the C&U regulations for carrying abnormal loads*.

Stock   Stock can be defined as: all the goods and materials stored by an organization and retained for future use. The quantity of goods between measuring points in a particular path, expressed in quantitative and/or financial terms. For example, the goods can be in a pipeline, in a warehouse or technical store, in reception, in production. Additional terms for stock are:

- All-time stock.
- Anticipation stock.
- Available stock.
- Buffer stock.
- Calculated stock.
- Capacity loading stock.
- Closing stock.
- Consignment stock.
- Cyclical stock.
- Decoupling stock.
- Economic stock.
- Effective stock.
- Free stock.
- Lot-size stock.
- Maximum stock.
- Norm stock.
- Obsolete stock.
- Opening stock.
- Physical stock.
- Pipeline stock.
- Reserved stock.
- Safety stock.
- Seasonal stock.
- Shortage stock.
- Speculation stock.
- Strategic stock.
- Surplus stock.
- Work-in-progress stock.

(Source: ILT Supply-Chain Inventory Management SIG)

Stock analysis   The process of analysing the stock position and the stock pattern as well as signalling differences with regard to the stock norms. *(Source: ILT Supply-Chain Inventory Management SIG)*

Stock carrying costs (or stock holding costs)   The total costs associated with holding stock. These costs consist of:

- The unit purchase cost.
- The reorder cost.
- The holding cost.
- The stockout or shortage cost. *(Source: ILT Supply-Chain Inventory Management SIG)*

Stock control   System for monitoring and replenishing stocks (eg in a warehouse) to ensure adequate levels to meet customer demand, but avoiding over-stocks which tie-up capital unnecessarily. *See also* Inventory control.

Stock cover   The current stock divided by the average weekly demand (weekly demand can be based on either past history or forward forecast). *(Source: ILT Supply-Chain Inventory Management SIG)*

Stock difference (or stock discrepancy)   The difference between the actual stock held and the calculated stock or registered stock. *(Source: ILT Supply-Chain Inventory Management SIG)*

Stock in transit/clearing   All materials, components or finished products in transit from one point in a supply chain to another supply chain destination, expressed in quantitative or financial terms. *(Source: ILT Supply-Chain Inventory Management SIG)*

Stock investment   The amount of money that is invested in all levels of stock at any given point in time. *(Source: ILT Supply-Chain Inventory Management SIG)*

Stock keeping unit (SKU)   A single type of product which is kept in stock; it is one entry in the inventory. *(Source: ILT Supply-Chain Inventory Management SIG)*

Stock location system   A system where all places within a warehouse are identified in some way to facilitate storage and retrieval of stock. *(Source: ILT Supply-Chain Inventory Management SIG)*

Stock management   The planning and control of the quantities, qualities and location of stocks. *(Source: ILT Supply-Chain Inventory Management SIG)*

Stock norm   A ratio of stock to, for example, sales, set as a standard and expressed as a percentage, or as a factor or as a number of days, weeks or months. The stock norm is determined by taking into account the:

- Safety stock.
- Production batch stock or shipment batch stock.
- Normal seasonal stock.
- Normative pipeline stock.
- Stock on order.

The quantity represented by the total of all out-standing orders for a particular item. The on order balance increases when a new order is released and decreases when an order is received or cancelled. *(Source: ILT Supply-Chain Inventory Management SIG)*

Stock point   A point in the supply chain meant to keep goods available. *(Source: ILT Supply-Chain Inventory Management SIG)*

Stock policy   The policy with regard to the level and location of stock to be held and where and how this should be done. *(Source: ILT Supply-Chain Inventory Management SIG)*

Stock position   The situation of a particular product, at a particular time, with regard to the relationship between the expected demand and/or requirement, the physical stock and the outstanding procurement orders. *(Source: ILT Supply-Chain Inventory Management SIG)*

Stock profile   Determination of the composition of stock, its quantity and flow. A technique for analysing product stock and throughput characteristics. Using computer data-base information or statistical summaries, the analysis considers lines, stockholding and throughput rate.

Stock site   A location at which stock is held.

Stock turn (1)   The rate at which warehouse stocks (ie inventory*) turns over (ie number of times replaced in a given period – usually one year). Generally, it is preferable to have a high stock turn: this indicates fast moving business.

Stock turn (2)   The number of times that an inventory turns over during the year and normally obtained by dividing the average inventory value into the annual cost of sales. *(Source: ILT Supply-Chain Inventory Management SIG)*

Stock turnover (or stock turn)   A widely used measure of inventory performance expressed as the ratio of the cost of units sold to the average value of stock. *(Source: ILT Supply-Chain Inventory Management SIG)*

Stock types   The products which are determined for delivery from stock. *(Source: ILT Supply-Chain Inventory Management SIG)*

Stockout   The situation when demand for a stock item is received but there is insufficient stock to satisfy the demand. *(Source: ILT Supply-Chain Inventory Management SIG)*

Stockout costs   The economic consequences of an internal or external stockout such as missed sales, delayed deliveries, anticipated lower sales in the future because of loss of goodwill, costs resulting from production stoppages and all kinds of associated costs. *(Source: ILT Supply-Chain Inventory Management SIG)*

Stockout percentage   A measure of the effectiveness with which a company responds to actual demand. The stockout percentage can be a measurement of total stockouts to total orders, or of line of items incurring stockouts during a period of total line items ordered. *(Source: ILT Supply-Chain Inventory Management SIG)*

Stockout risk   The accepted risk of having a shortage of stock of an item which is used in calculating the required level of safety stock. *(Source: ILT Supply-Chain Inventory Management SIG)*

Stocktaking   A physical count of products actually held in stock as a basis for verification of the stock records and accounts. *(Source: ILT Supply-Chain Inventory Management SIG)*

STOL   Short take-off and landing. Aircraft designed with short take-off capabilities, ideal for short-haul operations using city airports (eg the London City Airport in Docklands).

Stopping a moving vehicle   In GB, only a police officer in uniform is legally authorized to stop a moving vehicle (in NI* a DOE* enforcement officer* in civilian clothes may also do so).

Stored energy   Regarding vehicle braking systems, parking brakes must be capable of meeting efficiency requirement without the assistance of stored energy (ie without air/vacuum assistance). For these purposes, energy stored in a compressed spring is not counted as being stored – *see* Spring brakes.

Straddle carrier   Form of crane on wheels designed specially to lift and transport shipping (ie ISO*) containers (ie fitted with twist-lock fittings* at each corner) from road vehicles to rail, etc and capable of stacking such two/three high.

Straight-line depreciation   System whereby depreciation* is spread equally over a specified period of years (eg five years).

Strategic alliance   Term used in logistics operations when one company forms a relationship with another (ie an alliance) for the purposes of jointly exploiting business opportunities – but not a merger or takeover.

Strategic planning   Planning the long-term objectives of a business or a department within a company and the methods to be employed to achieve those objectives.

Strategic stock   The stock of goods of essential importance for the continuation of the production process and which is built up in order to compensate for long hold-ups of incoming goods (caused by strikes and political difficulties, etc in a particular country or region). *(Source: ILT Supply-Chain Inventory Management SIG)*

Strategy   A medium to long-term plan of action.

Streetcar   American term for a tram or trolleybus system.

Structure plan   A statutory development plan prepared by, for example, a County Council which sets out the policy for local land use and transport over a period ahead (eg 10 to 15 years).

Stuffing/stripping The process of packing or unpacking a trailer or container.

Sub-contractor A person/firm to whom the main contractor (ie the principal) has contracted work (eg haulage work). In law, the principal contractor remains liable to the customer if goods in the care of a sub-contractor are lost or damaged.

Subordinate legislation Legislation which is subordinate (ie lower in status) to the main provisions (eg regulations/orders made under powers given in an Act of Parliament).

Subrogation Term used in marine insurance whereby one person is substituted for another, inheriting the former's rights and liabilities in the process.

Subsidiary company A company of which another company (ie the holding/parent company) owns some or all (ie wholly owned) of the shares. Regarding 'O' licensing*, a company which may have its vehicles specified on the 'O' licence of or carry the goods of its parent company or vice versa (not to be confused with associate company* where this is not permitted).

Subsonic Travel at less than the speed of sound. *See also* Supersonic.

Sulphur A constituent of diesel fuel and a major contributor to so-called 'acid rain' which is detrimental to the environment. The EU proposes that the sulphur content of diesel fuel should be reduced to 1 per cent from 1 January 2003. *See also* ULSD.

Summary conviction Conviction of charged offender by court of summary jurisdiction (ie Magistrate's Court) – as opposed to indictment by judge and jury. Offences tried summarily carry lesser penalties than those on indictment, hence difference in system.

Summons Legal demand for offender (usually) to appear in court. Could also apply to witness. Not to be confused with subpoena whereby a person's presence in court is demanded by writ (written order to appear) – often served personally to ensure safe receipt.

Super singles Large size truck tyres usually used singly in place of a normal-sized twin wheel set. Although designed principally for rear axle use, many operators have adopted their use on front (steering) axles where they are said to provide greater directional stability and safety. However, experts advise that such use adds up to two per cent to the vehicle's fuel consumption.

Supercube   Term for high volume semi-trailer (frequently mounted on small wheels to give additional load height) offering substantial cubic capacity. *See also* High cube, Maxi cube, etc.

Superprix   Name given to truck Grand Prix race.

Supersonic   Capable of travelling at greater than the speed of sound as with the supersonic aircraft Concorde. *See also* Subsonic.

Supply chain (1)   The continuous link between the supply of raw materials through production to the finished product being delivered to the final consumer.

Supply-chain (2)   The total sequence of business processes, within a single or multiple enterprise environment, that enable customer demand for a product or service to be satisfied. *(Source: ILT Supply-Chain Inventory Management SIG)*

Supply-chain management (SCM) (1)   Logistics* industry term for management of the supply chain*.

Supply-chain management (SCM) (2)   Organization of the overall business processes to enable the profitable transformation of raw materials or products into finished goods and their timely distribution to meet customer demand. *(Source: ILT Supply-Chain Inventory Management SIG)*

Susie   Term for coiled (and colour coded) flexible hoses used on articulated vehicles (and drawbar combinations) to connect air supply for brakes (and electrics) between tractive unit and semi-trailer.

Sustainable development   The use of resources and the environment in a judicial manner so as to preserve their availability and quality for the use and enjoyment of future generations. Also defined as safeguarding the planet, its environment, its resources and its people.

Sustainable transport   Generic name given to low energy and mass transit modes (eg walking, cycling and the use of the bus and light rail systems).

Sustainable travel modes   The name normally given to walking and cycling and the use of public transport, or to modes which include low energy vehicles (eg mopeds and other small PTWs*).

SVDD   Speed violation detection deterrent. A new system for detecting speeding drivers with sensors (cameras) up to a mile apart which track every vehicle passing, registering its number plate and the time, and calculating how fast the vehicle has been travelling between the cameras. The camera sends a digital signal direct to a computer centre where the vehicle owner's details are checked immediately and a fine issued to those exceeding the limit.

Swan-neck trailer   Semi-trailer with low platform (eg for carriage of heavy or tall machinery/plant, etc) and swan shaped neck to higher level for coupling to fifth-wheel* on tractive unit.

Swap body   Interchangeable body between road vehicle/trailer and rail wagons. Built to standard lengths of 7.15 m, 7.45 m, 7.82 m, 12 m or 13.6 m. Can stand using built-in folding legs but not capable of being stacked. Used in distribution and intermodal operations. *See also* Demountable, Swop bodies and *Caisse mobiles.*

SWB   Short wheelbase (ie the distance between the axles on goods vehicles). *See also* LWB.

Swept circle   Legal requirement relating to use of longer articulated vehicles (ie up to 16.5 metres), such vehicles must be capable of turning within inner and outer swept circles of 5.3 metres and 12.5 metres diameter respectively.

Swingbed (swing-bed) wagon   Rail wagon designed for piggyback operations. Has a hydraulically-operated, hinged loading platform that swings out to the side and slopes down to allow semi-trailers to be loaded. Once the semi-trailer is in position the bed is swung back into position on the rail wagon and secured for transit.

Swivelling spotlights   Lamps (ie work lamps) fixed to top of vehicle/cab to give lights at scene of breakdown/accident/roadworks, etc. Must not be capable of being swivelled while vehicle is in motion (with exceptions) and may only be used for purposes stated. Must not cause dazzle to driver of any other vehicle.

SWL   Safe working load. The pre-determined safe level above which loading and lifting equipment must not operate. Indicated on cranes, hoists, lifting machines, vehicle hydraulic tailboards, etc by means of a plate where the driver/operator can readily see it. Usually a safety warning sound is emitted when the level is neared or exceeded, at which point damage may occur or the machine may collapse/turn over with a risk of injury to the operator and others.

Swop bodies   Term for demountable bodies* used on vehicles. *See also* Swap bodies.

SWOT   Strength, weakness, opportunity, threat. Management concept in which an organization's strengths, weaknesses, opportunities and threats are analysed.

Synchromesh   Motor vehicle gearbox in which the gear trains are synchronized to give easier, smooth and silent gear changes.

SYPTE   South Yorkshire Passenger Transport Executive (PTE*).

Tt

44 tonnes   Maximum permissible weight for goods vehicles in UK from February 2001 (apart from those operating under Special Types* legislation). Legislating for these vehicles is said to take the equivalent of 1,000 trucks off the roads, reduce CO^2 emissions by 80,000–100,000 tonnes and nitrous oxide (NOx) by 3,600–4,000 tonnes annually.

T   Ton*/tonne*.

T2000   Transport 2000. Campaigner against heavy lorries, albeit claiming to seek a coherent and environmentally sensitive transport policy

TAC   Type Approval Certificate. *See* Type approval.

Tachograph   Instrument (fitted mainly in heavy vehicles) for indicating and recording (on special charts – see below) time/speed/distance. Also records driver's other work activities/breaks/rest periods. Required on vehicles over 3.5 tonnes gvw under regulation *EC 3821/85* (unless exempt). *See also* Digital tachograph.

Tachograph chart/analysis   Special pre-printed circular disc with wax coated (ie pressure sensitive*) surface on which recordings are made. Such can be analysed with accuracy to determine basics of vehicle/driver activity (eg observance of EU hours' law) and by specialists in event of accident. Employer required to make periodic checks to ensure law is complied with under regulation *EC 3820/85*.

Tack-trak   Device (mainly intended for drivers) by which accumulated amount of driving/breaks/other work can be calculated – to avoid breaking law.

TAG (1)   Track access grant. Government grants towards the operating costs of rail freight services. Designed to encourage a switch of freight from road to rail. *See also* Section 8 grants and Freight facilities grants.

TAG/tag (2)   As in tag axle. Industry terminology for a trailing (ie non-driven) axle on a vehicle or semi-trailer.

Tailboard   The drop-down rear platform of a goods vehicle – to facilitate loading and unloading. May comprise a hydraulic tail-lift – see below. If tailboard is used to support the weight of goods while travelling, it counts as part of the overall length of the vehicle – such use may contravene the vehicle's overall maximum length limit.

Tail-lift   Handling equipment attached (mainly) to rear of delivery vehicles to enable driver (single-handed) to load/off-load consignments (frequently in roll-cages/pallets). Raised and lowered vertically or by cantilever, with hydraulic assistance.

Tallyman   Person on loading bay who checks off goods as they are loaded/ unloaded.

TAN (1)   Traffic Area Network. Great Britain is divided into eight Traffic Areas for goods vehicle and PCV* licensing purposes, each controlled by a Traffic Commissioner*.

TAN (2)   Transit advice note.

TAN21   Code name for the Government's new (2001) computerized O-licensing system. Operators will be able to conduct licensing business with the Traffic Area network (see above) by telephone or via the Internet, dispensing with a great deal of paperwork.

Tandem axle   Second axle in a tandem bogie (ie linked by suspension units). *See also* Trailing axle.

Tank inspecting authority   Authority approved (by DTLR* in UK) for testing tanker vehicles (and tank containers) used in international carriage of dangerous goods by road (ie under ADR*).

TAO   Traffic Area Office. Provides administrative support for the work of the TCs*. Eight such offices in the UK, one for each Traffic Area*.

Tare   The weight of a vehicle or loading unit before the load is added. The tare weight of the vehicle and the weight of the load together make up the gross weight.

Tare weight   Weight of vehicle in road going condition including weight of the driver, any passenger carried, a full tank of fuel etc prior to loading. Deduct this weight from pmw* to determine allowable payload.

TARIC   Code name for new EU integrated tariff (of duties, etc) used by Customs in conjunction with Harmonized Commodity Description and Coding System – HS re Standardization of Customs' procedures (including introduction of SAD* in 1988).

Tariff   Means a price list. Used in freighting to indicate such as Customs duties (see above) and minimum road haulage rates (eg as applied in Germany). In other transport spheres it means a list of fares for journeys.

Tariff terms   The conditions and scale of charges shown in a tariff.

Tariffication   System for establishing tariffs – *see* Tariff.

Tax relief   Approved expenses/charges that may be set against earnings/ profits to reduce liability for income/corporation tax, etc.

T&B   Tibbett & Britten Group plc. Major UK haulage and logistics group.

TBCF   To be called for. Term used mainly in parcels traffic where the customer calls at the local depot to collect goods rather than waiting for (or having missed) the delivery.

TBL   Too bloody late. Slang phrase used as a pejorative about failures in Just in Time (JiT*) deliveries in distribution. Likely to be increasingly common as road traffic congestion increases.

TBN   Total base number. A measure of the viscosity (ie internal friction) of oil.

TBV   *Telecommande de boite de vitesses.* Automatic gearshift system for heavy trucks – product of manufacturer Renault Trucks.

TC (1)   Traffic Commissioner. Authority for issuing goods vehicle and PCV 'O' licences* and monitoring LGV*/PCV* driver conduct. Formerly known as the Licensing Authority (LA*) when dealing with goods vehicle matters. Also responsible for the performance of operators of local services* (timekeeping, etc) and may require miscreants to repay some or all of FDR*.

TC (2)   Time charter. The hire of a ship for a period of time as opposed to a sailing from one port to another (ie voyage basis).

TCfL   Transport Committee for London. Operator of the London Lorry Ban.

TCM Convention   Convention on combined transport operations held in 1969 which agreed ground rules for such and, particularly, relative liabilities of the parties and use of combined transport documents.

TDA   Transport Development Area. Area designated for transport development (ie with funding allocation, etc).

TDC (1)   Top dead centre. A measure of when the piston in motor vehicle engine reaches the top of its stroke.

TDC (2)   Total distribution costs. The sum of order processing, local delivery, depot fixed costs, inventory and trucking costs.

TDG   Transport Development Group. Large and successful private UK group of transport and related companies.

TDI   Trade data interchange.

T&D   *Truck & Driver*. Monthly magazine for truck drivers and enthusiasts.

T&E   European Federation for Transport and Environment. Brussels-based organization which lobbies for an environmentally sound approach to European transport issues.

TE   Abbreviation often used for the term 'tonne' (ie a metric ton).

TE 160   Prohibition notice (formerly GV 160*) indicating that a vehicle is overloaded to the point of being unsafe. Issued by police and VI* enforcement officers. Vehicle must not be moved until excess weight is removed and clearance (Form TE 160C) is given. Prosecution may also follow.

TEC (1)   Total efficiency concept. Term used by Iveco Ford Truck in regard to its heavy vehicle cab design.

TEC (2)   Training and Enterprise Council. Body which provided funding for training and skills-related activities. Abolished in 2000 in favour of new body – NLSC (National Learning and Skills Council) – which is supported by local learning and skills councils. *See also* LSC.

Technobabble   Another term for technology jargon.

Telemarketing   Latest and, reputedly, the most dynamic form of marketing/ promotion of goods, previously called 'telesales'.

Telematics (1)   Defined in *Concise Oxford Dictionary* as: 'the branch of information technology which deals with the long-distance transmission of computerized information'. In the transport context, broadly, electronic systems for controlling and monitoring vehicle operations via cellular and satellite communication technologies.

Telematics (2)   Technology applied to road traffic and road vehicles. Computing and telecommunications systems established to promote the development and implementation of more efficient and safer transport (eg as in vehicle-to-base communication). Typical examples of such technology include: electronic tolling systems; smart card* ticketing; proximity stop information; on-board vehicle information and navigation systems.

Teleroute Powerful information system linking users and suppliers of transport services for the exchange of load and vehicle availability details (for finding return loads, etc). Operates throughout Europe with central computer in Lille, France. In UK contact Owner Operators Ltd or Routel (Maclean Hunter).

Teletext Information database available through normal television receiver.

Teleworking Working remotely at home but linked to an office by telephone/computer

'Telligent' Trade marked electro-pneumatic braking system on Mercedes-Benz 'Actros' range of disc-braked heavy trucks. A braking by wire system with no mechanical linkages, designed to ensure shorter stopping distances, greater stability under severe braking and uniform wear of disc pads through continuous monitoring.

Telma retarder Make of heavy vehicle retarder*. Gives additional retardation for safety reasons and to help preserve brake linings.

Temperature controlled Form of transport/distribution using refrigerated vehicles for the carriage of chilled/frozen foods.

Temperature recorder Instrument that records temperature (eg in a refrigerated vehicle body).

Temporary cover note Issued by insurance companies to provide immediate evidence of cover pending the issue of full certificate of insurance. Provides cover for limited period (eg 30 days) but acceptable to police and for VED application, etc. If sent by post cover is not effective until insured has document in his possession.

Temporary derogation Regarding 'O' licensing*, period when TC* may allow a standard licence to continue (one year plus possible further six months) for the replacement of a professionally competent person* (generally when such has died or become legally incapacitated*).

Temporary exemption Regarding goods vehicle plating and testing, period (not exceeding three months) of exemption from need to hold valid test certificate when for special reasons test cannot be carried out (due to severe weather, fire, epidemic, failure of essential services, etc – but not vehicle breakdown or operator convenience). Test station issues form VTG 33 confirming exemption.

TEN   Trans-European Network. A Euro-wide programme for identifying and improving key (transport) routes including 12,000 kms of new and upgraded motorways as well as linking with the networks of the 10 central and east European countries which have applied for EU membership.

TERFF   Trans-European Rail Freight Freeways (or Freightways in France which does not like the sound of anything 'free'). A trans-European rail network of routes along which any rail operator could operate a service over any other member state's infrastructure.

TERFN   Trans-European Rail Freight Network. A Euro-wide system of rail routes unencumbered with passenger traffic.

Terminal (1)   Depot/location where journeys begin and end and/or a change of mode (eg from road to rail or vice versa) takes place.

Terminal (2)   As in a computer terminal comprising the relevant hardware and software that facilitates electronic messaging and data interchange, etc.

Terotechnology   Term covering the concept of whole/total life costing* (of vehicles or plant, etc). In theory, rather than counting the price of a new vehicle, the idea is to calculate the costs over its whole life including purchase price – a quality/durable vehicle should work out cheaper in the long run.

TEU (usually written teu)   Twenty-foot equivalent unit. Term used in containerization and shipping as a measure of capacity or throughput related to a standard 20ft ISO* container (eg a 40ft container = two teus).

TfL   Transport for London. An executive arm of the Greater London Authority (GLA) reporting to the Mayor of London (not to be confused with the Lord Mayor of the City of London). Following election of the first ever Mayor for London on 4 May 2000, responsibility for London buses, Dial-a-Ride, Victoria Coach Station and London River Service was incorporated as Transport Trading Ltd and the Docklands Light Railway and the Woolwich Ferry were also transferred to TfL. It will assume responsibility for London Underground on completion of the PPP*. This body, comprising 14 board members and chaired by the Mayor, is responsible for delivering the capital's integrated transport policy.

TFT *Tele Formation Transports.* French transport training organization.

TGV *Train à Grande Vitesse.* French high-speed train.

TGWU Transport and General Workers' Union. Main trade union (Britain's largest) representing the interests of transport workers (drivers, etc). Also one of the bodies with rights of statutory objection to 'O' licences*.

Thatcham The Motor Insurance Research Centre at Thatcham, Berks (established 1993) where vehicle security devices are tested on behalf of insurers. Also publishes (via a Fax-Back system 0660 666680) a list of compliant security devices.

Third-party cover In connection with motor vehicle insurance, limited cover which meets legal requirement (ie *RTA 1988* s143) for compulsory cover against third-party liabilities (ie claims from third parties who suffer damage or injury).

Third-party (distribution) Outside specialist supplier of transport or distribution/logistics services, usually under contract. Alternative to own account* (ie in-house) operation of such services/facilities.

Third-party logistics (3PL) The provision of logistics services by an external provider (ie third-party contractor).

Third-party service provider Vehicle maintenance facility used by fleet operators wishing to contract-out their vehicle service and maintenance requirements – usually a main distributor for the make of vehicles operated or an independent repairer.

Three-line braking In goods vehicle air braking systems (mainly UK built), three air lines connected between tractive unit and semi-trailer to provide service (yellow), secondary (red) and auxiliary (blue) air supply.

Three-way tipper Tipping vehicle capable of tipping to the rear and to either side. Often found in local authority fleets.

Three-year rule Regarding automatic driving licence disqualification on accumulation of 12 penalty points, this applies if the 12 points are imposed within three years counting from date of offence to date of offence (ie not dates on which conviction and penalty points were imposed).

Ticket Voucher authorizing travel – usually in the form of a small slip of paper printed with details of the carrier and the journey (date, starting point, destination, route, fare paid, etc) and showing key conditions under which it is issued (ie the carrier's conditions of carriage*). Invariably paid for in advance in the case of train travel or on-board in the case of bus/tram travel, but not always – some train tickets are sold on-board and some bus tickets are purchased in advance.

TIDE   Tax, insurance, depreciation, establishment costs. A mnemonic used in vehicle costing matters as a reminder of the main constituents of an operator's fixed costs*.

Tilt   Canvas cover or tarpaulin. Term for vehicle/semi-trailer body with polyester tarpaulin cover supported on dismantable frames secured by cord through eyelets. Can be Customs sealed to meet TIR* requirements.

Tilt cab   Heavy vehicle cab which can be tilted forward to allow access to engine, etc for ease of servicing and repair.

TIMCON   Timber Packaging and Pallet Confederation. Trade association for firms in this business – runs the register of pallet trademarks and ownership markings as a means of combating pallet theft.

Time group recording   On tachograph chart*, recordings made in accordance with position of activity mode switch* (ie driving – unless made automatically – other work, breaks/rest period).

Time off   Under various provisions of employment law, employees are entitled to time off (with/without pay) for specified activities (ie trade union duties/activities/public duties/to seek work/training).

Time recorder   Instrument that records time (ie to monitor use of machine, engine running time, etc).

Time right   Phrase used in regard to tachographs. Namely, the legal need to ensure charts are put in instrument so recordings are made at the right time of day or night (am/pm).

TINA   Transport infrastructure needs assessment. A European Commission process to identify key transport links (ie roads, rail networks, airports, sea and river ports) within participating countries which link to form the Trans-European Network (TEN*).

Tip   Colloquialism for discharging a load whether from a tipper/tipping vehicle or other sort of vehicle.

Tipper/tipping vehicle   A vehicle designed and built to discharge its load (usually of bulk goods – sand, gravel, coal, grain, etc, or liquid or granular loads) by raising the front end of the body hydraulically.

TIR Transports International Routiers. Convention on the *International Transport of Goods by Road (TIR Carnets) 1959,* which allows goods in Customs sealed vehicles/containers (accompanied by TIR Carnet – see below) to transit countries and cross borders with minimum of formalities (ie inspection of goods). TIR cannot be used in inter-EU trade (where Community Transit* applies). Vehicles must be specially prepared and certified (ie by DoT in UK) and display plates (front/rear) with white TIR letters on blue background.

TIR carnet Approved customs document (printed in French) which accompanies TIR consignments showing full details of journey/load/ packaging, etc. Voucher removed and counterfoil stamped by Customs on departure, at each border crossing and on arrival. Carnets are issued by guaranteeing bodies (eg RHA*/FTA*) to whom they must be returned on completion of journey.

T/L Total loss. A loss or damage claim where the goods or vehicle/vessels is totally lost or damaged beyond repair/recovery.

TLC Total logistics concept. The concept whereby individual elements such as warehousing, inventory, order processing, transport, distribution, and many other key functions, are considered as a whole (ie the logistics function within the total supply chain concept).

TMC Traffic message channel. UK radio channel broadcasting road and traffic conditions. *See also* RDS-TMC.

TMOH Abbreviation for *The Transport Manager's and Operator's Handbook* written by David Lowe. Leading transport management reference book, published annually since 1970 by Kogan Page, London.

TNT Thomas Nationwide Transport. Originally an Australian transport group now merged into UK/European consortium (ie TNT Post Group – part owned by Dutch Post Office) including TNT Express parcels companies.

TOC Train Operating Company (providing passenger services). Under privatization, the TOCs are separate from the infrastructure provider (ie Railtrack).

Toll A charge, typically for the use of roads and bridges (eg the Severn, Humber and QE II bridge over the Thames). Many European motorways are tolled. Historically, in Britain, tolls were charged for the use of turnpike roads.

Toll gate   Point at which traffic must stop for the payment of tolls for the use of roads and/or bridges. Also called tollbooths, and where there are a number of them in a line, called toll plazas in the US.

Ton   Imperial measure of weight equalling 2,240 lbs (in shipping also referred to as a long ton). One ton equals 1.01605 tonnes.

Ton/tonne/miles/kms   A measure (either imperial or metric) of the utilization of a vehicle on the basis of the weight of load carried multiplied by the distance of the journey.

Tonnage   As in *Tonnage Convention 1994* adopted by IMO* to establish a universally recognized and standard system for measuring the tonnage of ships.

Tonne   Metric measure of weight equalling 1,000 kgs. One tonne equals 0.984207 imperial ton.

Top lift   Container, etc with capability (ie strength) for lifting from the top (ie by top-lift spreader* attachment on gantry crane*, etc).

Top sleeper   *See* Sleeper pod.

Top-speed limiter   *See* Road speed limiter.

Torque   The turning effort applied to a shaft. In motor vehicle technology, it effectively means the flexibility of an engine enabling it to pull well at low speed. Hence an engine's torque can be more important that its absolute power output.

Tort   Legal term for civil wrong (as crime is criminal wrong) such as trespass*/ private nuisance*, etc. Actionable by civil suit. If successful Court will make an award of damages (ie monetary compensation).

Total acquisition cost (TAQ)   The sum of all the costs to an organization of carrying an item in stock including reorder, carrying and shortage costs. *(Source: ILT Supply-Chain Inventory Management SIG)*

Total lead-time   The total time between the decision to place a replenishment order until its availability for use. That is, the sum of order lead-time, purchasing lead-time, transit time and any goods inward lead-time for that replenishment order. *(Source: ILT Supply-Chain Inventory Management SIG)*

Total life cost   *See* Terotechnology.

Total logistics solution   Modern jargon for service offered by consultants, etc to firms suffering problems with their logistics/distribution operations.

Total loss   When a vehicle is 'written off' following an accident.

Total operating cost   In connection with vehicle costing, a combination of fixed (ie standing)*, variable (ie running)* and overhead (ie establishment)* costs. In effect, the figure which indicates to an own-account operator what his vehicles cost to own and run and to a haulier the basis on which he calculates his profit margin.

Tower wagon   Legally defined as goods vehicle with built in expanding/extendible contrivance for inspecting/repairing, etc overhead structures or equipment and which carries no load other than its own articles. Special rate of VED applies.

Towing distance   Applies when one vehicle tows another by means of rope/chain/webbing strap, etc (but not when rigid two-bar used). Maximum distance between two vehicles must not exceed 4.5 metres. If distance exceeds 1.5 metres rope/chain, etc must be made clearly visible from either side.

Towing dolly   Term for towing device which lifts vehicles/trailers partially from ground. Legally defined as either towing implement (which raises other vehicles, eg when broken-down) or as converter dolly (on which is mounted a fifth-wheel* plate, etc to support and tow a semi-trailer*).

Towpath (towing path)   Footpath alongside canals and inland waterways – pavements of the waterways. Originally used by horses drawing barges. Now provide recreational access for walkers, cyclists, anglers and leisure boaters. BW* manages and cares for over 2,400 kms of towpaths.

Toxic gas/substance   Poisonous gas/substance carried by road and indicated by hazard warning symbol (ie diamond) showing skull and crossbones in black on white background.

TP (1)   Third party. Term used in insurance matters (eg motor insurance) when an accident occurs. The insurer (ie the insurance company) is the first party, the insured person/company/organization is the second party and anybody else involved (particularly if they make a claim for loss or damage) is referred to as the third party.

TP (2)   Third party (contractors). Distribution/logistics contractors providing either transport and/or warehousing (or both) or a total logistics service on a dedicated basis to retailers, wholesalers or manufacturers.

TPCS Tyre pressure control system. System whereby driver can monitor and control tyre pressures from the cab. Useful when pressures need to be lowered for off-road operations (eg in forestry work) – product of manufacturer Eaton.

TPP Transport Policies and Programme. PTA*, County Council and Unitary Authority annual planning document setting out transport policy and a programme of expenditure and a statement of progress. Now replaced by Local Transport Plans (LTPs*).

TPO Travelling Post Office. Royal Mail postal service on rail operated by EWS*.

TPR Transportable pressure receptacle. A receptacle used for the carriage of gas under dangerous goods legislation.

TPS Transport Planning Society. Society for professional transport planners.

TPWS Train protection and warning system. Advanced system to prevent trains passing signals set at red for danger. Using trackside sensors that act like a trip wire, detects when a train is travelling too fast to stop at a red danger signal and automatically applies the brakes. *See also* SPAD, ATP and ETCS.

TQM Total quality management. Concept for achievement of quality standards of service offered to customers. *See also* BS 5750/ISO 9000.

TR Nationality symbol for Turkey – to be shown on the rear of vehicles from that country.

Traceability The identification of goods or material used in manufacturing or processing to enable the relevant production batch and material source to be traced in case of subsequent defects. *(Source: ILT Supply-Chain Inventory Management SIG)*

Track access grant Government scheme to provide funds in support of a switch from road to rail. Specifically this grant covers up to 100 per cent of the track charges imposed by the rail track owners Railtrack. Provided for under the *Railways Act 1993*. *See also* Freight facilities grant, Section 8 grant and PACT.

Track gauge The distance between rail lines. For the UK and Europe the dimension is 1,435 mm (ie 4ft 8½ ins); Ireland, Spain, Portugal and Finland operate on different gauges.

Tracking (or tracing) system   Tracking by means of electronic communications systems and satellite tracking to identify location of goods and/or vehicles (in logistics may extend from tracing products from manufacturing source to final consumer, to determining the precise location of a road or rail vehicle).

Track-laying vehicle   Vehicle which travels on tracks or wheels and tracks (ie as with military tank, etc).

Traction (1)   Grip produced by tyre on road/surface. Essential for forward progress and stability of vehicle. For extra traction, goods vehicles often have twin drive axles*.

Traction (2)   Colloquialism for the provision of haulage with a tractive unit only (ie pulling client's semi-trailers).

Traction control   System used on motor cars to prevent driving wheels slipping or spinning (ie to lose traction). The system operates (in conjunction with the vehicle's anti-lock braking system) by rapidly and continuously applying and releasing the brake on that wheel, helping it to regain lost grip.

Tractionnaire   New fangled (Franglais) term for hauliers providing traction only (ie hauling only other firms' trailers).

Tractive unit   Drawing (ie motive) unit of articulated vehicle combination. Not to be confused with tractor.

Tractor   Vehicle intended for pulling rather than carrying. Legally defined as a motor tractor – vehicle not itself constructed to carry a load and with an unladen weight not exceeding 7,370 kg. *See also* Locomotive.

Trade licence   Licence which authorizes use of vehicle on road without payment of VED*. Only available to motor traders/repairers, etc and use restricted to specified purposes. Issued (in form of plates) by LVROs*.

Trade-off   An increase in cost in one area which may allow a greater reduction of cost in another area so producing an overall net benefit.

Trade plates   Number plates for attachment to vehicles used under provisions of trade licence. Numbers shown in red on white background. Plate with triangular licence holder must be carried at front of vehicle.

Trade protectionism   Action, usually by governments, to protect trade against unfair/excessive/foreign, etc competition.

Trading account   Document (usually prepared by accountant/auditor, etc annually for business) showing income and expenditure for year – same as profit and loss account*. Indicates gross profit/loss for year. Not to be confused with balance sheet*.

Trading Standards/Officer   Department of local authority (and officer of such) concerned with (among other things) vehicle weights (direction of vehicle by police for weighing and prosecution is on behalf of highway authority). Such have powers of prosecution for weight offences and can prohibit use of overloaded (ie unsafe) vehicle by issue of form GV 160*.

Traffic (1)   Vehicular traffic on a road or rail network, aircraft or ships operating along 'traffic lanes'. The more there are the greater the traffic congestion is said to be (ie the UK's M25 London orbital motorway is as congested with road traffic, as the English Channel is busy with shipping traffic, etc).

Traffic (2)   Goods or passengers carried by traffic (see above).

Traffic Area/Office   The UK is divided into a number of administrative areas (ie Traffic Areas) for 'O' licensing*, purposes under control of Traffic Commissioner*. Each has central office where forms are obtained/applications made, etc – see local telephone directory for address and telephone.

Traffic Commissioner   Statutory authority empowered to issue goods and passenger 'O' licences* and discipline operators (eight appointees currently, in UK) – previously called the Licensing Authority (LA*) when dealing with goods vehicle licensing. Also responsible for disciplinary matters regarding LGV*/PCV* driver licensing. Normally, one for each Traffic Area* appointed by Secretary of State* for Transport, to whom they report annually.

Traffic congestion   Situation where many vehicles on the same stretch of road, or in a town centre, result in congestion with consequent slow movement, frustration of drivers and excessive consumption of fuel and emission of vehicle exhaust fumes polluting the atmosphere – hence why traffic congestion is seen as an environmental evil to be eradicated.

Traffic jam   When traffic congestion gets to a point where vehicles come to a complete stop, or can only progress slowly in a stop-start fashion with the same environmental penalties as described above. The M25 London orbital route is frequently described as the world's longest traffic jam.

Traffic office   Superseded term meaning an office where traffic is planned (eg in a road haulage operation). Now largely replaced with terms like 'distribution' or 'planning' office.

Traffic warden   Person appointed by local police authority to act as such (ie when in uniform only). They have powers to enforce the law mainly in connection with stationary vehicle offences such as parking and causing an obstruction and at crossings and car pounds and can require a driver to give his or her name and address, but not produce their driving licence (except when on duty at car pound) or other vehicle documents.

Trafficmaster   Automated system of in-car reporting (via LED signal, screen or voice) of traffic delays, hold-ups, etc.

Trailer   Vehicle (mainly non-powered) towed by a motor vehicle but includes broken-down vehicles on tow, etc.

Trailing axle   Term for non-driven axle usually in a tandem bogie* on goods vehicle (ie provided to enable extra weight to be carried but not needed for traction* purposes).

Train weight   The weight of a drawbar* combination (ie drawing vehicle and trailer). *See also* GTW.

Trainee driving licence   Special heavy goods vehicle driving licence (now large goods vehicle entitlement*) for young drivers training under Young Driver Training Scheme*.

Trainferry   Cross Channel ferry ship fitted with rails to carry freight trains – operations ceased in 1993 when the Channel Tunnel opened.

Training Agency   Formed by government under provisions of *Employment and Training Act 1983* to assist people in training for employment and employers in finding suitably trained staff. Has two executive arms (ie Training Services Agency, which looks after training boards, and Employment Services Agency to run 'Jobcentres', etc).

Trainload   Rail freight service for larger volumes where a whole train of wagons is required – as opposed to wagonload* freight.

Tram   Light rail vehicle, usually runs singly or in articulated form on rails laid in town and city streets, not always segregated from other traffic and pedestrians. Common in Europe, but growing in popularity again in the UK (eg in Manchester, Leeds and Croydon).

Tramp   In the old days of road haulage, the practice whereby vehicles travelled the country seeking loads (ie tramping) as opposed to trunking* between two points. In shipping, a vessel engaged in bulk cargo or time chartering (ie not a liner* vessel) – the old-fashioned term was tramp steamer. A freight ship which sails neither to a fixed route nor schedule, but is available for hire or charter at negotiable rates.

Transaction   Recording of a material movement or an adjustment event that impacts on a stock position. *(Source: ILT Supply-Chain Inventory Management SIG)*

TRANSAID Worldwide   An independent charity aiming to alleviate poverty through transport solutions. It was set up in response to a challenge to the transport industry from HRH the Princess Royal and was run successfully on a voluntary basis for 10 years within Save the Children Fund. TRANSAID Worldwide is now established as *the* charity of the transport industry. More information is available at www.transaid.org.

Transducer   Re electronic tachographs* (and other vehicle equipment), device which converts (electronically) rotational speed, etc to give road speed reading at tachograph head.

Trans-European Networks (TEN*)   A Europe-wide system of networks for roads and for Combined Transport* proposed by the EU*.

Transfer of vehicles   Regarding 'O' licensing*, transfer of (over 3.5 tonne gvw) vehicles from licence in one Traffic Area* to another. Permitted for three months maximum before removing from original licence and adding to licence in other area (by use of form GV 80 in both cases). Not permitted if 'O' licence not held in other area (ie new application to be made at least nine weeks in advance).

Transfrigoroute   Commercial (trade) organization concerned with temperature controlled transport*.

Tranship   To transfer goods to or from one vehicle/vessel/rail wagon, etc to another, between modes or to a storage facility.

Transit (1)   Means carrying people or things from one place to another (ie in transit through – passing through). Used in connection with road haulage permits, etc – needed in some cases to transit (ie pass through) intermediate countries.

Transit (2)   Generic term for a van – any van, in the same way that 'all vacuum cleaners are Hoovers' (which in fact they are not). Everybody knows and loves the Transit van – conveyor of all things for all men. Product of Ford Motor Company.

Transit time (1)   The time taken to complete a journey. The time between a vehicle leaving base and arriving at its destination.

Transit time (2)   The time taken to move goods physically between different locations in a supply chain or laterally to another facility. *(Source: ILT Supply-Chain Inventory Management SIG)*

Transport   Means to carry or convey goods/people, etc. In the context of this dictionary, means anything and everything to do with operation of goods vehicles and movement of goods.

Transport 2000   Campaigning organization for environmentally sensitive transport policies.

Transport Action Clean Up   DTLR* programme aimed at cutting emissions pollution from vehicles in larger UK cities. Operators of older vehicles are offered grants towards the purchase of emission-reducing equipment such as catalytic converters and particulate traps.

Transport Kills   Report produced by HSE* on study of fatal accidents in industry which shows vehicles to be one of biggest killers (through loading, unloading, maintenance, movement and especially reversing of vehicles).

Transport Tribunal   Judicial body (under control of Lord Chancellor) constituted solely to deal with 'O' licensing* appeals. Comprises president (usually a judge) and at least two other sitting members – see booklet, *Appeals to the Transport Tribunal* available free from Traffic Area* offices.

Transportable pressure receptacles   Tanks and cylinders used for transporting gases.

Travel   To make a journey.

Travel card   An authority to travel usually sold in advance of the journeys to be made. Often representing reduced price for a number of journeys or concessionary rates for travel.

Travel demand forecasting   An exercise used to determine future travel patterns under given or hypothetical conditions. Used to plan the provision of public transport services or the need to build or expand road or rail networks.

Travelling height   Height required by law to be marked in vehicle cab when carrying containers, engineering plant, skips, etc which exceed 3.66

metres (ie 'travelling height'). Marking must show height to within plus/ minus 25 mm and be in letters at least 40 mm high. *See also* Height marking.

Travelling showmen   Person following the business of such. His vehicles (see also showmen's vehicles) are subject to special rates of VED*.

Tread   Part of a vehicle tyre which is in contact with the road surface. Has patterned grooves designed specially to provide grip/directional stability/disperse water, etc (racing cars and motorcycles use 'slick' tyres with no tread pattern which grip due to their soft texture when hot – ie at racing speeds).

Tread depth   Legal stipulation as to the minimum depth permitted for vehicle tyres, normally 1mm (but increased to 1.6 mm for new cars and light vans not exceeding 3,500 kg, from 1 January 1992) across three-quarters of breadth and around entire circumference.

Treaty of Rome   Historic treaty of 1957 bringing together the original 6 Common Market countries, now expanded to 15 EU member states, and from which has grown the SEM*.

Trefoil   A three lobed or leafed plant. Copied in stylized form for use as worldwide recognized symbol to warn of radioactive substances.

TREMCARD   Transport emergency card. Card (usually laminated) from CEFIC* which carries details of dangerous substance, the emergency action to be taken in event of spillage, etc and intended to be carried by drivers/ on vehicles carrying such. Meets legal requirement for information to be provided to driver in writing.

Trespass   The act of venturing on to somebody else's land without permission or remaining after permission to be there has expired. This is a tort* (ie civil wrong). However, only reasonable force (and no more) may be used to evict trespasser. Also owner of premises is liable if trespasser comes to harm (eg from dangers on premises – open trenches, etc – or from mantraps/guard dogs*, etc).

Triangular rear reflectors   Only to be fitted on rear of trailers – prohibited by law on other vehicles.

Tri-axle/bogie   Bogie* comprising a number of linked axles (usually on trailer). In this case three such axles linked by suspension.

Tri-deck (triple-deck) transporter   Vehicle transporter with three decks – often seen as car transporter or for carrying sheep.

Trip/s   A one-person one-way journey. A measure used in public transport planning (eg in calculating trip generation).

TRL   Transport Research Laboratory. Formerly the Government's Transport and Road Research Laboratory (TRRL) at Crowthorne, Berks. Now an independent, internationally recognized research establishment with, among other facilities, a test track for heavy vehicle testing.

Trolleybus   Passenger road vehicle (ie a bus) that takes its electric power from overhead cables. Quiet and more flexible in movement than a tram, but constrained by having to share road space with other vehicles. Popular in many UK cities until early 1970s.

Trombone trailer   Semi-trailer designed to be capable of extension (as with trombone) for carrying exceptionally long loads (pipes/girders/steel strip, etc).

Truck (1)   Common term for a heavy lorry.

Truck **(2)**   Leading monthly magazine for the truck industry and enthusiasts.

Truck mixer   Heavy vehicle with cement mixer unit (ie drum) mounted on chassis. Capable of continuing mixing process while travelling.

Truck rental   *See* Rental.

Trucking   Common parlance for road haulage operations.

Trucknology   Truck industry buzzword originally attributed to heavy vehicle manufacturer MAN* and taken up by Reed Business transport magazines as the title for a supplement issued with these journals.

Truckstop   Stopping places (usually on main routes) especially for goods vehicle drivers with all facilities for vehicle and driver (fuel, spares, food, refreshments, accommodation and showers, etc).

Trunk   A regular route or service with a constant or relatively high level of traffic flow. The main artery of the network (eg a motorway or main rail line). To trunk means to send traffic along the main leg of a journey, being supplied by a feeder* service at each end.

Trunker   A trunk vehicle (ie a vehicle used for long-haul journeys) or a trunk vehicle driver.

Trunking   The long haul leg of a journey between base and the delivery point. The leg of the journey between the local collection and delivery at either end of the journey.

TSG   Transport supplementary grant. Grant payable by the government via the DTLR* to local authorities in respect of the primary route network (PRN*) for major schemes (ie costing £2 million or more) on roads of more than local importance; assessment, strengthening and structural maintenance of bridges and other load bearing structures; and structural maintenance of the carriageway of primary routes and other A roads. Once started the Department continues to fund the project until completion.

TSO   The Stationery Office. Privatized successor to HMSO*. Publisher of parliamentary and statutory documents, plus EU and other official publications.

TSS   Turbine steamship. A ship powered by a steam turbine fuelled by coal or oil.

TT   Telegraphic transfer. A system for making international payments via a bank (ie the payment is telegraphed to the payee).

TTO   Through transport operator. A name given to a carrier who contracts to carry goods, but who only undertakes part of the carriage himself (for which he acts as the principal), contracting out the remainder of the carriage (acting only as agent) to one or more further carriers.

TUC   Trades Union Congress. Central body of trade unions in the UK to which most (but not all) are affiliated.

Tug (1)   Towing tractor (also called dock tractor). Used in moving trailers and semi-trailers in depots*/docks/marshalling areas*, etc.

TUG (2)   Transport Users Group. A group of individual transport users who meet to discuss transport issues, make suggestions for service improvements, and provide feedback on service levels.

TUPE   Abbreviation for the *Transfer of Undertakings (Protection of Employment) Regulations 1981* (implementing the EU directive on Acquired Rights) which safeguards employees' rights when they transfer to the new owner of their former employer's business.

Turbocharger   Engine component designed to force more air into engine by re-circulation to produce greater power.

Turbo-compounding   Latest technology in engine design (eg from Scania). System for increasing power output by converting heated exhaust (ie waste) gases into energy. Uses second turbine mounted 'downstream' from standard turbocharger*. Second turbine transmits power from exhaust gases via gear train direct to flywheel.

Turbofan   Type of jet engine used in aircraft where the jet engine drives a large propulsive fan and provides jet reaction at the rear.

Turbojet   Type of jet engine used in aircraft comprising a gas turbine which provides forward thrust from the exhaust gas.

Turboprop   Type of jet engine used in aircraft comprising a gas turbine from which the power drives a shaft carrying a propeller (ie prop).

TURERA   Abbreviation for *The Trade Union Reform and Employment Rights Act 1993.*

Turn around time (TAT)   The total time taken to repair a component at the repair location, including waiting time but excluding transit time. *(Source: ILT Supply-Chain Inventory Management SIG)*

Turning circle (1)   Articulated goods vehicles of 16.5 metres length must be capable of turning within minimum and maximum swept inner and outer concentric circles of 5.3 metres radius and 12.5 metres radius respectively.

Turning circle (2)   Buses first used since 1 April 1988 must be capable of turning on either lock so that no part of the vehicle projects outside a pair of concentric circles with radii of 12 metres for the outer circle and 5.3 metres for the inner circle. The outer rear corners of vehicles (ie the side opposite the direction in which it is turning) must not swing out more than 0.8 metres in the case of rigid buses and more than 1.2 metres in the case of articulated buses.

Turnover   The total revenue received by a business from its sales, etc. Usually measured annually.

Turnpike   Road on which tolls are charged (and collected at toll gates*). Historically such roads, administered by Turnpike Trusts, were created piecemeal in Britain from the late 17th century and disappeared with the coming of the railways.

Turns count   Regarding tachograph calibration*, a count of the drive wheels turning is made on a roller test rig (ie rolling road) to determine the characteristic coefficient of the vehicle (indicated by the symbol 'w' on the calibration plaque).

Turntable   Component part of fifth-wheel* coupling mounted on tractive unit* which carries the weight of the imposed semi-trailer and (greased) provides table on which trailer pivots (horizontally and vertically).

Turret truck   A type of fork lift truck on which the mast has a rotating head for pallet forks allowing stacking either side of the aisle. In narrow aisle applications, such trucks can operate up to 12-metre heights.

TÜV   Technischer Überwachungs Verein. German technical standards organization. Operates goods vehicle test stations akin to those operated in UK by the Vehicle Inspectorate (VI*). *See also* DEKRA.

TV in vehicles   Only permitted if driver cannot see screen (directly or indirectly) unless provided to give him road information or about his vehicle (when reversing, etc).

Twenty-eighty rule   *See* Pareto Principle.

Twenty-four/seven (or 24/7)   Marketing buzz words meaning open round-the-clock seven days a week.

Twin-splitter gearbox   Form of gearbox on heavy goods vehicle. Variation on splitter* g/box to give very smooth, clutch-less gear changes across range of many gear ratios and intermediate ratios to provide optimum truck performance (ie of speed/fuel consumption, etc). *See also* Range-change.

Twin-steer   Heavy vehicle with twin steering axles at front (ie as with rigid eight-wheeler and 'Chinese six' – no longer a popular vehicle configuration).

Twist lock (or twistlock)   Locking device fitted to vehicles/rail wagons, etc to secure shipping containers*. Locking pin in device is manually turned to locate in corner fittings on container to prevent movement in transit.

Two-dimensional bar code (2D bar code)   Codes in which information is placed in two dimensions and read from side to side, and up and down, by special scanning equipment and which can be read even if partially damaged. *(Source: ILT Supply-Chain Inventory Management SIG)*

Two-line braking   Braking system on articulated vehicles (mainly European) operated with two air lines only to semi-trailer UK system normally has three lines*.

Two-man instrument   Regarding tachographs*, instruments which have facility for accommodating two charts and providing two simultaneous recordings (for driver, time, speed and distance; for second man time only). Relevant modes selected by driver (number 1 mode switch) and second driver (number 2 mode switch). Charts have to be changed over when crew change position.

Two-speed axle   Rear axle of goods vehicle containing two crown-wheel pinions for changing between high and low ratios. Operated from cab by vacuum or electrically. No longer popular with advent of multi-ratio gearboxes.

Two-yearly inspection   Regarding tachograph* calibration, etc, statutory inspection required at approved centre at two-yearly intervals. Plaque* added to show when carried out. Illegal to miss this inspection.

Type approval   EU*-wide scheme whereby vehicles/components, etc are submitted to national authority (ie DTLR* – VCA* – in UK) for approval after which they can be sold as 'Type Approved', otherwise may not be sold. Vehicles without type approval cannot be registered in UK.

Type approval certificate   Type approved vehicles (see above) are issued with Certificate of Conformity* which is needed for first registration.

Tyre groove   Groove in vehicle tyre forming tread pattern. Must be at least 1 mm deep (1.6 mm for some vehicles from 1 January 1992) – *see* Tread depth. Base of the original groove over area of tread to which depth limit applies must remain visible. Grooves can be re-cut* on tyres for certain vehicles.

Uu

UAE United Arab Emirates. One of the Gulf states to which international road haulage vehicles regularly travel.

UIC Union International des Chemins de Fer. International organization representing rail operators. Equivalent to IRU* for road operations.

UICR Union International des Chauffeurs Routiers. International organization representing lorry drivers

UIR Union of International Road-Rail Operators. Organization concerned with encouragement of the use of road-rail* systems.

UIRR International Road-Rail Union. Organization concerned with road-rail* transport.

UITP International Union of Public Transport. Brussels-based organization representing national public/passenger transport associations.

UKASTA United Kingdom Agricultural Supply Association. Trade association for agricultural organizations concerned with, among other things, establishing a code of practice for road hauliers to improve cleanliness and safety in the carriage of food grains.

UKWA United Kingdom Warehousing Association. Trade association for warehousemen.

ULBC Ultra large bulk carrier. Ship for carrying bulk materials. *See also* ULCC.

ULCC Ultra large crude carrier. A large ship for carrying bulk products, usually crude oil or ore. *See also* ULBC.

ULD Unit load device. A unit for loading cargo (a container, pallet, stillage, airfreight igloo, etc).

Ullage Space above the level of the liquid in a tank/drum. Sometimes deliberately left to allow for expansion of the liquid. Usually expressed as a percentage of the total volume.

ULSD   Ultra low sulphur diesel. Type of diesel fuel (also known as City Diesel), which is claimed to reduce sulphur emissions by 90 per cent and dramatically reduce the emission of particulates (a harmful concoction of fine dust and black smoke). The EU proposes that the sulphur content of diesel fuel should be reduced to 1 per cent from 1 January 2003.

ULSGO   Ultra low sulphur gas oil. Environmentally-friendly form of rebated heavy oil (ie basically diesel fuel on which a lower rate of duty has been paid) used in fork-lift trucks, etc. Illegal if used in on-road vehicles. *See also* ULSD.

Ultra vires   Legal term meaning action beyond one's (legal) power or authority. Defined by the *Oxford Companion to Law* as 'a doctrine important in relation to the acts or contracts of public authorities, companies and others whose powers are limited by statute or constituting deed'.

ULW   Unladen weight. The weight of a vehicle inclusive of its body and parts normally used but exclusive of the weight of water, fuel, loose tools and equipment and batteries (but only where these power the vehicle). Use of the term ulw is gradually diminishing in UK legislation as metric measure is progressively introduced.

UN   United Nations. International body concerned with peace. Formed by the nations united against the axis powers (Germany, Italy, Japan) in World War II (1939–45). Sets legislative and other standards for shipping and for dangerous goods carriage.

UN number   Internationally recognized code numbers for dangerous substances established by the UN* (eg, for conveyance by road, as displayed on Hazchem* labels, etc).

Unaccompanied   Vehicle/trailer or semi-trailer shipped by ferry/rail without the driver. Collected at other end of transit by a local driver. In a passenger transport context it would mean the carriage of unaccompanied minors (ie children) by airlines for example.

UNCITRAL   United Nations Commission on International Trade and Law.

UNCTAD   United National Conference on Trade and Development. Organization concerned with developing trade between members nations of UN*.

Undertaking   Refers to the undertakings (ie legally binding promises) given by 'O' licence* applicants and holders to the Traffic Commissioner* in connection with their 'O' licence – penalties against the licence may follow if the law is broken or undertakings are not kept.

Undervalued currency A currency whose rate of exchange is persistently above parity.

UN/EDIFACT United Nations Electronic Data Interchange for Administration, Commerce and Transport. Internationally agreed standards and guidelines for the electronic interchange of commercial data.

UNICE Union of Industrial and Employers' Confederations of Europe. Europe-wide association of trades unions.

UNCTAD-MMO UNCTAD* Multi-modal Transport Convention.

Unfair contract terms *Unfair Contract Terms Act 1977.* Intended to eliminate from contracts clauses that aim to deprive parties (ie consumers) of their rights in law and of rights to duty of care. *See* Negligence.

Unfair dismissal Dismissal of an employee on grounds which are held to be not fair. Employees (after two years' service) have a right not to be unfairly dismissed and may complain to an Industrial Tribunal (within three months) if they are so dismissed. If case upheld, Tribunal will order reinstatement/re-engagement or award compensation.

Unfit driver Vehicle driver who is not fit to drive due to the effects of drink/drugs. Also, re LGV* driver entitlement, driver who by his conduct has shown himself not fit to hold an entitlement to drive heavy vehicles – decided by TC* who may penalize the entitlement.

Unified driving licence New form of driving licence in UK introduced in conformity with EU directives. Shows all of a drivers entitlements (ie ordinary/LGV*/PCV*) in a single document using EU system of categorization (eg Class I HGV licence becomes C+E entitlement).

Unit The standard size or quantity of a stock item. *(Source: ILT Supply-Chain Inventory Management SIG)*

Unit cost (1) In cost calculations, the cost of producing or moving a single unit as opposed to a whole batch or consignment.

Unit cost (2) The cost to an organization of acquiring one unit, including any freight costs, if obtained from an external source or the total unit production cost, including direct labour, direct material and factory overheads, if manufactured in-house. *(Source: ILT Supply-Chain Inventory Management SIG)*

Unit load   Load of goods unitized for transportation (in container, semi-trailer, on pallets, shrink-wrapped, etc) – not loose.

Unit of measure   The standard unit of an item used in the stock account and to construct order quantities. *(Source: ILT Supply-Chain Inventory Management SIG)*

Unitization   The system of forming unit loads by whatever method.

Unlit road   Road on which street lights are placed at intervals greater than 200 yards (in Scotland 185 metres). Vehicle headlamps must be used on such roads between sunset and sunrise.

UPC   Uniform product code.

UPS   United Parcels Service. American, reputed to be world's largest, express parcels carrier. Its characteristic brown coloured, standard design vehicles are recognized worldwide.

Urban Bus Challenge   Fund provided by government for which local authorities and other agencies can bid for improving public transport provision in these areas. *See also* Rural Bus Challenge.

Urban clearway   Section of highway marked as such by appropriate signs (illustrated in Highway Code*) and where vehicles must not park on carriageway during times shown on sign (except for as long as necessary to pick up or set down passenger). *See also* Clearway.

Urban test cycle   Regarding official tests to determine fuel consumption for new cars – one of three standard tests conducted to simulate urban driving and not exceeding 50 kph (other tests are constant speed at 90 kph and optional constant speed at 120 kph). Law requires such figures to be displayed on all new cars offered for sale (since 1978).

Urine-alcohol limit   Statutory limit for amount of alcohol in urine above which it is illegal to drive, etc – 107 mg of alcohol in 100 ml of urine. Normally, determination of a drink/driving offence is based on breath/alcohol test by breathalyzer* or blood alcohol test but where this is not possible for medical reasons the urine test may be applied.

URTU   United Road Transport Union. Trade union for transport drivers. Has statutory right of objection to 'O' licence* applications.

USDAW   Union of Shop, Distributive and Allied Workers. Trade union for shop staff and for distribution drivers. Has statutory right of objection to 'O' licence* applications.

User body   An organization (eg a consultative committee) representing the interests of a particular group of customers who use transport services (eg rail users). Some are statutory, having been set up through legislation, while others are voluntary.

User of vehicle   The person who drives a vehicle or who employs a person to drive it on his behalf (ie both driver and employer of the driver). Key term in transport law – most legislation is aimed at the 'user'. For example, 'O' licences* must be held by the user and most C&U regulations offences are committed by the user.

UTC   Urban traffic control. System for controlling traffic in urban areas.

UTI   *Unité de Transport Intermodal.* French term for Intermodal Transport Unit (ITU).

Utilization   Concept of achieving maximum use of warehouse space (vehicles, vehicle load capacity, labour, capital, etc). Measure of efficiency of use, which tells (among other things) whether there is over-capacity available, excess labour or whether capital expenditure has not been effectively used.

UTMC   Urban traffic management and control. Intelligent (modular) control systems to manage traffic in cities.

UTP   Urban transport planning. Urban planning concept mainly adopted in the USA.

Vv

V2 Take-off speed for an aircraft. Obviously varies with the size and type of aircraft.

Vacuum brakes Brakes on (heavy) vehicles operated by vacuum system – as opposed to air. Not found on modern vehicles.

Value added Concept whereby a service is given which adds value to a product. In theory distribution adds value because it puts the product into the consumer's hands.

Value chain Another logistics concept which represents the conversion of primary materials into the object desired by the consumer (ie the part of the logistics operation that actually adds value by making or converting something undesirable into a desirable object).

VAN (1) Value added network. Term used in computer technology.

Van (2) Goods vehicle with enclosed body, usually falling within small and medium weight categories.

Variable costs Accounting term denoting costs of operation which vary according to performance. In transport, the costs of running a vehicle (hence running costs) that vary with use (ie fuel, tyre wear, maintenance).

VASCAR Visual average speed computer and recorder. Machine fitted to police vehicles and used to trap speeding drivers (ie by recording the average speed over a measured distance).

VAT Value added tax. Tax added on to price of goods/services (eg transport) which seller/supplier has to recover from his customer and pass on to Customs & Excise (the dreaded VAT-man) – free tax collection service provided involuntarily by industry to government.

VBG Swedish manufacturer of vehicle towing equipment (drawbars*, etc).

VBRA Vehicle Builders and Repairers Association. Trade association for the vehicle body repair and commercial vehicle body building industry.

VCA (1)   Value chain analysis. Yet more distribution industry jargon.

VCA (2)   Vehicle Certification Agency. Vehicle and Component Approvals Division department within Vehicle Inspectorate* which deals with Type Approval*. *See* Vehicle Certification Agency.

VCRAT   Vehicle Crime Reduction Action Team. A Home Office initiative (started in August 1998) to ensure the Government's target of reducing all vehicle crime by 30 per cent by 2003.

VDRS   Vehicle defect rectification scheme. Operated by police when vehicle (car/light van only) found on road with defects that it is in the owner's best interest to have repaired. Defects form is issued and repairs must be carried out and certified on back of form by MOT test garage. Form then returned to police within 14 days. It is an offence to fail to do this.

VDU   Visual display unit. Computer screen on which the operator sees the data/work displayed.

VED   Vehicle excise duty. Payable for all motor vehicles kept on roads (unless exemption certificate* applied for) in accordance with duty rates based on vehicle type/number of axles, etc. Disc is issued to confirm payment, which must be displayed in windscreen. Failure to pay duty (or at wrong rate) can result in fines and need to pay back duty. *See also* GVED.

Vee (v) engine configuration   Vehicle engine where cylinders are formed in two banks at (usually) 60 degrees to each other (ie as in V6 and V8).

Veeder-Root   Scottish-based manufacturer of tachograph instruments (among other things). Now taken over by management and operating as TVI Europe Ltd.

Vehicle   A means of transporting goods or passengers, including lorries, buses and coaches, railway rolling stock, ships and inland waterway craft and aircraft.

Vehicle acquisition   Term to describe the process of determining the best (eg most economical) method of obtaining the use of vehicles (outright purchase/hire purchase/lease/contract hire/rental, etc). This procedure takes into account availability of capital, relevant tax positions and operational considerations.

Vehicle bans   Periods of time (usually at weekends) when goods vehicles (over specified weights) are banned from using roads (ie passing through).

Many EC states have such bans and international operators should be aware of these because of the delays they can cause to vehicle schedules. Also in UK, restrictions on vehicle above specified gross weights entering certain roads, areas, etc as shown on nearby signs.

Vehicle Certification Agency   Executive agency of the DTLR* responsible for carrying out tests on new vehicles, vehicle systems and components to ensure they meet international safety and environmental protection standards and for certification of vehicles under the type approval scheme. *See also* VCA.

Vehicle Enquiry Unit   A section within the DVLA* at Swansea which deals with enquiries about vehicle registration numbers, etc.

Vehicle Inspectorate   Executive agency of DTLR* which deals with vehicle testing and both roadside and on-premises inspection of goods and passenger vehicles.

Vehicle owner liability   *See* Owner liability.

VeMIS   On-board vehicle management data recording equipment. Product of Leafield AVM.

Vendor hub   Third party operation of a warehouse, funded by suppliers, containing vendor-owned stock for delivery to a customer (see lineside warehouse). *(Source: ILT Supply-Chain Inventory Management SIG)*

Vendor managed inventory (VMI) (1)   System whereby a supplier is responsible for maintaining pre-determined inventory levels.

Vendor managed inventory (VMI) (2)   An element of inventory stocked by one organization but where the forecast demand, and required stock levels to meet that demand, are calculated by the manufacturer or distributor of the stock items concerned. *(Source: ILT Supply-Chain Inventory Management SIG)*

Venture capital   Capital risked on new projects, setting up new businesses, or MBOs*, etc. Specialized firms (finance houses/bank off-shoots, etc) are set up to provide such.

VFR   Visiting friends and relatives. Term used in passenger transport analyses of the purposes for which journeys are made.

VG   Vortex generator. A device used to change the airflow characteristics of various surfaces (eg the frontal appearance of large vehicles to improve fuel consumption).

VI   Vehicle Inspectorate. Agency of the DTLR* dealing with vehicle standards and enforcement.

Vicarious liability   Legal term meaning that one person is held responsible for the (illegal/tortious) actions of another person. For example, an employer can be held liable for the actions of his employees.

Vicinity   In the context of 'O' licensing*, environmental representations may be made by those who own or occupy land in the vicinity of a vehicle operating centre. Vicinity is not defined as such but may be taken to mean 'near' or where affected by noise, etc from such a place.

Vienna Convention   *United Nations Convention on Contracts for the International Sale of Goods,* which came into force on 1 January 1988.

Vignette   In road transport context, a ticket or voucher confirming that charges for road use have been paid – currently Eurovignettes are in use in Germany, Denmark and the Benelux countries of the Netherlands, Belgium and Luxembourg.

VIN   Vehicle identification number: 17-digit international number given to vehicles and recorded on computerized DVLA* owner file. Duplicated on the PNC* to give the police 24-hour access to relevant details of all vehicles registered on the DVLA computer.

Virage project   Experimental vehicle of manufacturer Renault Trucks.

Visa   *See* Entry visa.

Viscosity   A measure of the internal friction of a fluid (eg engine oil). A typical diesel engine oil would rate 5W/40, but the latest Euro III* diesel engines use synthetic oils rated at 0W/40 – very thin in the cold and very thick in hot temperatures (and usually only changed at 100,000 km intervals). *See also* ACEA.

Vision requirement   Medical requirements for drivers: they must be able to read a number plate in good daylight at distance of 75 yards (with glasses or contact lenses if worn). More stringent standards are applied to LGV*/ PCV* drivers.

VGT   Variable-geometry turbocharger. In layman's terms, a system to make smaller turbocharged diesel engines perform like huge naturally-aspirated diesels (ie to give them more 'grunt' at low engine revolutions).

VLBC   Very large bulk carrier. Tanker ship built purposely to carry bulk oil.

VLCC   Very large crude carrier. *See also* ULBC and ULCC.

VMI   Vendor managed inventory. Logistics buzzword for a system by which inventory costs are (hopefully) reduced.

VMS   Variable message signs. Electronic signs seen mainly on motorways to convey up-to-date information to drivers (eg on traffic conditions ahead).

VNA   Very narrow aisle. Racking with an aisle width of 1.8 metres or less. Often combined with 'high bay' racks up to 35 metres. Because of the height racks are often constructed from structural steel sections.

VOC (1)   Vehicle Observer Corps. Voluntary group of hauliers, etc formed under auspices of RHA* to combat lorry thefts.

VOC (2)   Volatile organic compound. Constituent of partially burnt fuel from vehicle exhaust. Also vapours emitted during distribution of petrol – to be channelled back into underground storage tank of the service station and stored until they can be transferred back into the delivery tanker.

Vocational driving entitlement   Means driving licence needed for a person's work. Under new EU driving licence scheme, drivers who qualify to drive large goods/passenger carrying vehicles (LGV*/PCVs*) will be given a 'vocational driving entitlement' on their new 'unified'* licence.

Vocational licence   Correct name for separate LGV/PSV drivers licences which are now being phased out with the introduction of new EC scheme for unified licences.

Vodafone (Racal)   One of licensed operators (by government) providing UK cellular telephone network – another is Cellnet (British Telecom).

Voith   Manufacturer of vehicle retarders (ie braking systems), etc.

VOR   Vehicle off road. Term usually applied when spare parts are urgently required for vehicle out of service.

Vorad   Eaton Vorad collision warning system. Product of Eaton designed to reduce accidents by the fitment of radar scanner to vehicles to warn drivers of potential collisions. *See also* AICC, CoPilot and Prometheus project.

VPD   Variable power drive train.

VRN   Vehicle registration number. Shown on plate (ie number plate) affixed to front and rear of registered vehicles (with exceptions, eg motorcycles which only require rear number plates).

VRO   Vehicle Registration Office. *See* LVRO.

VSIB   Vehicle Security Installation Board. National accreditation body for vehicle security installers/installations. Publishes a Code of Practice for the installation of anti-theft devices in vehicles.

VTC   Vocational Training Certificate. Proof of qualification achieved by special training and examination – eg as with DGSA qualification.

VTOL   Vertical take-off and landing. Aircraft capable of taking-off and ascending vertically and also descending and landing vertically. Mainly confined to military applications as with the Harrier, the so-called 'jump' jet.

Ww

WA   With average. *See* Average.

Wagon and drag   Old haulage industry term for lorry and trailer (ie drawbar combination*).

Wagonload   Rail freight service for individual wagon loads or to meet less than full trainload* requirements.

Waiting period   Period required for offenders to wait before penalty points can be removed from their driving licence/counterpart.

WAN   Wide area network. A system for linking computers located at different sites to enable them to share information and peripherals like printers.

WAP   Wireless application protocol. Used in connection with mobile telephone technology.

War risk   An exclusion clause found in contracts and insurance policies which absolves the party (eg the insurer) from meeting claims arising from the perils of war, strife, riots, hostilities, etc.

Warning triangle   Reflective red triangle to be placed on roadside to warn approaching drivers of a vehicle stopped on the road ahead. Legal requirement to carry and use such in many EU states (eg France, Germany; Spain requires two).

Warranty   A guarantee or implied condition of sale (eg in respect of a vehicle or items of plant and equipment). Also in marine insurance policies.

Warsaw Convention   International convention (signed in 1929) governing the carriage of cargo and passengers by air.

Way   The road or track on which vehicles travel – hence roadway or highway and railway. Can also include a canal or river. Ways may be natural (ie river or sea), natural but artificially improved (ie a river with navigation improvements) or artificial (ie roads and railways).

Waybill Non-negotiable document which is evidence of a contract for the transport of cargo. *See also* Air waybill.

Wayleave Term that relates to a situation where the right to use a way* is granted by the owner (eg the land owner) in return for a payment. Typical use would be to erect pylons and run telephone wires or power cables along the way.

Way marker A sign on a track or path indicating the route to follow (or a choice of routes) and possibly the distance to the next key point ahead or the final destination.

Way point A point or stopping place on a road, path or track. Often where a journey is, or may be broken, or from which route distances are measured.

WDA Writing down allowance. Accounting term referring to a tax allowance under which a 25 per cent per annum allowance is made on the residue of capital expenditure (on vehicles, plant and equipment, etc) brought forward from the previous accounts period.

Web site A specific site on the World Wide Web exclusive to a firm or organization providing information on its products/services/activities and giving it a 24-hour global presence. Usually prefaced by a 'home page' and comprising a number of linked Web pages and may offer links to other associated or relevant Web sites.

Webasto Manufacturer of vehicle cab heaters (among other things).

Week Under EU drivers' hours law, fixed period from 00.00 hours Monday until 24.00 hours on following Sunday during which the driver may drive for six shifts after which he must have a weekly rest-period.

Weekly rest Rest period to be taken by goods vehicle driver under EU law once each week and following six daily driving shifts. Must amount to 45 hours normally but may be reduced to 36 hours when driver at base and 24 hours elsewhere. Reduced time must be made up en bloc by end of the following week.

Weigh out Where the weight capacity of a vehicle/container is reached before the volumetric capacity is filled.

Weight limit Restriction on use of certain road sections/bridges by vehicles exceeding specified maximum gvw as shown on road sign (black vehicle, showing weight limit, on white background within red circle).

Weight not to be exceeded in GB   Weight shown on DTLR plate* for vehicle which indicates the maximum weight for vehicle/trailer and its axles permitted on the road in Great Britain – this may be less than manufacturer's design weight but takes priority. *See also* PMW.

Weight tolerance   No tolerances are allowed in observing permitted maximum vehicle weights but when subjected to dynamic weighing*, axle and gvw are determined to within +/– 150 kg per axle (for vehicle 150 kg x number of axles).

Well Driven   A campaign to monitor safe and considerate lorry driving. Stickers on the backs of some lorries give a telephone number to ring if you wish to praise or berate the driver.

Wharfage   A fee charged to a ship owner/operator for the use of a wharf for mooring and loading/unloading cargo.

Wheel clamp   Device used by authorities (ie police) for immobilizing illegally and obstructively parked vehicles. Driver has to make contact and pay fixed penalty fee plus release charge to recover vehicle. Also used (controversially in many cases) by private contractors.

Wheelbase   Distance between centre line of front and rear axles of vehicle. In case of three axles (ie one front /two rear), distance between the front axle and a point 110 mm behind centre line between two rear axles.

Wheels and sheds   Term used by logisticians (usually derogatively) to describe fundamental aspects of the supply chain, namely lorries and warehouses.

White goods   Distribution term for domestic appliances/equipment.

White Paper   Government document setting out proposals for action/ legislation for consultation with interested parties (usually preceded by a Green Paper* and followed by the publication of a Bill* and subsequently an Act of Parliament*). In the transport context, the best known White Paper of recent times was that of 1998 on the future of transport, *'A New Deal for Transport: Better for Everyone'*, commonly referred to as the Integrated Transport White Paper. *See also* Green paper.

White ticket   In connection with fixed penalty* system, ticket issued by police or traffic warden* for non-endorsable offences.

White van (man)   White painted, mainly small, delivery vans invariably showing no owner/operator livery (ie unmarked). Notorious for being driven aggressively by drivers who exhibit road rage tendencies. Most, however, are used legitimately and driven in a sensible and considerate manner.

Whole life cost/costing   System for counting the cost of buying and operating a goods vehicle or plant* over its whole life (including its value at final disposal) when making purchasing decisions, rather than just comparing initial prices of one vehicle against another. *See also* Tero-technology.

Wide tyre   Vehicle (ie lorry/trailer) tyre which has area of contact with the road of at least 300 mm wide measured at right angle to length of vehicle.

Wide-angle mirror   Mirror on goods vehicles designed to give the driver wide angle vision along the side of his vehicle, usually combined with close-proximity mirror* to show side of the vehicle near to ground at front. Required on vehicles over 12 tonnes gvw first used since 1 October 1988.

WiP   Work in progress*. An expression used to describe work processes prior to their completion.

Wipe the slate clean   Term used in connection with the driving licence penalty points scheme whereby once 12 points have been accumulated within a three-year period a mandatory disqualification has been imposed; the driver's 'slate' in this respect will be wiped clean for a fresh start. Also, at one time a term used to describe the driver's need to take breaks during or after a driving spell driving, but this interpretation has since been rescinded.

WMS   Warehouse Management System. Computer software.

Woolf Reforms   Also known as Civil Procedure Rules. A procedure introduced in 1999 for speeding-up civil claims through courts, particularly the pre-trial procedure, and reducing the cost of litigation. Established a three-track procedure system: small claims, fast track and multi-track depending on the size of the claim.

Work in progress (WiP*)   The total amount of work in process, between production stages or subject to a waiting time. *(Source: ILT Supply-Chain Inventory Management SIG)*

Work-in-progress stock   The stock of products and/or materials and components which are still in the production department and are not, or are no longer, included in the stock in the store. *(Source: ILT Supply-Chain Inventory Management SIG)*

Working capital   Funds needed by a business to meet its day-to-day expenditure (ie operating expenses).

Working stock   The stock of materials, components and subassemblies (excluding safety stock) held in advance of demand so that ordering can be done on a lot size rather than on an as-needed basis. In other words, the normal stocks formed by products arriving in large regular orders to meet smaller, more frequent customer demand. Also known as cycle stock or lot size stock. *(Source: ILT Supply-Chain Inventory Management SIG)*

Works truck/trailer   Legally defined as truck/trailer designed to be used in private premises and used on road only for delivering goods between or to or from premises or vehicles in the immediate neighbourhood. Special rate of VED* applies.

Write-off   When a vehicle is damaged beyond repair in an accident and constitutes an insurance claim on this basis. *See also* Total loss.

Writing down allowance   Term used in depreciation calculations to indicate the amount to be 'written down' for this year (ie the amount by which the value of the asset is to be depreciated for one year's life).

Written off/down   Accounting term referring to an asset which has been fully depreciated in the books of account.

Written plea of guilty   Offender summoned to appear in Court to answer for alleged offence may instead write pleading guilty (but possibly stating mitigating* circumstances) and asking the Court to deal with the case in his or her absence. The Court may accept this or may adjourn the case for a personal appearance. Where applicable the offender would need to submit his/her driving licence to the Court prior to the hearing.

WTO   World Trade Organization. Established in 1995 to ensure a new era of global economic cooperation and a more open multilateral trading system.

WTR   *Working Time Regulations 1998* as amended 1999. Imposes limitations on weekly working and minimum break and holiday requirements, etc.

WWDSHEX   A charter shipping term meaning 'Weather working days Sundays and holidays excepted'.

WWW   World Wide Web. The link to sources of information via the Internet.

WYSIWYG   What you see is what you get. Computer term describing that what is seen on the VDU screen is exactly what is printed out on the 'hard' copy*.

Xx

Xenon   As in high intensity discharge xenon headlamps. *See* HDIX.

Xenophobia   Word which describes the attitude of certain people who dislike all things 'foreign' including foreign food, foreign customs and foreign people – and, for many British people, especially anything to do with the EU.

Yy

Yellow ticket   Re fixed penalty* notice scheme, ticket (issued only by police) which denotes a driving-licence endorsable offence and therefore one where police must take the driver's licence. Appropriate number of points are added to licence and it is returned when fixed penalty fee is paid (or following conclusion of Court hearing if this is elected).

York Antwerp Rules   A set of rules in marine insurance relating to the adjustment of general average*.

Young LGV Driver Training Scheme   Scheme established by RTIETB* (run by NJTC*) for training young HGV (now LGV) drivers with progression through the various classes of licence (ie Class III/II/I) to produce a qualified driver at age 21 years.

Your Lorry Abroad   Free booklet available from IRFO* Newcastle upon Tyne, which explains requirements for taking a goods vehicle abroad. Full title: *A Guide to Taking Your Lorry Abroad.*

YU   Nationality symbol for Yugoslavia – to be shown on the rear of vehicles from that country.

Zz

Zero defects   Term used in connection with quality management*. Aim is to produce goods/services with no defects rather than try to remedy defects later.

Zero inventories   Part of the principles of just-in-time which relates to the elimination of waste by having only required materials when needed. *(Source: ILT Supply-Chain Inventory Management SIG)*

ZEV   Zero Emissions Vehicle. Vehicle powered by hydrogen fuel cell (HFC) which emits virtually no harmful emissions into the environment – in effect a clean air vehicle.

ZF   Manufacturer of vehicle gearboxes/transmission systems, etc.